KATHLEEN PALMER CLEVELAND

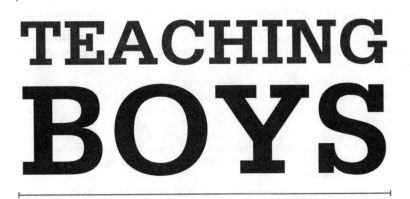

TEACHING BOYS

WHO STRUGGLE IN SCHOOL

STRATEGIES

THAT TURN

UNDERACHIEVERS

INTO SUCCESSFUL

LEARNERS

ASCD | Alexandria, Virginia USA

ASCD®

1703 N. Beauregard St. • Alexandria, VA 22311-1714 USA
Phone: 800-933-2723 or 703-578-9600 • Fax: 703-575-5400
Web site: www.ascd.org • E-mail: member@ascd.org
Author guidelines: www.ascd.org/write

Gene R. Carter, *Executive Director;* Judy Zimny, *Chief Program Development Officer;* Nancy Modrak, *Publisher;* Scott Willis, *Director, Book Acquisitions & Development;* Julie Houtz, *Director, Book Editing & Production;* Miriam Goldstein, *Editor;* Sima Nasr, *Senior Graphic Designer;* Mike Kalyan, *Production Manager;* Valerie Younkin, *Desktop Publishing Specialist;* Sarah Plumb, *Production Specialist*

All web links in this book are correct as of the publication date below but may have become inactive or otherwise modified since that time. If you notice a deactivated or changed link, please e-mail books@ascd.org with the words "Link Update" in the subject line. In your message, please specify the web link, the book title, and the page number on which the link appears.

ASCD Member Book, No. FY11-6 (Apr. 2011, PSI+). ASCD Member Books mail to Premium (P), Select (S), and Institutional Plus (I+) members on this schedule: Jan., PSI+; Feb., P; Apr., PSI+; May, P; July, PSI+; Aug., P; Sept., PSI+; Nov., PSI+; Dec., P. Select membership was formerly known as Comprehensive membership.

PAPERBACK ISBN: 978-1-4166-1150-9   ASCD product #111028

Also available as an e-book (see Books in Print for the ISBNs).

Quantity discounts for the paperback edition only: 10–49 copies, 10%; 50+ copies, 15%; for 1,000 or more copies, call 800-933-2723, ext. 5634, or 703-575-5634. For desk copies: member@ascd.org.

Library of Congress Cataloging-in-Publication Data
Cleveland, Kathleen Palmer.
    Teaching boys who struggle in school : strategies that turn underachievers into successful learners / Kathleen Palmer Cleveland.
        p. cm.
    Includes bibliographical references and index.
        ISBN 978-1-4166-1150-9 (pbk. : alk. paper) 1. Boys—Education. 2. Underachievers—Education. 3. Academic achievement. I. Title.
    LC1390.C54 2011
    371.823'41—dc22

                                                                                    2010051018

20 19 18 17 16 15 14 13 12 11   1 2 3 4 5 6 7 8 9 10 11 12

To Bret and Ian,
whose experiences as learners
inspired me to write this book

TEACHING BOYS
WHO STRUGGLE IN SCHOOL

Acknowledgments

The work of Harvey Silver, Richard Strong, Matthew Perini, Thomas Dewing, and J. Robert Hanson has contributed greatly to the ways in which we know and understand our students through the lens of style. In equal measure, the studies about boys' underachievement coming out of Australia and England during the past decade have transformed our ability to understand and respond effectively to this issue. Were it not for all of these resources, this book could not have been written.

I would like to thank the amazing students and teachers in elementary, middle, and high schools across the country with whom I have worked during the past 30 years, each of whom has been my teacher. I owe a special debt of gratitude to my many graduate students, whose shared ideas and stories illuminated and gave voice to each of the principles in this book. Their "pictures" of underachievement among boys informed my own understanding of this issue and helped me define the complex mosaic of factors and influences it encompasses.

Thanks also to Scott Willis of ASCD for seeing the potential of this book and for his supportive guidance as I prepared the manuscript for submission, and to Miriam Goldstein, whose wise and skillful editing burnished its rough edges and made it shine.

Finally, I wish to thank Bernie Cleveland, Laurie Beck, Elaine Duff, Ingrid Flom, Laurie Hager, Emily Hurst, and Ruth Palmer for their indefatigable support and invaluable feedback during the writing and revision of the manuscript.

Introduction

In recent years, I have watched with concern the steady increase of claims regarding a crisis in boys' achievement. Magazine covers, television programs, and books paint a grim picture of "a stunning gender reversal in American education" (Conlin, 2003) that is characterized by an alarming decline in boys' scholastic prowess in every grade level, kindergarten through postgraduate (MSNBC, 2006; Tyre, 2006). Some authors refer to emerging neuroscientific findings and suggest that boys and girls—by virtue of each gender's brain- and hormone-based differences—actually learn in different ways (Gurian & Stevens, 2005; Sax, 2005) and thus also need to be taught in ways that are selectively gender-friendly, even if this means a return to the single-sex classrooms of old.

As an educator and researcher, I looked for ways to confirm or deny what I was reading and to make sense of what sounded like a massive problem requiring an immediate, nationwide response. My background in brain-based learning, learning styles, and multiple intelligences made me both skeptical and curious about underachievement perspectives based primarily on differences between boys and girls.

I sought clarity about this issue with the same process of inquiry I use in my work, which is to say that I was alternately confused, excited, frustrated, overwhelmed, and illuminated in nearly equal measure. After many months, I arrived at a perspective about underachievement in boys that I believe addresses the complexity of the issue, yet also offers workable solutions that don't further stereotype the problem or disenfranchise the very learners for whom they are designed. In this book, I will introduce you to the questions I asked, the information I examined, the conclusions I eventually reached, and the potential solutions I found along the way. I invite you to discover them much as I did, by exploring the ideas, stories, and resources herein.

Ultimately, I realized there is no magic, one-size-fits-all-boys solution, but I firmly believe (as I hope you will come to as well) that there are many potential responses that can, indeed, be quite magical, especially where underachieving boys and school are concerned. This book is meant to explore those responses and offer each reader a degree of understanding that is deep enough to support change, flexible enough to encompass many variables, and broad enough to serve as a viable framework for practical decision making. It is not an instructional recipe book filled with strategies, nor is it solely a book about ideas; it is, rather, a bit of both. I wrote it for the many educators who want to take part in solving the problem of "boys and school," and its ultimate effectiveness as a tool will be determined by the unique experience and expertise each educator brings to its reading.

PART I

Boys and School

CHAPTER 1

Framing the Issue of Underachievement

Start painting with fresh ideas, and then let the painting replace your ideas with its ideas.

—Darby Bannard, artist and professor

Where to Begin?

As is often the case when an area of inquiry appears straightforward and simple at the outset, my goal of sorting through the various claims about a crisis in boys' academic achievement proved far more challenging than I initially imagined it would be. During the first few months of exploration, it became clear that essentially two perspectives frame this very public debate, the proponents of which each cite research-based evidence yet reach vastly different and conflicting conclusions (see Figure 1.1, p. 6).

Supporters of Perspective A suggest the existence of a genuine crisis in boys' education that requires a major shift in American educational policy to overcome recent gains in girls' overall achievement (which are viewed as having been made at the expense of boys' achievement). Suggested solutions

FIGURE 1.1

Two Conflicting Perspectives

Group A*		Group B**
• Boys' education is in crisis.	← Perspective →	• Hispanic, black, and low-socio-economic groups of boys and girls are in crisis, primarily in large metropolitan inner-city schools. There is no crisis among white middle- and upper-class boys.
• By almost every benchmark, boys across the nation and in every demographic group are falling behind.	← Evidence →	• Boys' achievement levels have increased continuously in all subject areas over the past 30 years of national testing, with the exception of a slight but steady decrease in 12th grade reading scores since 1990, which is also seen in girls.
• Recent gains in girls' achievements were made at the expense of boys'.		• Overall, there has been no radical or recent decline in boys' scores relative to girls' scores. There is no trend; boys score higher in some areas, girls in others. • Boys' scores increased when girls' scores increased. However, girls' scores increased more.
• Today's classrooms, pedagogies, and teachers favor girls. • Boys' brains are hardwired to require a different kind of learning than girls' brains do. • This is the major reason boys are underachieving.	← Conclusions →	• There is wide variation among individuals of the same sex. • It is inappropriate to draw causal links between observations about brain structure or activity and human behavior. • Boys' rates of achievement are caused by multiple factors.
* Conlin, 2003; Gurian & Ballew, 2003; Gurian & Stevens, 2005; Sax, 2005; Tyre, 2006		**Alloway et al., 2002; Barnett & Rivers, 2006; "Canberra," 2002; Corbett, Hill, & St. Rose, 2008; Eliot, 2009; Mead, 2006; Reichert & Hawley, 2006; Salomone, 2003, 2006a, 2006b; Toch et al., 2006

Source: From *Boys and School: Challenging Underachievement, Getting It Right!* by K. Cleveland. © 2008 by TeacherOnlineEducation.com. Reprinted with permission.

include increasing boy-specific teaching strategies in coed classrooms (to counterbalance a presumed overabundance of girl-friendly pedagogy) or separating boys from girls altogether and offering the former instruction perceived as more friendly to boys' brains (Conlin, 2003; Gurian, 2001; Gurian & Ballew, 2003; Gurian & Stevens, 2005; Sax, 2005; Tyre, 2006). The major assumptions underlying this perspective are that boys' brains are hardwired differently than girls' brains, that all boys share this difference, and that the instructional strategies that help boys learn differ from those that help girls learn.

In contrast, supporters of Perspective B conclude that there is no unilateral crisis in boys' achievement, though they readily agree that achievement levels are at a crisis point among several subgroups of the male population (specifically Hispanic, African American, and economically deprived youth, particularly in major urban inner-city settings) (Alloway, Freebody, Gilbert, & Muspratt, 2002; Barnett & Rivers, 2006; "Canberra," 2002; Corbett, Hill, & St. Rose, 2008; Eliot, 2009; Mead, 2006; Reichert & Hawley, 2006; Salomone, 2003, 2006a, 2006b; Toch et al., 2006). In response to the concern that boys' learning needs have been undercut as a result of the attention given to girls' needs, Perspective B proponents point to statistics from the Department of Education showing quite the opposite: namely, that there have been no dramatic changes in boys' achievement levels during the last 30 years and that in many areas, boys' achievement has actually increased, occasionally eclipsing that of girls.

Insights from Both Perspectives

Though clearly at odds, these two perspectives each informed my inquiry in an important way. Perspective A heightened my awareness around the issue of boys and academic underachievement. The proliferation of published books and articles on this topic and a concurrent increase of attention paid to it by other mass media suggested to me that, at some level, concern about boys' underachievement was resonating strongly with the general public as well as with educators. Some perceived "truths" expressed in these publications were connecting with people deeply enough that they were buying into claims of a crisis taking shape in our schools, despite ample evidence to the contrary. I wondered what those "truths" were.

Perspective B engaged me in exploring more deeply the research used to justify conclusions on both sides of the debate. I realized that even though there might not be a genuine crisis, there were, nonetheless, specific aspects of the American education system with which many boys still struggled. Achievement trends aside, too many boys were not reaching expected levels of success, and the problem was both widespread and serious.

When in frustration I eventually abandoned my fruitless attempts to reconcile these two opposing perspectives, a gift emerged from the detritus of my efforts. I realized that the problem of underachievement was not a gender-wide crisis needing a gender-wide one-size-fits-all-boys solution. Indeed, the problem didn't even encompass all boys. Instead, the real issue was finding ways to identify and respond to the specific reasons for under-achievement among the boys still struggling in our classrooms and schools despite our best efforts: the boys who fall behind and stay behind, the boys who drop out too soon, and the boys we just never seem to reach. There had to be a way to help these specific boys without jeopardizing the achievements of other, more successful learners (boys and girls), and this would turn out to be a vastly different proposition than the one I had originally envisioned.

This shift in my perspective also altered the trajectory of my inquiry. As my focus moved away from all boys and toward struggling boys in particular, I recognized that I needed to learn more about the specific ways in which boys struggle in our classrooms. I also wanted to examine how the way we "do school" might be interfering with an underachieving boy's potential for achievement. And with the latter consideration came a secondary realization that the solutions used by each teacher would need to be as different as the teachers and their students. In other words, their problems were unique, and the solutions to those problems must necessarily be unique as well. Finding solutions would mean helping educators find ways to respond flexibly and effectively to the challenges their underachieving boys were facing in their classrooms.

A Look at the Problem Through Educators' Eyes

To reframe my understanding of these complex issues, I acted much as an artist might when nothing seems to be working: I went back to the proverbial drawing board and began anew with a fresh canvas. I consulted educators currently working in the field, who deal with the problem of boys' underachievement on a daily basis, hoping that a new "rough sketch" of the issue might emerge from their shared observations. I asked these classroom teachers, administrators, and counselors from all grade levels and subject areas to answer the following questions about underachievement among boys, based on their own experiences. I encourage you to take a moment to answer these questions for yourself before you read on.

1. What characteristics distinguish the struggling boys in your classroom?

2. By contrast, what skills, attributes, attitudes, or behaviors do you see in boys who are successful in your classroom?

3. What do boys in your classroom say they love about school?

4. What do boys in your classroom say they hate about school?

5. What would boys in your classroom say they are most successful at?

6. Are there any aspects of the subject you teach that seem to be obstacles to academic success for a large number of boys?

7. What aspects of teaching boys are most challenging for you?

The collective responses I gathered uncovered valuable clues in four key areas regarding the dilemma of academic underachievement among boys (see Figure 1.2, pp. 10–11).

Clue No. 1: The influence of nonacademic factors on academic success. With regard to differences between academic skills, there were no surprises when I compared responses to the first question (What characteristics distinguish the struggling boys in your classroom?) with those to the second question (By contrast, what skills, attributes, attitudes, or behaviors do you see in boys who are successful in your classroom?). The descriptions of successful boys included critical academic skills such as listening, organizing, focusing, using time wisely, paying attention to details, reading and writing well, and finishing assigned tasks.

What I found especially interesting, though, were the nonacademic factors teachers mentioned when characterizing their high-achieving boys. These factors fell into three general categories: *social confidence* (e.g., "has

FIGURE 1.2
Survey Responses

Question No. 1
What characteristics distinguish the struggling boys in your classroom?

- Afraid of failure
- Apathetic
- Attitude that "school is stupid"
- Can't stay on task
- Careless
- Confrontational
- Disinterested in school
- Disorganized
- Disruptive
- Distractible
- Doesn't plan
- Doesn't respond to help
- Easily discouraged
- Hurries to finish
- Immature
- Impatient
- Impulsive
- Inattentive
- Indifferent
- Insecure
- Lack of athletic ability
- Lack of motivation
- Lack of perseverance
- Lack of self-control
- Lack of support
- Low self-esteem
- Negative home life
- No positive male role model
- No work ethic
- Passive
- Resistant
- Short memory
- Struggling in multiple classes
- Unwilling to ask for help
- Unwilling to compromise
- Upset by mistakes

Question No. 2
By contrast, what skills, attributes, attitudes, or behaviors do you
see in boys who are successful in your classroom?

- Can be creative without having to be right or wrong
- Confident
- Enjoys challenges
- Focuses well, refocuses more quickly
- Gets along with most others
- Gets work done
- Has circle of close friends
- Has parental involvement and support
- Has vision of the future
- Less concerned with what others think
- Listens well
- Mature
- Organized
- Participates in organizations
- Pays attention to details
- Persistent
- Proud of achievements
- Self-motivated
- Sets goals
- Strong reading and writing skills
- Surrounds self with positive influences
- Uses time wisely
- Willing to ask for help
- Willing to ask questions

Question No. 3
What do boys in your classroom say they love about school?

- Acting stuff out
- Building/making/competing
- Choice
- Computers
- Doing experiments
- Field trips
- Food rewards
- Friends
- Learning something "cool"
- Lunch
- P.E.
- Physical activities
- Recess
- Social time
- Sports
- Working in groups

FIGURE 1.2
Survey Responses (*continued*)

Question No. 4
What do boys in your classroom say they hate about school?

- Being told what to do
- Boring classes
- Doing the same thing every day
- Everything
- Grades
- Homework
- Inconsistent teachers
- Learning useless stuff
- Negative teachers
- Reading uninteresting books
- Sitting still
- Studying
- Taking notes
- Taking tests
- Too many rules
- Unfair grading
- Writing
- Writing essays

Question No. 5
What would boys in your classroom say they are most successful at?

- Class discussions
- Debates
- Doing things with their hands
- Group work
- Lunch
- Math
- P.E.
- Problem solving
- Science
- Shop
- Sports
- Subject areas in which they felt successful
- Video games

Question No. 6
Are there any aspects of the subject you teach that seem to be obstacles to academic success for a large number of boys?

- Complexity
- Composition writing
- Content vocabulary
- Details
- Explaining thought processes
- Finishing work
- Grammar
- Group projects—staying on task and being responsible
- Inferential reading
- Journals
- Reading
- Seat work
- Sequencing
- Social skills for group work
- Spelling
- Sustained reading
- Technical writing
- Writing

Question No. 7
What aspects of teaching boys are most challenging for you?

- Aggressive behavior
- Arguing
- Bullying
- Competition for attention
- Constant teasing
- Demand for relevance
- Disregard for reading

Source: From *Boys and School: Challenging Underachievement, Getting It Right!* by K. Cleveland. © 2008 by TeacherOnlineEducation.com. Reprinted with permission.

circle of close friends," "gets along with most others," and "participates in organizations"); *attitudes about self and learning* (e.g., "enjoys challenges," "confident," "persistent," "proud of achievements," and "willing to ask for help"); and *access to support systems* (e.g., "has parental involvement and support" and "surrounds self with positive influences").

I wondered if the familiar negative behaviors we view as causes for underachievement might, in fact, diminish if underachieving boys were privy to the protective benefits that these seemingly nonacademic factors offer to their more successful male peers. Were underachieving boys disruptive, resistant, confrontational, or uninterested, for example, because "that's just how some boys are and there's nothing one can do about it," or were these behaviors the result of *not* having access to support systems that could build social confidence and positive attitudes about self and about learning? Could these missing or undeveloped attributes provide educators with a road map for helping struggling boys?

Clue No. 2: Factors contributing to the "experience" of school. Among the responses to questions three (What do boys in your classroom say they love about school?), four (What do boys in your classroom say they hate about school?), and five (What would boys in your classroom say they are most successful at?), I caught glimpses of several additional factors with the potential to affect a boy's academic success.

It was evident that what was alternately valued or reviled by many boys had much to do with the *experience* of school. The type and qualities of their interactions with peers and teachers seemed to affect boys' perspectives about school in general. On the one hand, what seemed to make school worth their time and effort revolved around the quality and frequency of interactions with friends. On the other, what made school a less than welcoming experience had to do with the teacher-student relationship, the kinds of instruction used, and the classroom setting itself. I wondered how much a feeling of belonging had to do with an underachieving boy's ability to engage in academic learning and if an absence of this feeling might negatively affect his behavior, his attitudes about school in general, and his perceptions about himself as a capable learner.

I noticed, too, that lack of success in certain content areas contributed to the degree of a boy's negativity about school in general. I wondered if there might be ways to help underachieving boys feel more successful as learners and how significant a piece of the equation this was. Were there ways to "do school" differently that might catch more boys before they fell through the cracks and make them want to stay?

Clue No. 3: How competence can enhance persistence. The responses to question six (Are there any aspects of the subject you teach that seem to be obstacles to academic success for a large number of boys?) seemed to home in on how hugely important literacy skills (i.e., reading, writing, grammar, composition, vocabulary, spelling) are to academic success, regardless of a teacher's subject area or grade level. These responses raised two additional questions for me. I wondered, first, why so many boys struggle with literacy and if there were approaches that might help these literacy-challenged learners find more success with this crucial task. Second, I wondered how strongly a boy's feelings of inadequacy about his literacy skills affected his willingness to persist in acquiring them. Would addressing literacy in ways that a boy could more fully embrace improve his overall feeling of competence and his willingness to persevere? Would this, in turn, affect a boy's attitudes about learning in general and about himself as a learner?

Clue No. 4: How a classroom's physical arrangement impacts a learner's success within it. The responses to question seven (What aspects of teaching boys are most challenging for you?) brought a final, equally important consideration to the fore. I wondered how factors within the physical environment of the classroom (e.g., lighting, seating, room arrangement) might affect a boy's academic achievement. Were aspects of the physical arrangement of the classroom exacerbating the problems of underachieving boys, and were some of the characteristic negative behaviors we associate with them the result of these elements? Could the classroom be reconfigured to allow underachieving boys to function better within it?

A New Direction

Social confidence, attitudes about self and learning, access to support, connections between competence and persistence, and a classroom's physical configuration—these were very different considerations than those proffered on the exhaustive lists of purportedly brain-based explanations for boys' underachievement I'd been reading. And though I had more questions than ever, I recognized that addressing the question of academic underachievement in boys would not be as simple as identifying gender-specific factors (i.e., boys' brain chemistry or hormones) or the academic part of the equation (what and how we teach). It would be about comprehending how a host of factors come together to support a struggling boy as a learner and the ways in which his needs are met in the contexts of school, classroom, relationships, and learning experiences.

To this end, a set of overarching goals emerged that provided a pathway for leading the struggling boy away from underachievement and toward his potential, not by catering to his deficits, but by building on his strengths:

 • *Replace* his negative attitudes about learning with productive perspectives about the role of risk (and even failure) as a necessary and valued part of the learning process;

 • *Reconnect* him with school, with learning, and with a belief in himself as a competent learner who is capable, valued, and respected;

 • *Rebuild* life skills and learning skills that lead to academic success and also lay the groundwork for success in life; and

 • *Reduce* his need to use unproductive and distracting behaviors as a means of self-protection.

With these four goals in mind, I finally had a way to look at the issue of boys' underachievement without stereotyping or overgeneralizing boys as a gender, the problems involved in underachievement, or potential solutions to those issues.

Milepost

In this chapter, I traced the discovery process that gradually led to my shift in perspective about how to approach the issue of underachievement among boys. An examination of two conflicting perspectives brought clarity about the scope of the problem as well as potential solutions. I realized that the problem of underachievement among boys is widespread and serious but that it is neither a crisis nor the result of efforts over the past 30 years to help girls be more successful.

A review of educators' responses to questions about their personal experiences with underachieving boys highlighted several potential avenues of inquiry that framed the problem of underachievement in a new way. As I compared the negative behaviors that so often characterize underachieving boys to those of boys who are successful in school, I realized that the issue of underachievement might well be contextual in nature, that is, more about how we "do school" than about any gender-wide limitation resulting from differences between boys' and girls' brains or hormones. I recognized that academic achievement involved many factors: attitudes about self, the experience of "doing school," the importance of literacy skills (and the mountain of woe heaped on boys who aren't successful in acquiring them), and the ways even the physical attributes of our classrooms can limit a boy's potential to be a more successful learner.

As guidelines for the solutions I ultimately hoped to find, I set forth four criteria that focused on helping struggling boys reach their potential, so that like their more successful male peers, they, too, might experience academic success.

What's Next?

In the remaining chapters of this book, I will present data from relevant research studies; provide information and insights from resources created by dedicated educators and community leaders; and illuminate strategies and stories shared by the teachers across the country who—united in their concern about underachievement in too many boys—generously shared their experiences, ideas, and successes. I invite you to join me in exploring these varied resources as a way of understanding and responding to the problem of underachievement that "gets it right" for the struggling boys in our classrooms, not because they are boys, but because they are learners whose needs we have not yet successfully met.

CHAPTER 2

The Pictures Within the Picture: The Style Dynamic

I always wondered in school, why has nobody discovered me? Didn't they see that I was more clever than anybody in the school? That the teachers had trouble learning, too? That all they had was information that I didn't need? It was obvious to me. Why didn't they train me? I was different. I was always different. Why didn't anybody notice me?

—John Lennon

Have you ever seen a mosaic picture created from dozens and dozens of miniaturized images? At first glance, the image simply looks as though it was created using artfully organized dots of color. It is only upon closer investigation that you see that the larger image is actually a collection of tiny, complete images: the pictures within the picture.

In so many ways, the issue of underachievement in boys is like this mosaic. Within the larger picture of underachievement, we can see the faces of individual boys who make up this population. And if we look still more closely, we see that each boy is a mosaic himself, created from the many "pieces" of who he is, how he learns, and what he needs in order to succeed in our classrooms. Simply put, the issue of underachievement in boys is more complex than it first appears, and the more closely we look at it, the more complexity we see.

As I continued to examine the issue from numerous angles—painstakingly teasing apart a daunting pile of potential causal factors—I came to agree with the opinion offered by University of North Dakota associate professor Marcus Weaver-Hightower. Weaver-Hightower, whose research focuses on issues of boys' education and policy, among other areas, argues that understanding who underachieving boys are and how to help them lies in examining the context of the problem, that is, the manner in which social and academic factors within the classroom affect an underachieving boy's ability to function as a learner within it (Weaver-Hightower, 2005).

The Style Dynamic

Initially, I was drawn to a consideration of style as a classroom-based factor influencing a boy's underachievement by educator Harvey Silver (2007a, 2007b), who uses the lens of style as a framework for explaining why students learn and respond to instruction in different ways. Silver's work, in turn, led me to the seminal research of J. Robert Hanson and Thomas Dewing (1990), which identifies these four distinct styles and their correlating degrees of risk for academic underachievement. In Figure 2.1, you will find a description of the four styles, which are derived from the four "core functions" of the Myers-Briggs Type Inventory: how one takes in information—i.e., via (1) sensing or (2) intuition—and how one makes decisions—i.e., by (3) thinking or (4) feeling. You will also find the percentage of each style type within the at-risk population (derived from Hanson and Dewing's data) and the name I have given each style and used throughout the book (the Sensing-Feeling SF/Interpersonal, the Intuitive-Feeling NF/Self-Expressive, the Sensing-Thinking ST/Practical Doer, and the Intuitive-Thinking NT/Thinker-Knower).

Upon seeing the data displayed in Figure 2.1 for the first time, I was immediately struck by the disproportionate percentage of at-risk learners with the SF/Interpersonal style (63 percent). Nothing I had read previously had presented such a clear connection between one specific and well-defined group of students and their status as at-risk learners or offered more potential for getting a handle on the context of underachievement of which Weaver-Hightower speaks. At the very least, the data suggested the utility of examining the SF/Interpersonal style in greater depth. And, further, I hoped that by understanding the classroom-based conflicts experienced in general by these learners—both boys and girls—I might be able to isolate any factors that especially affected boys with this learning style.

A Closer Look at the Four Styles

Of course, to fully understand the SF/Interpersonal style, I needed to explore all four styles. To assist you in the same task, I have included four

FIGURE 2.1
MBTI Core Functions and Associated Styles

Style (MBTI Core Functions)	Name	Priority During Learning	Percentage of At-Risk Population
ST (Sensing-Thinking)	**ST/Practical Doer**	**Mastery:** Motivated by getting it right and the joy of collecting and sorting information	12%
NT (Intuitive-Thinking)	**NT/Thinker-Knower**	**Applying Logic:** Motivated by mastering knowledge and the joy of intellectual challenge	1%
SF (Sensing-Feeling)	**SF/Interpersonal**	**Connecting:** Motivated by interacting with others, providing practical service, and using resources to be helpful	63%
NF (Intuitive-Feeling)	**NF/Self-Expressive**	**Imagining:** Motivated by making a difference in people's lives and the joy of growth through empowerment and artistic self-expression	24%

Source: Adapted by Kathleen Cleveland from data from the following sources: *GSU Master Teacher Program: On Learning Styles,* by H. J. Brightman, n.d., Georgia State University. © by Harvey J. Brightman; *Research on the Profiles of At-Risk Learners: Research Monograph Series,* by J. R. Hanson and T. Dewing, 1990, Moorestown, NJ: Institute for Studies in Analytic Psychology. © 1990 by Hanson and Dewing; *MBTI Manual* (3rd ed.) (p. 298), by I. Briggs Myers, M. H. McCaulley, N. L. Quenk, and A. L. Hammer, 2003, Mountain View, CA: CCP. © 2003 by Briggs Myers, McCaulley, Quenk, and Hammer; and *The Strategic Teacher: Selecting the Right Research-Based Strategy for Every Lesson,* by H. F. Silver, R. W. Strong, and M. J. Perini, 2007, Alexandria, VA: ASCD. © 2007 by Silver, Strong, and Perini. Adapted with permission.

descriptions that provide brief but thorough breakdowns of each style. In addition, I have listed three recognizable figures who fit the basic mold of each learning style. By imagining these individuals as children in the classroom, you may more quickly understand the differing needs and abilities that learners of each style possess.

The ST/Practical Doer

Focus: Mastery

Exemplars: Henry Ford, Teddy Roosevelt, John Wayne

A boy of this style lives in the concrete world of fact-based knowledge and physical action. He tends to have a practical nature that serves him well in completing the physical tasks that often occupy his attention. He excels in acquiring and applying procedural skills and approaches problem solving in a linear, step-by-step fashion. As a rule, an ST/Practical Doer prefers to stay busy (and is easily bored if not busy); seeks immediate feedback as recognition of his accomplishments; and memorizes well. He dislikes long explanations (which he is inclined to tune out), along with unclear directions (which compromise his ability to achieve mastery), open-ended questions (which conflict with his preference for factual accuracy), and discussions about ideas or theories with no concrete basis in reality. He has great respect for rules and procedures as well as a high ability to understand and recall detailed, factual information. Epitomized by Sgt. Joe Friday's familiar and laconic request for "Just the facts, ma'am" in the 1950s *Dragnet* television series, this learner wants to know the "who-what-when-where-how" of each learning experience.

The NT/Thinker-Knower

Focus: Applying Logic

Exemplars: William F. Buckley, Albert Einstein, Mr. Spock (Leonard Nimoy's character in the *Star Trek* saga)

A boy with this primary style thrives in a world governed by logic. He is often at his best when classroom learning involves acquisition and demonstration of knowledge (versus an accumulation of information) for the purpose of solving problems or generating hypotheses to be tested and explored. He is the quintessential deductive problem solver, able to draw conclusions by forming patterns and making inferences from observations of seemingly disparate facts and details. His notable skills in subject areas that rely on the use of abstract symbols (i.e., language, mathematics, and science) result in academic achievements in advanced course work, and this becomes more apparent as the grade level increases. With high personal expectations for accuracy, he wants to know that his teacher is skilled and knowledgeable in his or her field and will question the teacher as a means of affirming the teacher's competence. His disdain for busy work coupled with his strong verbal skills can be especially challenging to accommodate when other learners in a classroom are at lower levels of academic readiness. Like the ST/Practical Doer, the NT/Thinker-Knower often prefers to work alone and is highly competitive.

The SF/Interpersonal

Focus: Connecting

Exemplars: Garrison Keillor, Charles Kuralt, Ronald Reagan

A boy with this primary style flourishes by connecting with others, which allows him to share and discuss ideas and experiences with them. His focus and motivation during learning comes from the nature of the interactive experience and his enjoyment of the person-to-person interchange rather than from the information and procedures he acquires as a result. As a learner, he is at his best in a collaborative, noncompetitive learning environment, able to acquire and understand facts and procedures by voicing them aloud in his own words, sharing his perspective with other learners, assimilating their responses, and then consolidating his understanding in a highly personalized way that makes sense to him. Like the ST/Practical Doer, the SF/Interpersonal prefers the concrete aspects of learning (i.e., information versus theory and principle), but whereas the ST/Practical Doer is attracted to factual and procedural information for its ability to help him master tasks, the SF/Interpersonal is attracted to information that offers him a vehicle for understanding people's needs and wants. By understanding how it changes others' lives or affects them personally, he connects with the information. As a poor memorizer, he may find it useful to "make sense" of procedures, facts, or abstract information by embedding them in stories or scenarios whose characters or action sequences provide a context for understanding and remembering the information.

The NF/Self-Expressive

Focus: Imagining

Exemplars: Dr. Martin Luther King Jr., Steven Spielberg, Robin Williams

At first glance, these three figures might seem to have very little in common, yet each demonstrates a distinguishing characteristic of the NF/Self-Expressive learner: a focus on the larger issues of human existence, an appreciation for aesthetic elements of human creativity and expression, and an acute awareness and sensitivity to the emotions and motivations of others. This is the learner who sees every shade of gray between the black and white of facts and procedures, and his associative, random way of processing information and ideas makes it especially difficult for him to focus and learn detailed information or to apply sequential procedures. As an inductive problem solver, his brain generates continuous possibilities, often producing intuitive leaps in logic and insight that he is then at a loss to explain sequentially to others. Whereas the NT/Thinker-Knower collects information and organizes it systematically to arrive at a conclusion based on his observations, the NF/Self-Expressive uses the conclusions of others as a springboard to generate new ideas and solutions. Like the SF/Interpersonal learner, he enjoys group work, but is most in his element when given the opportunity to choose or develop solutions to problems that connect to his values and have social significance.

I continued to have "style revelations" when I compared the distribution of each style within the *at-risk* population to its distribution within the *general* population (see Figures 2.2 and 2.3, pp. 23 and 24). I was startled to discover, first, that percentages of *both* the SF/Interpersonal and NF/Self-Expressive styles are proportionally overrepresented within the at-risk population.

When I looked at these two styles together, I was further taken aback to see that the SF/Interpersonal and NF/Self-Expressive styles' combined 59.8 percent of the general population jumps to 87 percent of the at-risk population, while the ST/Practical Doer and NT/Thinker-Knower styles' combined 40.2 percent of the general population accounts for a mere 13 percent of the at-risk population. Why were SF/Interpersonal and NF/Self-Expressive learners proportionally at so much greater risk in the same schools in which the ST/Practical Doer and NT/Thinker-Knower learners experienced a reduced risk?

FIGURE 2.2

Comparing Style Percentages in At-Risk and General Populations

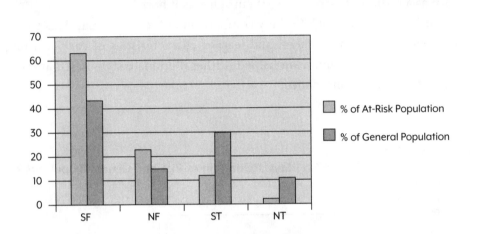

Note: SF/Interpersonal: 63% of at-risk vs. 43.4% of general population; NF/Self-Expressive: 24% of at-risk vs. 16.4% of general population; ST/Practical-Doer: 12% of at-risk vs. 29.9% of general population; and NT/Thinker-Knower: 1% of at-risk vs. 12% of general population.

Source: Data from *MBTI Manual* (3rd ed.) (p. 298), by I. Briggs Myers et al., 2003, Mountain View, CA: CCP. © 2003 by Briggs Meyers, McCaulley, Quenk, and Hammer; and *Boredom and Its Opposite* (presentation at the ASCD Conference on Teaching & Learning, Atlanta, GA, Oct. 20, 2007), by H. Silver. © 2007 by H. Silver. Adapted with permission.

I wondered what competencies might so consistently protect students with the ST/Practical Doer and NT/Thinker-Knower styles from risk. In what ways did their gifts and abilities *match* the essential skills that students must have in order to achieve success in today's schools, given the manner in which that success is most often measured and quantified (i.e., as the result of the abilities to acquire, organize, memorize, and express knowledge in written form; to function well in a structured classroom; to cope successfully with objective assessment and procedural skills; and to work well independently) (see Figure 2.4, pp. 26–27)? By contrast, how were the needs and abilities of SF/Interpersonal and NF/Self-Expressive learners *in conflict* with this essential skill set? Was it that the SF/Interpersonal or NF/Self-Expressive learner was unable to acquire these essential skills, or that he was unable to learn as a result of having to use them? Or was it both?

In Figure 2.4, you will find my comparison of these essential skills to the inherent abilities, preferences, and learner characteristics of each learning style. Making this comparison helped further illuminate style-based areas of conflict as well as congruence.

FIGURE 2.3

Comparing SF/NF and ST/NT Style Pairings in At-Risk and General Populations

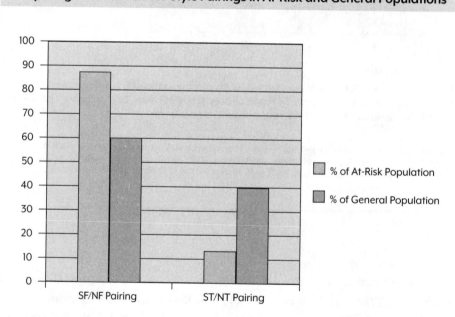

Note: The SF/NF style pairing represents 87% of the at-risk population; the ST/NT style pairing represents 13% of the at-risk population.

Source: Data from *MBTI Manual* (3rd ed.) (p. 298), by I. Briggs Myers et al., 2003, Mountain View, CA: CCP. © 2003 by Briggs Meyers, McCaulley, Quenk, and Hammer; and *Boredom and Its Opposite* (presentation at the ASCD Conference on Teaching & Learning, Atlanta, GA, Oct. 20, 2007), by H. Silver. © 2007 by H. Silver. Adapted with permission.

It was immediately evident that the needs and abilities of learners with the ST/Practical Doer style and the NT/Thinker-Knower style are highly congruent with the essential skills students need to achieve academic success. Students with these learning styles are knowledge-oriented, work well independently, and deal competently with objective assessments. Both respond with a high degree of proficiency when asked to learn and demonstrate information acquisition or skills in an objective format that is logically organized. Conversely, the characteristic needs and abilities of learners with the SF/Interpersonal style or NF/Self-Expressive style may put them at risk in the same classrooms where many ST/Practical Doers and NT/Thinker-Knowers thrive. SF/Interpersonal and NF/Self-Expressive learners acquire and process information in markedly different ways than do ST/Practical Doer and NT/Thinker-Knower learners, and this makes "doing school" a challenge, especially as the grade level increases.

The primary reason for this school-versus-style conflict resides in an SF/Interpersonal or NF/Self-Expressive learner's need to connect with what he is learning before he learns *so that he can learn it*, a process that takes extra time for both the student to do and the teacher to accommodate. Although an SF/Interpersonal or NF/Self-Expressive learner can accomplish this task in a number of ways, the following three are perhaps the most typical: (1) by working interactively with others, which generates an interpersonal connection that provides an opportunity for these learners to develop personal meaning as a result of dialogue and shared experience; (2) by forging a personal connection to the information itself (i.e., linking it to his experience, values, or a larger purpose that holds personal meaning); or (3) by engaging with the information in a manner that is aesthetically pleasing and which results in a personal expression of the content or skill. Regardless of the approach, however, these kinds of connections are the means by which these learners are best able to engage in the process of learning.

In the story following Figure 2.4 on page 27, notice how Zak, whose learning style profile includes both SF/Interpersonal and NF/Self-Expressive characteristics, attempts to engage in a math lesson by personalizing the information (SF/Interpersonal), connecting it to his inner emotional framework and interacting with it in an aesthetically pleasing way (NF/Self-Expressive).

FIGURE 2.4

Style Strengths Compared with Essential Skills for Academic Success

SF/Interpersonal CONNECTING

· Focused on interacting
· Interested in facts about people
· Learns by talking, sharing, and completing tasks with others
· Makes sense of information by forging personal connections
· Provides "service" through personal support
· Sympathetic, supportive, loyal
· Wants contributions to be recognized
· Wants to be appreciated for self

↑

Shared "F" Qualities

· Cooperative (dislikes competition)
· Decisions based on feelings (relative values or merits)
· Desire for harmony
· Difficulty justifying decisions logically or sequentially
· Likes to work with others
· Personal warmth
· Relies on relational skills
· Responds to learning through feelings, values, personal interactions
· Sensitive to reactions of others; needs to feel liked and safe

↓

←Shared "S" Qualities→

· Fact-oriented
· Focuses on the here and now
· Linear (step-by-step)
· Makes sense by making connections to reality
· More successful during steady work (tasks and information chunked)
· Perceives concretely through senses
· Preference for learning through action
· Service-oriented
· Strong observational skills

Essential Skills for Academic Success

The following skills support academic success as measured in our schools:

· **Comfort with acquisition of decontextualized facts, information, and skills**
· **Digests information by reading**
· **Facility with objective assessment**
· **Follows written directions**
· **Organized, sequential**
· **Self-directed, task-oriented**

ST/Practical Doer MASTERING

· Comfortable with routine
· Focused on doing well
· Interested in facts about things
· Makes sense of information by forging mechanical/systems-based connections
· Pragmatic
· Provides "service" through task completion
· Responsible, steady
· Systematic
· Wants immediate results and feedback

↑

Shared "T" Qualities

· Analytical, organized
· Competitive
· Dispassionate
· Interested in and capable of handling details
· Likes to work alone
· Logical, cause-and-effect thinker
· Needs to be treated fairly
· Objective and logical decision maker (nonpersonal, impartial, neutral; bases choices on criteria or standards)
· Strong need for accuracy

↓

FIGURE 2.4

Style Strengths Compared with Essential Skills for Academic Success (continued)

NF/Self-Expressive IMAGINING	←Shared "N" Qualities→	NT/Thinker-Knower APPLYING LOGIC
· Enthusiastic · Focused on complexities of human interaction, insight · Highly attuned to emotions and motivations of others, empathetic · Inductive problem solver · Looks beyond facts to symbolic meaning · Makes sense of information by forging connections to human values/larger purposes in life · Thinks metaphorically	· Approaches tasks with bursts of energy · Bored by routine · Delights in problem solving · Gift for spoken and written word · Global (holistic, conceptual) · Pattern seeker · Perceives intuitively by making mental connections · Prefers to do things in "own way" · Seeks possibilities (associations, future potential) · Thinks abstractly	· Analytical · Deductive problem solver · Enjoys knowing and passing knowledge to others · Focused on intellectual prowess · Makes sense of information by forging theoretical connections · Skilled at strategic planning · Systems thinker · Sets high standards and expectations for self and others

Source: Data from *MBTI Manual* (3rd ed.) (pp. 40–44, 64), by I. Briggs Myers et al., 2003, Mountain View, CA: CCP. © 2003 by Briggs Myers, McCaulley, Quenk, and Hammer; and *Learning Styles & Strategies* (p. 57), by H. F. Silver and J. R. Hanson, 1996, Ho-Ho-Kus, NJ: Thoughtful Education Press. © 1996 by Silver and Hanson. Adapted with permission.

Zak

Zak is creative and inventive, and always produces original work. He often responds to what we are learning in a different way than other kids do. When he's working on a math word problem, for example, he turns it into a story (in which he is often the main character). Somehow, this helps him to make sense of the problem and helps him "get into it." He has a strong need for fairness in the way he and other students are treated, and this comes out even in math! He might comment that it just doesn't seem fair that "x is less than y." And when we are making graphs or other representations of data, he never wants to make the graph just about the data. He will get out colored pencils and make the data more interesting visually by adding colors or patterns in some way. It's not that he's "decorating," but more that he's using color and patterns to make working with the data more palatable. I think it helps him remember it, too. It's not unusual, in fact, for him to explain something in class by drawing a picture of it rather than using numbers or words.

Source: Adapted from an original submission by Lori Downer, Columbus, OH. Used with permission.

As the grade level increases and the content and skills become more difficult to master, we further limit the opportunity for SF/Interpersonal and NF/Self-Expressive learners to "do school" successfully by eliminating chances for learners like Zak to develop these essential connections (Hanson & Dewing, 1990).

The Teacher-Student Style Dynamic

Looking at school-versus-style factors from a slightly different perspective, I also realized that style conflicts within the teacher-student relationship might undermine a learner's ability to function successfully in the classroom. Simple as the following scenarios are, each illuminates how style conflicts between the teacher and the student may unwittingly lead to a boy's misbehavior and underachievement (as well as the teacher's frustration).

For each scenario, I have chosen one exemplar from each of the style descriptions introduced previously to "play" the part of the student: Robin Williams as the NF/Self-Expressive student, Garrison Keillor as the SF/Interpersonal student, William F. Buckley as the NT/Thinker-Knower student, and John Wayne as the ST/Practical Doer student. I encourage you to replay each scenario imagining both male and female teachers for each style.

Scenario 1

Student:

  Style: NF/Self-Expressive

  Exemplar: Robin Williams

Teacher:

  Style: ST/Practical Doer

In Teacher ST's 3rd grade math classroom, the mastery of facts, memorization of algorithms, and practice, practice, practice are the focus of daily instructional routines. Teacher ST might see NF/Self-Expressive learner Robin as a daydreamer with poor study skills and a lack of motivation. Robin's seemingly endless "What if?" questions might be viewed by Teacher ST as pointless and irrelevant attempts to distract or even embarrass him or her. Robin's earnest attempts to work sequentially might be overlooked by Teacher ST when Robin is still unable to demonstrate mastery during homework, quizzes, and tests. Even though Robin is getting better at remembering the steps he needs to use, he still forgets sometimes. This doesn't make sense to Teacher ST, who believes that once a procedure is learned, it "stays learned." Because Teacher ST doesn't give credit for partially correct work, Robin's efforts are not valued. Lack of measurable success equals failure, and failure is attributed to lack of effort. At some point, Robin may stop trying, turning his remarkable brain toward causing trouble instead of learning math. Teacher ST might believe that Robin is a lazy learner who doesn't care about learning math and who disrespects both the discipline of mathematics and Teacher ST.

Scenario 2

Student:

Style: SF/Self-Expressive

Exemplar: Garrison Keillor

Teacher:

Style: NT/Thinker-Knower

Teacher NT is a 12th grade history teacher who focuses classroom learning activities on examining the principles of historical conflict. Teacher NT engages students in extensive study of historical documents, Socratic discussion, and debate as a means of examining the theories of cultural change and the role of conflict in human history. SF/Interpersonal learner Garrison would probably long to put a human face on the principles and ideas about which Teacher NT so often talks. At first, the small-group discussions and debates might be fun and energizing for Garrison. He might even begin to make sense of the complex ideas that Teacher NT values so highly when he is able to process what he hears and reads via discussion with other students in his group. His ability to lighten things up with a story or a joke solidifies his position as a contributing member of his group, something especially important to Garrison when he starts to feel that his peers don't have the same problems that he does understanding the reading assignments. But when Teacher NT announces that group work isn't about having fun, and when his chance to take part in a debate depends on outlining his position in detail before ever getting the opportunity to discuss it with others, Garrison might begin to lose interest and find the work and the written documentation overwhelming. Without the opportunity to bounce his thinking off of his peers, he might have trouble figuring out what he wants to say, and his work might seem incomplete and disorganized as a result. Once he falls behind, Garrison might begin to take some pleasure in upsetting Teacher NT, and his trips to the office would relieve his boredom and give him some social status.

As these first two scenarios suggest, SF/Interpersonal learners and NF/Self-Expressive learners may be especially at risk in classrooms run by teachers with opposing styles. It would be easy for these teachers to misinterpret the SF and NF students' behaviors and attitudes because they are so different from their own.

Although the SF/Interpersonal or NF/Self-Expressive learner is more at risk in general, the ST/Practical Doer or NT/Thinker-Knower can experience equally debilitating teacher-student style conflicts in the classroom. These learners—who typically find the experience of "doing school" to be a good fit for their abilities—may nonetheless encounter difficulties if their styles do not match those of their teachers. Consider the next two teacher-student scenarios.

Scenario 3

Student:

 Style: NT/Thinker-Knower

 Exemplar: William F. Buckley

Teacher:

 Style: SF/Interpersonal

Teacher SF's 6th grade classroom interactions are built around collaborative group work, during which students routinely process their thinking and develop their writing skills in the context of cooperative learning activities. In variously structured small groups, students generate ideas, edit one another's rough drafts, and share their finished work. Imagine what it might be like for young NT/Thinker-Knower William F. Buckley to function as a learner under these conditions. Though William would be much happier working independently, Teacher SF requires all students to work in small groups, a situation that William might dread for several reasons. He might dislike letting others (whom he considers less well-informed than he) see his work or give him feedback. Neither would he be likely to enjoy spending his time giving feedback to other students if he feels they cannot understand or appreciate his perspective or insights. It might seem illogical to William to repeat what he views as an unproductive learning experience—and even a colossal waste of his time—again and again. He might express his frustration passively by becoming intentionally obstinate or aloof in his groups, either refusing to give his classmates help or doing so in a manner designed to confuse or mislead them, hoping that if he alienates others, he will be allowed to work alone. Teacher SF and many of William's classmates might view him as selfish and uncooperative. William would have difficulty understanding why Teacher SF lowers his grades for something as trivial as his lack of participation, and Teacher SF might eventually find it hard to remain patient and understanding with this boy, who seems to value his own possession of knowledge more than sharing it in a community of learners.

Scenario 4

Student:

  Style: ST/Practical Doer

  Exemplar: John Wayne

Teacher:

  Style: NF/Self-Expressive

In Teacher NF's 9th grade science classroom, students are urged to see science's potential for solving real-world issues that are important both globally and locally. Teacher NF believes that by providing a platform for experimentation and trying out new ideas, students will find personal meaning during the learning process. In this classroom, science is viewed as a springboard to creativity and self-expression through the use of projects, experiments, and problem-based learning. Currently, Teacher NF's focus is on using science to promote and support "green" or ecological living. ST/Practical Doer John might cringe each time he hears Teacher NF say something like, "Try something new and see what happens. Use your imagination!" As someone who values clear goals and directions, John might well be frustrated by what seems to him to be a disorganized free-for-all. Although it feels risky to question his teacher, John nonetheless is compelled to ask Teacher NF what is right or wrong about his work. When Teacher NF responds with a question of his own (e.g., "Well, John, what do you think is right or wrong?"), John might feel embarrassed or angry that he can't get a straight answer about what he's supposed to be doing and how to do it. When others receive praise from Teacher NF, John might try to model his work after theirs, using their ideas as his framework for achieving success. He might feel confused when his strategy receives the opposite of his hoped-for reaction from his teacher, who would likely view John's efforts as "copying" rather than as "modeling." During discussions or brainstorming activities, John might feel safer just clamming up and saying nothing, drawing pictures of the motorcycle he wants to build instead of listening. Teacher NF might see John as a slow and uninspired learner with little hope of thinking on his own.

As Abraham Maslow once famously said, "If you only have a hammer, you see every problem as a nail." In other words, if we, as educators, view our underachieving boys' behaviors, attitudes, and choices through the narrow lens of our own style, we can aggravate the teacher-student style conflict by attributing negativity where none is intended or interpreting behaviors to be the result of attitudes that don't exist. When we take into consideration the elements of power and control inherent in the teacher-student relationship, it is easy to see how a conflict of styles might amplify the traits of the involved styles as each party attempts to respond to the other, in some cases increasing the conflict.

I want to emphasize that the classroom conflicts you observed in these four scenarios are the result of style dissonance rather than gender-based discord between teacher and boy. As I hope to make clear in many ways throughout the following chapters—and as research bears out—the ability to reach and teach underachieving boys is not dependent in any way upon a teacher's gender. Just as I do not pit boys against girls in describing potential reasons for the underachievement of many boys in our schools, neither do I wish to suggest that a teacher's success in responding to underachieving boys is dependent on his or her gender. There is no innate "mismatch" between male students and female teachers (or between male teachers and female students), any more than there is a magical "match" between male teachers and male students (or between female teachers and female students). A teacher's gender does not guarantee that a boy will be able to learn from him or her better or less well. The research, in fact, indicates that few boys believe that gender has any bearing on a teacher's effectiveness (Alloway et al., 2002; "Canberra," 2002). As we will explore in depth in Part II of this book, "excellent teaching style 'is not dictated by gender' but [by] a range of attitudes and abilities" ("Canberra," 2002, p. 160).

Milepost

The more I examined the possible connections between style conflicts and underachievement in boys, the greater my belief that it was essential to seek a broader perspective about the school-versus-style dynamic. It also seemed plausible that some of the acting out, disrespect, or shutting down we see among our underachieving boys of all learning styles might be the result of a style conflict. At the very least, broadening our perspectives about the motivations behind boys' behaviors—especially those we view as irritating or intentionally disruptive—is helpful because it allows us to understand these behaviors in ways that are both less negative and less judgmental.

At this point in my research, I couldn't yet say with certainty that the apparent conflict between style and the way we "do school" was causing so many boys to underachieve, but I felt there were compelling reasons to continue exploring the connections between being a boy, his style, his risk as a learner, and his academic underachievement.

First, it seemed increasingly evident that the combination of gender and style could put a boy at risk—especially if that style was either SF/Interpersonal or NF/Self-Expressive. Looking over data related to gender distribution among the various learning styles, I noted that 1.5 times as many girls as boys fall under the SF/NF pairing (Myers et al., 2003). So if "being at risk" were simply a matter of school-versus-style conflicts, we would logically expect to see more SF/NF girls than boys experiencing difficulties in our classrooms. Yet this is plainly not the case, as evidenced by the preponderance of boys at risk in our schools—in special education classrooms, identified as having learning disabilities, named on retention lists, and populating our detention halls and dropout rosters (Alloway et al., 2002; "Canberra,"

2002; Eliot, 2009; Rennie Center for Education Research and Policy, 2006; Younger & Warrington, 2005). I wondered why having either the SF/Interpersonal or NF/Self-Expressive style might cause problems for boys in the school setting that are apparently not experienced to a similarly detrimental degree by girls with these styles. What other factors might be at work?

Second, it became increasingly clear that boys with the SF/Interpersonal and NF/Self-Expressive styles are more often at odds with the experience of "doing school," in contrast to their ST/Practical Doer and NT/Thinker-Knower counterparts, who frequently thrive in the school setting. Although the various styles are represented almost equally within the general population (Myers et al., 2003), the at-risk status among the groups is wildly disparate.

Third, I came to see how educators might be as much a part of the problem as we are the bearers of its solution. Our style-based preferences and resulting instructional choices may well affect the learning success of our underachieving boys in ways many of us have not previously considered, particularly in regard to how these learners experience school. The more we understand about both, the greater our chances of effecting positive change for them.

Finally, my purpose here is not to use style to label or to separate boys and their particular needs in a manner that demeans or suggests that one style is better than another. Rather, I use these style groupings to identify and illuminate one reason why some boys struggle when others don't and to help explain why those who struggle do so in different ways and for different reasons. Remember that all learners possess characteristics of each style to some degree. With a basic understanding of the various learning styles and how their dominant characteristics might affect behavior and academic comprehension, we have a common language to discuss the problems of underachievement and understand the nature of seemingly contradictory achievement outcomes. As you go through this book, you will find many illustrations and explanations that will help you to differentiate among the relevant characteristics of each style and see how those characteristics contribute to or interfere with a boy's ability to function successfully in the classroom.

Note to the reader: If you are interested in learning more about your own style, several inventories are available on the Internet. The Kiersey Temperament Sorter (www.kiersey.com) is based on the Myers-Briggs Type Inventory core functions, and the Kiersey site offers several inventories. You may also wish to visit the Cognitive Profile website (www.cognitiveprofile.com), where you will find another inventory based on the MBTI core functions as well as additional information regarding learning needs, preferences, and habits characteristic of each style.

What's Next?

In addition to the style dynamic, a second, equally important factor emerged from my research: a gender-based factor with nearly universal influence on learning. Whereas the underlying style dynamic between teacher and student helps us to understand conflicts between how we teach and how students learn, an exploration of the cultural influences surrounding masculine identity building helps us understand conflicts within the social fabric of our classrooms, especially in regard to peer-to-peer influences. Like the style dynamic, this classroom-based factor encompasses multiple facets of the classroom context and illuminates new perspectives about how and why some boys are unable to reach their potential as learners.

CHAPTER 3

The Invisible Background: Cultural Expectations for Masculine Identity Building

I worry about bullies. I worry about the narrow construction of masculinity in our culture that views deviance as "queer." I worry about hierarchies that always put athletes on top. I worry about the boys who don't fit this narrow definition, who are oppressed by the "boy code." I worry about schools so big that kids get lost in them.... But my main worry is about boys who are alienated from school itself.

—Thomas Newkirk, author and professor
at the University of New Hampshire

In addition to the style dynamic, a second and equally important "contextualization of the situation for boys" (Weaver-Hightower, 2005, pp. 2–3) exists within a set of cultural expectations for masculine identity building that I would never have dreamed could affect boys' achievement in school so significantly. The influence of these expectations stretches across demographic, racial, and socioeconomic divides (Pirie, 2002) and is often unknowingly reinforced by teachers themselves. The result is an entrenched and socially codified force that works against boys' academic achievement. Like a detailed transparency laid over an original image, this second classroom-based factor adds clarity to the dynamic that results from conflicting styles, furnishes additional ways to discern more fully why boys are struggling, and helps us to more clearly appreciate why the SF/Interpersonal and NF/Self-Expressive boy may experience the negative impact of these cultural expectations even more intensely.

As is true for almost any consistent yet largely unexamined element of our daily lives, this classroom-based factor has a heightened ability to exert its influence steadily—almost without notice—because of its accepted normalcy. It simply does not register on our radar when thinking about academic underachievement. Unlike learning styles, it is not linked overtly to how or what we teach, rendering it nearly invisible, which makes its influence even more detrimental to learning, especially among boys who are already struggling in other ways.

The following excerpt from an Australian report on improving educational outcomes for boys provided my first glimpse at what these cultural expectations were all about and how they affected a boy's ability to function as a successful learner in the classroom:

> The issue of fear of failure is particularly pertinent to boys and their construction of gender. For boys, fear of failure operates across a number of domains. It relates to fear of not living up to popular images of masculinity, fear of being labeled a sissy or seen as feminine in any way, fear of powerlessness, and fear of having their sexuality questioned. In the learning domain, boys have been found to be unwilling to attempt new learning when they are uncertain of success and are less likely to re-attempt something that they had previously been unsuccessful at....Many of the problems boys experience during their education can be traced to their frustration and feelings of inadequacy in attempting to live up to what they believe their peers and society generally expect of them as males. (Martin, 2002, p. 62)

Armed with this new awareness of how trying to live up to society's definition of masculinity can affect boys academically, I eventually identified three interrelated factors, one primary and two secondary. Both of these secondary factors feed off of and support the primary factor, but all three affect boys' ability to learn in potentially devastating ways.

Factor No. 1: The Boy Code

From the minute boys enter our classrooms, masculine identity building is taking place in one form or another. At some level, teachers and students, both male and female, often act in accordance with a set of unspoken tenets that are subtly or explicitly reinforced through tacit approval, willing indifference, or a lack of awareness. William Pollack (as cited in Neu & Weinfeld, 2007) calls this set of culturally embedded expectations about masculinity the Boy Code. An examination of this "code" yields new insights about the troublesome behaviors exhibited by many struggling boys in our classrooms and reveals why boys with certain styles (SF/Interpersonal and NF/Self-Expressive, specifically) might experience its negative impact more deeply than their peers.

In their book *Helping Boys Succeed in School*, educators Terry Neu and Rich Weinfeld (2007) capture Pollack's Boy Code in the form of a "dos and don'ts" poster.

1. Do not cry (no sissy stuff).
2. Do not cower, tremble, or shrink from danger.
3. Do not ask for help when you are unsure of yourself (observe the code of silence).
4. Do not reach for comfort or reassurance.
5. Do not sing or cry for joy.
6. Do not hug your dearest friends.
7. Do not use words to show tenderness and love. (2007, p. 24)

As a female who grew up without brothers or close male friends, I had never given much thought to how boys are affected by society's restrictive set of "rules" regarding acceptably masculine behavior. Further, I was disturbed by the extent to which I and so many other educators tacitly accepted these rules—though we might not have been able to express them as clearly as Neu and Weinfeld—as representative of how "real men" are supposed to behave. A real man "likes to drive fast and take risks.... He likes to display his muscles, not his emotions...and he certainly doesn't cry.... He's not a sissy and gets insulted if you call him a 'girl' or a 'woman.' Soldiers, athletes, and superheroes are the archetypes of his dreams.... He would rather fight than talk because he likes action better than words. And he knows that reading books is something girls do" (Pirie, 2002, p. 16). This caricature of a "real man" would be laughable were it not for the fact that television shows, movies, video games, and cartoons also model these behaviors over and over. In a typical boy's life, similar messages are reinforced thousands of times. And I was discomfited by the realization of how little effort we spend on discounting or diminishing the veracity of such expectations in the eyes of those most susceptible to these unexamined "truths" about male behavior.

The following vignette, as do the others presented in this chapter, illustrates one aspect of the Code's influence. Each story describes a real-life scenario as related by the boy's teacher or parent. To maintain the anonymity of these boys, I changed their names and have listed their teachers or parent separately from the vignettes they contributed (which is unlike the pattern of attribution you will find in the remainder of the book.) The names of the educators who generously gave permission to share their stories in this chapter are as follows: Diane Bolles (Enumclaw, WA); Lynnett Burroughs (Williamsburg, KS); Rob Erhart (Middletown, OH); Kimberly Gessler (Camas, WA); Laurie Hager (Williamsburg, VA); Joy Kiedrowski (Cleveland, OH); Suzanne Obuchowski (Newburyport, MA); Nate Parsons (Crestline, OH); Cynthia Scott (Middletown, OH); and Christopher Ward (Grove City, OH).

Toby, Grade 5

Toby was on his scooter this past summer, playing with a group of neighborhood kids. He did some sort of jump and landed squarely on both knees. He immediately jumped up and yelled, "I'm OK!" and then proceeded to casually saunter to our house with blood running down both legs. As soon as he was inside, he began crying and telling me how much it hurt. But he certainly didn't want anyone outside to think he couldn't handle pain. He also has an extreme aversion to going to the nurse at school. When he fell at recess and his elbow was bleeding, his teacher insisted he go to the nurse. Knowing he'd rather collapse on the floor than go to the nurse, I asked him what he did and he said, "I went to my locker, put on my sweatshirt, used that to soak up the blood and went back to the classroom." He also added that he spent a long enough time at his locker to make it seem as though he had been all the way to the nurse's office and back!

I discovered that the greater danger in regard to the Code's impact on learning is that these stereotypical expectations do not solely affect everyday, on-the-street, how-to-be-a-boy behaviors. They also send a message about how real men, and thus boys who want to be real men, are supposed to view school and learning. According to the Code's expectations, not only are boys supposed to behave like superheroes and hide their emotions, but they also do not want to be perceived as smart, always fight instead of talking through a conflict, and do not enjoy reading or writing. Displaying any of these "unmanly" behaviors—demonstrating intelligence, being articulate or adept at conflict resolution, showing emotional sensitivity, reading and writing well—results in a boy being labeled a sissy.

One of the more compelling explanations for the prevalence of this stigma consists of four linked factors, each of which reinforces negative attitudes toward literacy from a slightly different perspective: (1) the growing absence of positive male role models, (2) a concurrent overabundance of hypermasculine, antihero models in the media, (3) an unspoken understanding that boys who follow the Code are never homosexual, and (4) an acute fear of being labeled as different. Without the benefit of a counterbalancing model of masculinity from which to gain perspective, the definition of acceptable masculine behaviors increasingly narrows, and the differences between what females do and what males do become even more rigidly prescribed (Martin, 2002). One author used the phrase "dichotomized gender absolutism" (Jackson, 1998, pp. 91–92) to describe this phenomenon, in which anything "not overtly male"—overtly male including "such qualities as restrictive emotionality, concern with power and status, excessive self-reliance, homophobia, anti-authoritarian bravado, anti-intellectualism, and non-relational attitudes toward sexuality" ("Canberra," 2002, pp. 59–60)—is by definition feminine.

Sadly, because many girls are successful at tasks requiring literacy skills—reading, writing, and speaking among them—boys often purposely shun such tasks in order to avoid being associated with anything feminine or "girly," thereby stunting their ability to master the kind of skills necessary for success in school and, arguably, outside of school as well. Boys who possess a natural affinity for literacy-based tasks are often rejected, labeled, and isolated if they demonstrate interest or ability in using these "feminine" skills, because it means they are acting like a girl and, by association, might be "gay."

Early on in a boy's school experience, he hears the word "gay" used to label other boys in the most derogatory way possible and to set them apart as different. Thus, before they know what the word really means, even the youngest learners understand that being gay is seen as something negative, something they do not want to be associated with, and they quickly figure out what behaviors will result in being labeled as gay. Accordingly, they come to believe that following the rules laid out in the Code will protect them from such teasing and rejection.

Raphael, Kindergarten

I had one little boy who had trouble with writing and basic letter sounds and soon fell behind. He knew he was already being labeled as "dumb" by some of the boys, so he tried unsuccessfully to fit in by doing some of the competitive things he saw them doing, like turning his work in first. When he realized that racing to finish first had no value unless he also did his work correctly, he became even more agitated and looked for a different way to gain status.

He began to call the girls names with the hope that this would somehow give him status with other boys. This backfired, too, for when the smarter boys he so longed to associate with distanced him even more as a result of his behavior, he was again desperate to find a way to fit in somehow.

His next tactic was to turn against the smarter boys who had shunned him and get some of the other struggling boys to call them "gay." This really hit the mark. He was especially vociferous about these labels on the playground, where kids from other grades might hear him, and this began to give him the status he wanted. The "smarter" boys in his class did not like this, and some of them even began to act out themselves.

When I talked to Raphael about his behavior, I can remember him asking me emphatically, "Don't you know it's not cool to act like a girl?"

The fear of not belonging, and the accompanying anxiety of being different or of being labeled gay or a sissy, is so strong that in and of itself it can, and often does, seriously compromise a boy's ability to function in school

(Reichert & Kuriloff, 2004). Belonging, in fact, is so important that some boys will do almost anything, endure almost anything, and inflict on one other almost anything in order to be "part of the group."

Grade 6 Bullies

I remember a group of older boys in my class who had failed several times and felt that education was a waste of their time. Through bullying, they were able to influence almost every boy in my class. Those students who wanted to learn found it hard to stay focused with this group of five boys consistently harassing them. Several of the boys' grades began to fail in one particular class, which was being taught by a first-year teacher. Several times throughout the year, she left the class unsupervised for short periods of time, but it was long enough for the bullies to walk around hitting and smacking the other less popular, less "macho" boys. Several of these boys became edgy and some began to act out in order to get kicked out of the class themselves and escape the situation without losing face.

Kindlon and Thompson (2000) refer to the behaviors perpetuated in the previous two vignettes as a "culture of cruelty," which is depicted in popular media as normative and then acted out among peers within schools and classrooms. Cruelty, among other behaviors, is permitted, even expected, because it is seen as the price of acceptance (Younger & Warrington, 2005).

If a boy cannot be part of the group or desires to further protect himself from humiliation, he may attempt to set himself apart in ways that are accepted and encouraged by the Code. How better to cover up one's inability to function in an academic setting than by becoming the class clown ("Canberra," 2002) or adopting disruptive, "hyper-masculine" behaviors (Martin, 2002)?

Olin, Grade 7

Olin was in my 7th grade choir class a few years back. He hated choir. He told one of his other teachers at an early point in the year that it was his goal to get in trouble every day. He and a small group of boys would make it a point several times a week to try to do distracting things in choir class. For example, at 12:28 every day, Olin and some other boys would start coughing. One time Olin started passing yarn around the room to make a giant "loom." I did notice, however, that not all the boys were involved, and the boys who either ignored what was going on or failed to participate usually got a "You're so gay" after class.

Paramount among the many fears generated by the Code—fear of being different, fear of being rejected by one's peers, fear of being viewed as weak or a sissy, etc.—is the fear of failure (Martin, 2002). This is especially detrimental where learning is concerned because as a result of this fear, not only are boys less likely to reattempt something at which they have previously been unsuccessful, but they are also less willing to try something new because of the possibility that they *might* fail. By assuming failure before trying, a boy avoids his fear and is excused from the failure itself. Not trying becomes acceptable because it is better than trying and failing, and, consequently, learning is stopped in its tracks before it even has a chance to take hold. Even when a boy does try, he may limit his chances of success by employing defensive pessimism (setting unrealistically low expectations) and self-sabotage (setting obstacles in the path to success).

But what happens if a boy actually *wants* to achieve in school? How does the Code work in this situation?

Daniel, Grade 11

Daniel is an African American boy who grew up in the slums of a nearby metropolitan area. From the time he was little, drugs were prevalent in his environment. Preteen boys in his neighborhood could always earn money by running drugs or by standing watch at a corner while a drug deal went down. The problem for Daniel was that he liked school from the time he started. School made sense to him, and it offered an opportunity to get away from the turmoil of his broken home, where his father was long gone and his mother spent such long hours at work that she had no time, patience, or energy for her five children when she got home. Success in school came fairly naturally to Daniel, and because the other boys didn't see him putting much effort into his work, they joked around about Daniel doing well but left it at that.

As the years passed, however, it became evident that Daniel was actually working to succeed, and the teasing grew harsher. Making matters worse, his teachers were usually white women, so Daniel was perceived as being submissive to the "oppressive race" and the "weaker sex." Initially, Daniel was able to control the situation through the use of his quick humor. When he would play the role of class clown, he appealed to the Boy Code notion that acting out in school is masculine.

But as junior high rolled around, another factor related to race came into play. The boys began to notice that Daniel did not talk like them. Instead, he talked like the white people he watched on television. At this point, he lost his friends and his safety. Although he was routinely attacked, the beatings just convinced him that the boys in his neighborhood were fools. Ironically, it would seem that the torment he received at the hands of the Boy Code actually motivated him to succeed. The effects of the Boy Code are not easily diminished, however; he is still scarred by the sense that his experiences have left him without a race and a culture.

As Daniel's situation indicates, if the boy is smart and African American, the Code makes it especially difficult for him to survive in school (Boyd-Franklin, Franklin, & Toussaint, 2000; Kunjufu, 2007). In addition to the typical exclusionary labels such as nerd, geek, or sissy (and the many other less palatable variations), these boys are often accused of "acting white," and like other boys who choose to do well academically despite enormous and often dangerous peer pressure, they must learn to use coping strategies to avoid the worst of the negativity aimed at them, even to the point of not carrying books or backpacks and refusing to study in public places, fighting, and forming servant-master relationships with bullies (e.g., doing homework or taking tests for bullies in exchange for reduced hazing).

A startling picture emerges regarding the complex ways in which the Code affects learning by playing into a boy's natural need to build and protect his burgeoning masculine identity. It negatively affects his attitudes and willingness to engage in learning on many levels: by labeling literacy or being smart as feminine and, thus, something to be avoided at all costs; by emphasizing being tough and uncommunicative; and by convincing boys to adopt a host of counterproductive hypermasculine behaviors and defensive maneuvering, including the willingness to fail in order to secure a sense of belonging. Its influence is as pervasive as it is pernicious.

Factor No. 2: The Code and Boys' Emotional Fragility

One of the most unexpected insights I encountered in attempting to understand the full impact of the Boy Code is that many boys experience emotions every bit as strongly as girls do (Eliot, 2009). And although boys are expected to "act tough," they are often more emotionally fragile than girls.

Nolan, Grade 11

Nolan was very easily frustrated and was one of those boys who would ball his paper up and throw it away if he made one mistake. He would often tease other boys and engage in what I would call horseplay before class, even though I would constantly tell the boys not to do this. On at least one occasion, he ended up getting hurt and then became quite upset and would not talk for the rest of class. He would also shut down if someone teased him too hard, even though he had no problem saying obnoxious things to other boys in the class.

We've all seen boys like Nolan, who are often on edge, ready to explode at the slightest provocation, unable to handle routine interactions, and overly reactive to slights, either actual or perceived. But we rarely add emotionally fragile to that list.

Saying the words "emotional fragility" in the same breath with "boys" seems like a contradiction in terms when positioned against the common mental image of skinned knees, rowdiness, and physicality. We think of girls as emotionally fragile but rarely boys, and we have been well trained to accept this perception.

Wyatt, Grade 9

I have a student who had a very traumatic experience involving a death in his life who usually acts out very physically when his emotions get the best of him. We have some shared experiences in this regard, so he will talk to me about what is really going on. This has, unfortunately, always come after the physical outburst. Our goal has been to discuss the situation before it becomes too much for him to handle. Today, his emotions were swirling, and I just happened to notice and quickly pulled him out of class to talk to him. I asked him why he did not ask to speak to me as we had discussed. He said he didn't want to get made fun of for asking to speak to me because he couldn't handle his emotions. Here is a boy who would rather end up in a physical restraint situation than break the Code and admit he needs help.

Yet when the Boy Code is in effect and acting tough is reinforced as a boy's only option, the result for many boys is, indeed, emotional fragility. The irony, of course, is that what we perceive as emotional fragility in girls—the frequency and ease of their emotional expression—actually helps girls as a group to develop emotional strength and resiliency. And by contrast, what is often perceived as signifying emotional strength in boys—their stoicism and toughness in the face of fear and pain—is actually a barrier to the healthy development of emotional strength and resiliency. A boy's suppression of his emotional self actually makes it even harder to remain stoic or tough in the face of fear or pain because he is most vulnerable to his emotions under duress, especially if he does not understand what they mean or how to control them (Kindlon & Thompson, 2000):

• He must function with a limited repertoire of emotional responses and consequently is less able to understand or deal with the inevitable conflicts, problems, and changes that he encounters on a daily basis. Molehills become mountains.

• He is less able to interpret and respond appropriately to others, making it impossible to develop the meaningful relationships that are so important to his sense of safety and need to belong. A boy has difficulty maintaining equanimity when he doesn't understand what other people's words and behaviors mean, and that imbalance is exacerbated when he responds inappropriately based on misperceptions of their intentions.

• He is constrained from understanding his own pain or getting help to assuage it, and may therefore turn inward and isolate himself or, conversely, turn outward and act with cruelty, both of which generate further shame, self-hatred, or anger.

• In relation to his ability to learn and process information, such enforced stoicism prevents him from accessing his emotions and feeling empathy, both of which are hugely important to understanding and interpreting literature. Further, the less he communicates, the more he stunts the development of the language skills he needs in order to express himself both verbally and in writing, skills critical to academic success.

Thus, adhering to the Code not only limits a boy's engagement with learning by heightening his fear of being labeled a sissy, but it also heightens his fear of failure, spurs self-protective or deflective behaviors to avoid such failure, and squashes his social skills and emotional resiliency, all of which affect his ability to learn.

Factor No. 3: The Code and the Lack of Positive Male Role Models

As a third avenue of exploration, I considered how a lack of positive male role models might contribute to the Code's pervasiveness and largely unchallenged hold on the lives of many boys.

Joey, Grade 8

Joey grew up in an urban setting with an emotionally distant father and a mother overwhelmed by raising seven children. The neighborhood took care of the family, bringing clothes and food to help them survive. Joey had only one new piece of clothing prior to entering his teens: a new pair of pants for his First Communion. The hand-me-down clothing was the source of his first Boy Code conflict. On his first day of gym class, he showed up to school wearing "girl's" tennis shoes passed down from one of his six sisters. Joey didn't know the difference; he had played with his six sisters for years and didn't have a brother. His mother didn't know the difference, either. But all the other boys knew, and Joey was immediately labeled a "sissy." It didn't help that he was tiny and the youngest boy in his class. For the next eight years, Joey was called progressively worse names, until he came to believe that he must indeed be a "fag," even though he was too scared to ask anybody what one was. He tried sports, but without help from a father, brother, or other role model, he was doomed to failure, and he quickly learned that even trying sports set him up for more ridicule. Any boy who needed to gain status would pick a fight with him; he was the perfect target for bullies.

Multiple researchers point to a boy's lack of male role models as a major factor in his underachievement in school and in life (Alloway et al., 2002; "Canberra," 2002; Martin, 2002; Younger & Warrington, 2005). One author describes what can happen to a boy when he has no mitigating influences on the Code's effects:

> There are now more boys who lack adult male role models, or whose experiences of adult men have been limited to those who are uncommunicative, uncaring, or violent and abusive.... Their exposure to the types of male images available through film, television, magazines and popular sport are not being compensated for by the role of the real-life male figures in their lives. As they get older they will gravitate towards those negative male mentors, peers and behaviors who are best able to duplicate the unrealistic images they may associate with a strong male identity. The media depictions of many sporting heroes and the limited range of masculine values these public images present (strength, toughness, winning) may affect the self-esteem of those boys who do not, or cannot, identify with this type of masculinity. ("Canberra," 2002, pp. 59–60)

In other words, the negative impact of the Code increases when a boy lacks a strong, positive male role model to demonstrate on a daily basis that being a man involves more than adhering to the Code's simplistic, stereotypical version of masculinity. And this is especially true for SF/Interpersonal or NF/Self-Expressive boys, whose self-image can be particularly vulnerable, given their natural inclination toward interests and learning approaches that may not as readily align with the Code's version of masculinity.

Hal, Grade 4

Hal is sensitive, caring, artistic, and struggling since the recent divorce of his parents. His older brother is athletic and tough, and according to Hal, he does not seem to be upset by the family changes. When the boys visit their father, the father and older son choose dark and violent movies; the little guy hates them and is called a sissy when he cries and reports having nightmares brought on by watching these movies. Both the father and older brother tell him that he needs to "man up." When his dad and brother play football and video games and Hal pulls out his drawing materials, he is laughed at by both

older males. Sometimes he tells me he feels sad more days than not. He is certain that his father does not love him and his brother thinks he is a loser. I am
talking about a good-looking, smart, talented kid who is clinically depressed
because of the cruel "boy code."

Further, a boy can experience tremendous confusion when he receives
mixed messages about what being masculine means.

Brent, Grade 1

It seemed like Brent had a split personality. One week, he loved school and did
his best; the next week, he hated school and wouldn't do a thing. I remember
a day when he had been acting out all morning and was spending a good
deal of time in the "thinking spot." The next day, his parents came in for their
scheduled conference. Mom was very sweet and supportive. Then there was
Dad. He was the epitome of macho, dressed in a camouflage sweatshirt and
sporting a chew wad in his cheek. It became very clear why Brent's behavior
was so changeable. He spent one week with Dad and the next with Mom. Dad
was more interested in hunting and sports, and if Brent was having problems
with school it was because his mom and I were too easy on him. During the
conference Brent was really detached and wouldn't talk with me. Then Dad
left. Brent immediately started crying and apologizing. He really did like school
and me, but he knew his dad wouldn't want him to show it. It was a rough year
with Brent. Lots of ups and downs. He ended up going to another school for
2nd grade, and I often wonder what became of him.

A Continuum of Violence and Disengagement

Although every source I consulted when writing this book offered me
valuable insights, an article by Robert K. Pleasants (2007), an educator working in the juvenile justice system, proved to be one of the most illuminating
resources. Pleasants offers suggestions for how teachers might respond to
the many issues at play in the development of their male students' gender
identity, making an essential connection between the violence and disengagement experienced and exhibited by the incarcerated boys with whom
he works and the boys who struggle to achieve in our classrooms. Namely,
the issues that begin in kindergarten and even preschool are at one end of

the same continuum that leads to underachievement, disengagement from school, dropping out, and, all too often, incarceration.

Pleasants asks us to see with the clarity of his experience and perspective that we need to pay attention to this continuum, specifically "the intersections of masculinity and violence, the social networks that positively and negatively affect young men, identity construction, emotional expression, and literacy in the lives of male youth" (2007, p. 249). Boys in traditional schools confront the same issues as their counterparts behind bars—the effects of the Boy Code, emotional fragility, issues of literacy, and the lack of positive male role models—as they struggle to build their identities and learn in our classrooms. It's just a difference of degree and duration.

The implication of Pleasants's message is that if we understand the gravity and scope of the process unfolding in our classrooms, we can intervene and find ways to disrupt the negative influences of the Code, counterbalancing the absence of positive male role models and helping our boys to build academic and social skills along with emotional resilience. This is, in fact, what we will be exploring in the remainder of this book, learning how to help one boy at a time, one teacher at a time, one classroom at a time.

Your mind may well be buzzing right now with questions about what we can do to address a problem that is so entrenched in our culture. As you might suspect, there are no easy solutions, but the good news is that even in the face of a problem with enormous power to influence learning in a negative manner, we can still make a difference. The following chapters hold many ideas about how to address this issue from multiple perspectives. In the meantime, I will leave you with one final story that illustrates how even the simplest efforts to help a struggling boy can have lasting and meaningful results.

Safe Haven

I had a young African American boy in my 9th grade world history class. He never had homework to turn in, and it was affecting his average. I used homework as a way to take the fear out of tests and quizzes. All of my assignments were weighted equally, and so for the poor test taker, there was always a way to bring up the average. I also accepted late homework and redos of any assignment my students completed outside of class. But for this young man, my strategy was not having the desired effect. His test scores were abysmal and he seemingly cared little to raise them by following through with any other assignments. It didn't take me long into the school year to decide I needed to get a grip on this situation.

I saw him before school one day and asked if he would mind talking with me. He was nervous, and I tried to allay his fears as I sat down next to him, explained my worries, and asked him what I could do to help. He seemed thunderstruck that I wasn't blaming him and that I was extending a hand. I started with my usual troubleshooting dialogue that helps me to understand students' organizational habits (or lack thereof), backpack and locker status, as well as the places they choose to study in the evenings. It became quickly apparent that my words were gaining no ground and he looked ahead vacantly. "So let's start with your backpack," I said. "Can I take a look and see how you have your notebooks together?" He replied that he had a backpack, but that he couldn't bring it to school. "Any reason why?" At this, he pretty much scoffed at me and finally turned to look me in the eyes: "Do you know what the kids on my bus would do to me if I carried a backpack? I'd get beat."

Literally, kids who brought school work home on this particular bus route were physically accosted by other kids. It certainly wouldn't take *me* long to figure out that trying to do well at school had harsh physical and mental consequences. I knew from his address that he lived in the public housing projects, and my mind began spinning. How could I beat this system? I told him we could get around this, and he smiled rather sadly at my lack of understanding. "You just don't get it," he said. And he left.

Over the next few weeks, I started to change the way I ran my class. Without singling him out in any way, I let it be known that I was always here in the mornings early, and that anyone was welcome to come in, study, or just put their heads down on the desks until the first bell rang. No pressure, no questions, and I was here if they needed help. Gradually, I also let it be known that I had this big file cabinet available and nothing to put in it. If anyone wanted to keep work in there just as a sort of temporary storage, it was available. And then in this cabinet, I also stuck extra copies of assigned work.

My class stood empty for the first few weeks, and I felt as though my signals to this student and anyone in his same situation were not being heard. And

> then the morning came. He shuffled in, mumbled, "Hey," and headed to the
> file cabinet. To say my heart was in my throat would be no exaggeration. It
> took time, lots of time, but we worked our way into a quiet connection and
> sometimes he even asked for help. He'd always sit far from the door when
> he came in. I suspect he did not want to be spotted, but I tried not to pry. I'll
> never forget his efforts to control his face when I told him that he had passed
> (barely) for the year.

Was this a perfect ending? A warm and fuzzy greeting card moment? Not
exactly, but with a file cabinet and an invitation to be safe, one teacher made
a real difference in one boy's life as he struggled to succeed academically
within the strictures placed on him by the Code. This teacher didn't do the
work for him or promise him anything she couldn't deliver. But she worked
within the limitations of the situation to offer him a way to do his work and
still stay safe. The choice was his to make, and because he made it, he also
owned its positive outcome.

I'd like to think that, just as I did, Robert Pleasants would smile at hearing
this story, which holds seeds of hope for this boy, his teacher, and for all of
us who try each day to make a difference. It is my hope that the remainder of
this book will offer many more such seeds.

Milepost

In this chapter, I shared my explorations into the question of why so many
boys are struggling in our schools by looking closely at the cultural expectations surrounding masculine identity building. Many of the interfering
and unproductive behaviors that characterize the underachieving boys in
our classrooms may now be more clearly understood as very individualized
responses to teachers and peers that depend upon an array of different influences. Style and the expectations laid down by the Boy Code intersect to pre-
dispose boys with the SF/Interpersonal and NF/Self-Expressive styles to be
especially vulnerable to the negative effects of the Code. Further, the absence
of positive male role models intensifies its pervasive negative influence, hob-
bling boys as they are beginning to develop and understand their emotional
selves by restricting them to a narrowly conceived image of masculinity that

interferes with both their academic learning and their ability to embrace the risks necessary for continued growth and ongoing learning, both in and out of school.

We have begun, then, to define what Weaver-Hightower calls "a true contextualization of the situation for boys" (2005, pp. 2–3), realizing in this quest that helping our struggling boys is a complex problem demanding a multifaceted solution. There is no one-size-fits-all-boys solution. Each teacher who reads this book will need to find a different set of possible solutions, because his or her boys struggle in different ways and for different reasons. The blessing hidden within this challenge is that when we are able to see each boy's challenges as unique, we are freed to find and use a whole range of solutions, addressing the larger issue of underachievement in boys as we build a repertoire of effective approaches, one boy at a time.

What's Next?

With a new and broader perspective on who is struggling and why as the foundation, the next chapter offers the decision-making framework I eventually developed for addressing the complexities of the issue in a way that is at once flexible, effective, and practical.

CHAPTER 4

A Long-Term, Integrated, Multifaceted Approach

....

We cannot hold a torch to light another's path without brightening our own.

—Ben Sweetland, author

....

Research for a New Framework

Having found seemingly plausible explanations for why and how boys struggle in school, most notably conflicts among learning/teaching styles and the pernicious effect of the Boy Code on masculine identity building, I next sought research in support of these emerging perspectives. A combination of patience and good fortune led me to a set of invaluable resources that I will henceforth refer to as the "Big Four" (see Figure 4.1). These four large-scale studies address underachievement among boys with both rigor and a breadth of perspective. Throughout the rest of the book, you will find references to the remarkable wealth of information they provided me.

The "Big Four"

Boys: Getting It Right
(aka the Canberra study)
House of Representatives Standing Committee on Education and Training, Parliament of Australia
(2002)

Boys, Literacy and Schooling: Expanding the Repertoires of Practice
(aka the Alloway study)
Australian Government, Department of Education, Employment and Workplace Relations (2002)

Improving the Educational Outcomes of Boys
(aka the Martin study)
Australian Capital Territory, ACT Department of Education, Youth and Family Services (2002)

Raising Boys' Achievement
(aka the Younger & Warrington study)
University of Cambridge Faculty of Education, England (2005)

Three of these resources resulted from massive efforts conducted on behalf of various governmental agencies in Australia, and the fourth was conducted on behalf of the University of the Cambridge Faculty of Education in England.

The first, *Boys, Getting It Right* ("Canberra," 2002)—henceforth, the Canberra study—was undertaken in response to a growing concern among Australian parents and educators regarding an alarming rise in boys' underachievement and disengagement. The study examined these issues from educational, social, and economic perspectives and across grade levels and subject areas. Its authors took care to assert that their examination of boys' underachievement in no way assumed that boys were suffering as the result of previous efforts to increase girls' achievement, nor would any recommendations seek to undermine those hard-won successes. Rather, the study's purpose was threefold: (1) to gain insight about the causes of the problem, (2) to seek out successful strategies used by teachers with boys and girls alike, and (3) to share that knowledge and expertise.

Boys, Literacy and Schooling: Expanding the Repertoires of Practice (Alloway et al., 2002)—henceforth, the Alloway study—focused specifically on difficulties that boys experienced with literacy-related tasks in school. Like the Canberra study, the Alloway study's goal was to identify instructional strategies and interventions with proven success among boys. These key strategies were then implemented across varying educational settings and evaluated for their effectiveness.

Improving the Educational Outcomes of Boys (Martin, 2002)—henceforth, the Martin study—analyzed motivational data from nearly 2,000 boys of middle school age who completed the Student Motivation Scale, an instrument that measures six supportive factors related to learning (self-belief, value of schooling, learning focus, planning and monitoring, study management, persistence) and four factors that undermine learning (anxiety, low control, failure avoidance, self-sabotage). The goal of this study was to prioritize the impact of these 10 factors on boys' academic outcomes and use this information to build a list of recommendations that might either reinforce the positive influence or minimize the negative impact of the factors during learning as a means of improving the educational outcomes of underachieving boys.

Raising Boys' Achievement (Younger & Warrington, 2005)—henceforth, the Younger and Warrington study—examined boys' underachievement during a four-year project that spanned two specific intervals, Stage 2 (elementary school) and Stage 4 (high school), during which test results indicated a marked decline in boys' achievement as compared to girls'. Like the Martin study, the Younger and Warrington study endeavored to pinpoint strategies with the potential for enhancing boys' motivation and engagement during learning.

Three overarching aspects of these studies made their collective findings particularly significant to this book:

• **Scale and rigor.** In Australia, especially, the amount of time, effort, and expertise expended upon the Canberra, Martin, and Alloway studies (whose pages total in excess of 800) confirmed the seriousness with which the country's government approached the issue of underachievement. Considerable effort was made to arrive at an informed decision regarding recommended solutions by looking at a wide range of potential influences, without stereotyping boys' needs or abilities.

• *Breadth and relevance.* The timing of these reports coincided with the proliferation of popular media reports in the United States about boys' academic underachievement, but all four of these reports took a much broader approach to seeking solutions to the problem than anything I saw in any U.S.-based studies or reports. The inclusion of both research and anecdotal evidence culled from extensive interviews with teachers, administrators, parents, and the students themselves underscored the complexity of the issue and the attendant need for a multifaceted response.

• *Credibility.* The degree of congruence among the four reports lent credibility to both the recommended strategies and the findings upon which they were based.

Although I initially doubted that boys in Australia or England experience problems similar to those experienced by boys in American schools, I quickly realized my skepticism was unfounded. The United States, Australia, and the United Kingdom share not only a common language but also a very similar approach to public-funded schooling. Each country requires compulsory attendance through at least age 16. Each also has a mix of public and private schools, and public schools greatly outnumber private schools in all three countries (just 10 percent of schools are private in the United Kingdom, while approximately 25 percent are private in both the United States and Australia). All four studies focused on public rather than private schools, and although both the United Kingdom and Australia have a higher rate of single-sex schooling than the United States, the schools included in the Big Four studies represented a negligible proportion of such institutions. Thus, the overall educational experience examined by the Big Four lined up to a substantial degree with the experience of American students.

Further, educational statistics from all three countries reflect similarly stagnant levels of achievement among boys. These lowered levels of achievement are seen across all demographic groups, from urban to rural settings, with boys from minority populations and low socioeconomic settings most at risk. Teachers and parents express similar concerns about absent fathers, high levels of truancy and grade retention, changes in family structures, the influences of media stereotypes, and too many boys dropping out or in juvenile correction centers (Alloway et al., 2002; "Canberra," 2002; Martin, 2002; Younger & Warrington, 2005). Significantly, the behaviors, attitudes, and learner characteristics mentioned in the Big Four frequently mirror those identified by teachers in the United States (see Figure 1.2, pp. 10–11). Clearly, regardless of the country in which they attend school, many boys are struggling with underachievement in similar ways and their teachers and parents all share similar concerns and offer similar insights about the problem (Alloway et al., 2002; "Canberra," 2002; Martin, 2002; Younger & Warrington, 2005).

Interestingly, I found that the biggest difference between the U.S., Australian, and U.K. educational systems was not related to the boys, their schools, or their problems, but rather to the degree of governmental commitment to addressing the issue of underachievement. In short, both Australia and the United Kingdom outstrip the United States in terms of mounting concerted efforts to find the reasons behind the problem as well as workable solutions with a demonstrated ability to make a difference. Australia's efforts, in particular, remain unparalleled, and the resources available to educators worldwide as a result of its tremendous, long-term investment are invaluable.

A Long-Term, Integrated, and Multifaceted Approach

As thorough and informative as the data in the Big Four were, simply having access to the data provided only the first part of the solution. Although both plentiful and intriguing, the information I had gleaned still needed to be organized and made sense of in a manner that could lead to its flexible use in classrooms at all grade levels and in any subject area. My eventual solution was the gradual development of a decision-making framework that I call "Pathways to Re-Engagement." It takes into consideration the factors I shared in Chapters 2 and 3 (school-versus-style dynamics and masculine identity building), and it provides a means by which each educator can organize, make sense of, and integrate the new ideas he or she finds relevant throughout this book (see Figure 4.2).

FIGURE 4.2
Pathways to Re-Engagement

PATHWAY **1**

Support

Access Points:
- Trusting Relationships
- Nonthreatening Learning Environment

Tools:
Teacher Actions That Build Trust
Leader Coach Model
A Climate of Safety
Shared Principles
* *The 8 Keys of Excellence*
Guidelines for Classroom Policies

PATHWAY **2**
Guide

Access Points:
- Clear Expectations
- Informational Feedback
- Positive Reinforcement

Tools:
Basic Requests for Communicating
Effective Directions in a Nutshell
* *Medals & Missions*
* *Super Strokes*

PATHWAY **6**
Empower

Access Point:
- Engaging Literacy-Building Activities

Tools:
* *Graphic Novels*
* *Enactments*
* *Talking Cards*

PATHWAY **3**
Reinforce

Access Points:
- Tools for Communication
- Tools for Collaboration

Tools:
* *Pragmatic Communication Skills*
* *Roles, Gambits, & Structures*

PATHWAY **5**
Ignite

Access Point:
- Active Learning

Tool:
* *Principles of Active Learning*

PATHWAY **4**
Adjust

Access Point:
- Zones of Comfort

Tools:
Strategies for:
Increased Physical Movement
Increased Social Interaction
Reduced Distraction
Physical Comfort

* *Key Resources*

Source: © 2010 by Kathleen Palmer Cleveland, Big Canoe, GA. Reprinted with permission.

Pathways to Re-Engagement

Responding to underachievement is an ongoing process, for our under-achieving boys as well as for us. Alongside the initial awareness of the complexity of the task comes a secondary realization that, regardless of what we try, not every underachieving boy will respond to the same approaches or become engaged in learning for the same reasons.

As my own response to the enormity of this challenge, I developed the Pathways to Re-Engagement decision-making model. This straightforward and practical model consists of three components: Pathways, Access Points, and Tools. It is designed to help you identify general initial approaches to meeting the needs of underachieving boys (the Pathways); to help you then choose more specific, related approaches that might be most effective (the Access Points); and to provide classroom-based interventions and strategies that address specific problems your underachieving boys may be experiencing (the Tools). Together, the Pathways, Access Points, and Tools may help you to re-engage boys in every aspect of the learning experience.

Pathways. By addressing a general need or shortcoming, each of the Pathways provides an overarching focus for moving an underachieving boy from a position of academic weakness toward his potential strengths as a learner. The six Pathways—Support, Guide, Reinforce, Adjust, Ignite, and Empower—establish the foundation for the Access Points and Tools within that particular Pathway. Choosing a Pathway is a bit like using a cookbook's table of contents to plan a menu. It helps you to get started by organizing your choices into groups of recipes defined by their function (e.g., appetizer, breakfast, entrée, vegetable, dessert). Similarly, the Pathways organize sets of responses to underachievement that share common qualities, and you know that by choosing a particular Pathway, you will locate just what you need without expending unnecessary time and energy.

Access Points. Each Pathway has at least one Access Point. Choosing an Access Point allows you to narrow your focus to a course of action that research has proven to be successful in addressing the larger need pinpointed by the Pathway. For example, under the Support Pathway, you might focus on building trusting relationships with students or creating a nonthreatening learning environment. Think of Access Points as the key recipes within each category of the cookbook, the ones that the experts indicate are essential for any cook to master. They are the foundation for many other recipes, and in learning to use them, the cook builds an essential repertoire of skills that lead to flexibility and expertise. In a similar way, the more Access Points you understand and can use effectively, the greater your ability to respond to emerging problems experienced by the underachieving boys you teach.

Tools. Within each Pathway and its associated Access Point(s), you'll find Tools from which to choose. Tools provide the practical means by which you can actively respond to the needs associated with a Pathway or Access Point. Each Tool offers one or more classroom-based strategies that are easily adapted to multiple grade levels and subject areas. For example, if you want to create a nonthreatening learning environment (Access Point), you might turn to the Tool that offers suggestions for creating a climate of safety or the Tool that provides guidelines for establishing clear and fair classroom policies. Think of Tools as the ingredients for the key recipes. They are the individual components of the recipes that will enable your struggling learners to succeed.

Milepost

The issues of masculine identity building and school-versus-style dynamics—so central to our understanding of how and why the contexts of our classrooms may place some boys at greater risk than others for underachievement—are primary considerations when deciding which Pathway to pursue. The four goals I introduced in Chapter 1 take into consideration both the Boy Code and the school-versus-style conflict and serve as unifying criteria for the Pathways to Re-Engagement:

• *Replace* the struggling boy's negative attitudes about learning with productive perspectives about the role of risk (and even failure) as a necessary and valued part of the learning process;

• *Reconnect* him with school, with learning, and with a belief in himself as a competent learner who is capable, valued, and respected;

• *Rebuild* life skills and learning skills that lead to academic success and also lay the groundwork for success in life; and

• *Reduce* his need to use unproductive and distracting behaviors as a means of self-protection.

Meeting these goals requires reexamining, reframing, and rethinking the problem of boys' underachievement. The ideas, examples, and resources found within each Pathway help us to respond to the needs of these boys, in part, by requiring us to look in new directions, think about familiar problems in new ways, and find new solutions based on our growing insights.

Although each Tool is offered as a means to meet the needs of struggling boys, the benefits of applying these strategies extend to all students—boys and girls alike. It is the inclusive applicability of all the Tools that characterizes this book's approach. It is not necessary to separate boys from girls in order to help underachieving boys. Further, in using these Tools, no learner's prior success (girl or boy) is diminished or undermined. By implementing a Tool, we actually enhance our ability to support *all* students.

You will also discover that the elements within and between each Pathway are connected as well as independent. Do not feel constrained to using just one Tool when it seems as though two or three used in conjunction will more readily achieve the desired results. The lines between Pathways, Access Points, and Tools are not concrete, and overlap, where effective, is highly encouraged. As you work through the Pathways, you will discover what combinations of strategies work best and which strategies work better when employed singly.

What's Next?

The remainder of this book is organized by Pathway. The process of exploring each Pathway and building one's own repertoire of responses is not intended to be quick. It is my hope that you will explore one Pathway at a time, not moving forward to the next until you have savored the first one a bit, allowing its ideas to truly sink in. Talk about the ideas and tools found within this book with your peers, but also be sure to take time to reflect on your personal practices in light of what you learn. It is during such moments of sincere introspection that the deepest insights are sometimes gleaned.

As you explore each successive Pathway, you will encounter four recurring resources designed to gradually deepen your understanding of how best to help your struggling learners: (1) additional insights and research from the Big Four that further illuminate how boys learn best; (2) guidelines for building your professional expertise and skill set; (3) Key Resources you can explore further in an effort to expand both your knowledge and your expertise; and (4) classroom-based stories, examples, and strategies from other teachers that may help or inspire you.

Above all, remain attentive to the message of hope that infuses the whole of the Pathways to Re-Engagement model: hope that despite the complexity of the problem at hand, it is indeed possible to make a difference for our academically struggling boys.

PART II

✖

Pathways to Re-Engagement

CHAPTER 5

Pathway No. 1: Support

....

In order to discover new lands, one must be willing to lose sight of the shore for a very long time.

—André Gide, French writer, 1869–1951

....

Support is the first and most essential of all the Pathways. In many ways, it defines what the Pathways to Re-Engagement model is all about, in that it addresses the overarching question of what we must provide if we want our struggling boys—many of whom have years of failure under their belts—to willingly re-engage in the learning process.

We know from developmental psychologist Lev Vygotsky's work (1978) that optimal learning takes place when a student is able to stretch just beyond his current level of understanding or proficiency. In this new territory lies an optimal degree of challenge that stimulates learning without overwhelming the learner. But a learner who is sensitized to the perils of this stretch by his prior lack of success may feel vulnerable. For him, this stretch into new and unknown territory—where his lack of knowledge or skill might be made painfully public—may appear both greater and more difficult than it really is. His perception is distorted.

We also know, however, that what often helps an underachieving learner overcome the anxiety inherent in this "stretch" is his awareness that there will eventually be a reward for accepting the risk. The feeling of accomplishment that results from accepting the risk and seeing it through balances the initial discomfort (Bernard, Mills, Swenson, & Walsh, 2005).

The obstacle for a struggling boy is that too often he experiences the discomfort of the initial risk without the benefit of the eventual relief of accomplishment. As his experiences with failure continue to diminish his hope for eventual success, it becomes harder for him to willingly re-engage and try again (Black & Wiliam, 1998b). It is no wonder, then, that a struggling boy might be skeptical that "this time will be different." Even a teacher's well-meaning words of encouragement may not be enough to counteract the reality of his past experience.

So, our first task is to help the underachieving boy—who is often highly sensitized to failure—feel safe enough in our classrooms to willingly re-engage in learning. If we can find ways to make him *want* to take that first step back into learning, then we increase the odds that he will continue on until he experiences the joy of accomplishment and recognizes that it is within his grasp. And herein, of course, lies the rub for any reader still hoping for a simple solution to this challenge. There isn't one. The plain truth is that these kinds of intrinsic changes take time because they must happen within the learner. It's hard work, for us and for them.

Though re-engaging an underachieving boy may seem like a nearly impossible task, building trusting relationships and creating a nonthreatening learning environment offer two essential Access Points that scaffold the process in two ways: first, a secure teacher-student relationship encourages the underachieving boy to accept the risks of learning, and second, a supportive classroom culture encourages him to persist through both the trials and the errors of learning without shutting down.

Access Point: Trusting Relationships

We do not believe in ourselves until someone reveals deep inside us that something is valuable, worth listening to, worthy of our trust.... Once we believe in ourselves we can risk curiosity, wonder, spontaneous delight or any experience that reveals the human spirit.

—e. e. cummings

As far as the Big Four are concerned, the quality of the teacher-student relationship is the gateway to helping an underachieving boy find success in the classroom (Alloway et al., 2002; "Canberra," 2002; Martin, 2002; Younger & Warrington, 2005). The powerful force within the teacher-student relationship that swings open that gate is *trust*. Despite initial fears, a struggling boy may be more willing to re-engage if he trusts in two things: first, that his teacher believes he can succeed, and second, that his teacher will provide the support he needs while he is trying.

In Figure 5.1 (p. 70), boys tell us exactly what teacher qualities communicate a supportive attitude and allow this trust to develop.

"The quality of the relationships between students [and] teachers... is crucial to achieving optimal educational outcomes for all students, and this is particularly true for boys" ("Canberra," 2002, p. xx).

"As far as boys were concerned, motivation, engagement, learning, and achievement would go a long way if significant time, energy, and resources were directed to strategies to enhance and then maintain a good relationship between students and teachers" (Martin, 2002, p. 126).

"If a teacher met even one of these conditions in the eyes of the students, the boys tended to respond positively and to learn from and work hard for that teacher. When teachers failed to hold up their end of the bargain, the students echoed Herb Kohl's famous book title: 'I won't learn from you'" (Smith & Wilhelm, 2002, p. 99).

FIGURE 5.1

Tool: Teacher Actions That Build Trust

Teacher-to-Boy Interactions

- Attends to my interests in some way
- Cares about me individually
- Easy to talk to
- Helps me feel OK about myself
- Knows how I learn
- Knows me personally
- Knows what I'm feeling
- Listens to me; is understanding
- Listens when I have a problem
- Respects me
- Talks to me about what interests me outside of school

Responses to Misbehavior

- Doesn't hold a grudge
- Fair
- Gives me a second chance
- Has no negative expectations
- Likes me even if I mess up
- Shows no favoritism

Support During Learning

- Encourages me to try again
- Explains work carefully
- Helps me learn and makes sure that I get it
- Helps me learn from my mistakes
- Makes work interesting
- Passionate about and committed to what is being taught

Fear Reduction

- Doesn't humiliate me in front of the class
- Explains policies and why they are being enforced
- Relaxed and can laugh at own mistakes

Source: From *Boys: Getting It Right. Report on the Inquiry into the Education of Boys* (pp. 135–136), by the House of Representatives Standing Committee on Education and Training, 2002, Canberra, Australia: Australian Government Publishing Service. © 2002 by the AGPS; *Teaching the Male Brain: How Boys Think, Feel, and Learn in School* (p. 162), by A. N. James, 2007, Thousand Oaks, CA: Corwin. © 2007 by A. N. James; *"Reading Don't Fix No Chevys": Literacy in the Lives of Young Men* (p. 99), by M. W. Smith and J. D. Wilhelm, 2002, Portsmouth, NH: Heinemann. © 2002 by Smith and Wilhelm; and *Raising Boys' Achievement* (Research Report No. 636) (p. 73), by M. Younger and M. Warrington, 2005, Cambridge, UK: Department for Education and Skills. © 2005 by Younger and Warrington. Adapted with permission.

Trust building isn't solely the result of overt teacher-to-student actions, though these are an invaluable and requisite foundation. From an under-achieving boy's perspective, trust is also measured by a teacher's general reactions to student misbehavior, the kinds of support offered during learn-ing, and the ways in which a teacher understands the fear of failure and helps boys to deal with it.

Thus, rather than thinking of trust building as the result of any specific set of teacher actions, behaviors, and words, we become aware that it is possible to weave a message of trust into virtually any teacher-student interaction—what-ever form it might take—by keeping the qualities laid out in Figure 5.1 in mind. And even though individual educators' behaviors, attitudes, and words may differ greatly, if each educator is proceeding with these qualities in mind, the message received by the struggling boy remains consistent: You can trust me.

Tool: The Leader Coach Model

If the word "coach" came to mind as you read through the list in Figure 5.1, you've identified yet another facet of a trusting teacher-student relation-ship where underachieving boys are concerned. From the world of athletics, we find a model for teacher-student interaction that offers an additional clue about what helps boys feel supported while they learn.

> The leader coach leads by example and gains the trust and dedication of his players....Boys favor a coach who demonstrates a concern for the welfare of individual athletes, promotes a positive group atmosphere, and has warm interpersonal relationships with athletes. This style may mean that the development of a successful athletic program turns into a longer process, but among our interviews with athletes, this style was preferred for the lessons learned beyond the sport. The leader coach actively encourages his athletes on and off the field....The leader coach demands academic excellence in addition to athletic excellence, because his chief goal is for his athletes to succeed in life. (Neu & Weinfeld, 2007, pp. 146–147)

Underlying the primary teacher-student interactions described by Neu and Weinfeld is a complementary focus on building positive life skills. The neces-sity of acquiring life skills along with academic learning is a recurring theme among the Big Four studies (Alloway et al., 2002; "Canberra," 2002; Martin, 2002; Younger & Warrington, 2005), and encouraging and helping boys to master such skills is one of the most purposeful ways in which an educator (male or female) can build rapport and communicate interest in the underachieving boy as a learner *and* as a person. When trust building is combined with an intentional effort to help a struggling boy succeed in life as well as in school, his perception of support is enhanced along with his belief in his competence as a learner.

A leader coach in action. In the following story shared by high school science teacher Lou Kristopson, academic achievement and teacher-student trust grow alongside the life skills his students are practicing.

Building Learners and Leaders

Within each group of two or three students, one student would be the "lab leader," and this role rotated continually. The leader was responsible for conducting the lab; discussing the lab questions, graphs, etc.; understanding the concept behind the lab; and reteaching it to the other members. The leader (as "boss") was also responsible for making sure that when the lab was done, everything was clean and put back exactly as it was found. When a group finished its lab, the leader would call me over for a final inspection. If I was dissatisfied, the leader either resolved the problem or asked one of the other group members to help him or her resolve it. Because I shared responsibility in this way, my labs always went smoothly. The only problem was when more students clamored to be the boss than there were spots available!

Source: Original submission used as adapted with permission from Lou Kristopson, Stow, OH.

In Lou's story, we see a leader coach's support for academic excellence enhanced by the simultaneous development of students' life skills: leadership, responsibility, self-direction, collaboration, and organization (to name a few). His students are jointly empowered as both learners and leaders, developing their competence in two ways, each supporting the growth of the other.

The leader coach role might look very different in an elementary classroom, as we can see in Jan Williams's 4th grade class.

"Growing" Individual Skills

I teach 4th grade. I've always loved having boys in my classroom and thought I was doing a really good job at connecting with them. In the past, I would often share stories about my two sons' athletic experiences (and successes), thinking that all of my boys would relate to sports. I gradually noticed, though, that the more I talked about sports, the more withdrawn several of my boys became. It dawned on me that they were the ones for whom sports was but another challenge they'd never be able to meet (or at least they thought so), so I started to make it a habit to find out the interests of all my students. I started the year with several "all-about-me" kinds of activities and developed a list of student interests that I used throughout the year, intentionally building them into our learning as well as employing them during the informal chats I liked to have.

I also realized that because of my particular learning style—I'm strongly ST (Sensing-Thinking)—I focused a lot on the task at hand and my feedback was mostly corrective. I noticed that when I made a point of commenting on what students were doing well before I suggested a correction, they were more likely to actually listen, and whatever I affirmed became a point of pride that was often intentionally repeated. I also started to take the time to notice and affirm the kids for displaying unique skills that weren't necessarily academic and so weren't often rewarded (e.g., helping someone without being asked, encouraging others during their group work, or just being sensitive when someone was feeling bad or angry). Somehow, even this simple recognition seemed to mean a lot, and though I couldn't prove it, I really think that because the kids felt better about themselves, they were willing to work harder on other things.

I also tried to help students develop new skills. Everyone had a chance to do the class jobs. Because I knew some of the kids would struggle with these tasks, I always spent time teaching the skill explicitly before any student took on the responsibility. In the beginning, I assigned two students to the same task so that if one struggled, the other could support him or her. Gradually, I eliminated this as a requirement and made it into an option. I was surprised how often students still chose to work together and equally surprised about the ways they negotiated the responsibility.

Source: Original submission used as adapted with permission from Jan Williams, Kent, WA.

For Jan, being an effective leader coach meant becoming aware of her own learning style and finding ways to support the styles of her students in new ways. An underachieving boy in Jan's classroom has the opportunity to recognize and appreciate his own individual gifts, develop his skills, and learn how to act responsibly within a community of learners. His trust in Jan's willingness to support him as a learner grows, in part, because the strength of their relationship does *not* depend on how well he does as a student. Paradoxically, this frees him to be more willing to take the risks that will help him develop as a learner, knowing that he will be supported in the process and valued regardless of the outcome.

The leader coach sets high expectations and offers support to the struggling boy as he endeavors to meet them, but the relationship itself is not dependent on the student's academic success. And as the leader coach communicates a genuine concern for the boy as a person, he or she creates conditions for the boy to re-engage in learning. In this seemingly simple cycle, we see the power of the teacher-student relationship to help an underachieving boy move from a position of weakness toward his potential as a successful learner.

Access Point: A Nonthreatening Learning Environment

As both Lou's and Jan's stories indicate, the teacher-student relationship not only builds trust, but it also sets the stage for maintaining a supportive, nonshaming learning environment for underachieving boys. I also hope that you are seeing with ever-increasing clarity that the ability of a teacher to reach and teach an underachieving boy is not a matter of the teacher's gender. What makes a teacher effective is his or her ability to understand the issues a struggling boy may be facing, to build a trusting relationship, and to support him so that he feels safe enough to re-engage in learning.

"Supportive environments require an informed coach-teacher to set the stage and maintain a nonshaming environment for boys. This type of environment accepts the boy for who he is, supports him when he struggles, and lets him know that it is OK to fail, but also challenges boys to succeed" (Neu & Weinfeld, 2007, p. 238).

Establishing a nonthreatening learning environment is an extension of the first Access Point, developing trusting relationships with students. With this second Access Point, however, the relationship exists within the larger context of the struggling boy and his ability to interact, succeed, and feel safe while learning. In short, this Access Point addresses the relationship between the struggling boy and the learning environment, and it expands the concept of relationships into a larger arena that includes social and academic interactions among students and the potential effect of peer influences on the quality of those relationships. Both the Boy Code and style dynamics inevitably come to the fore, influencing how these relationships play out during learning activities as well as within the social exchanges that occur alongside and between structured interactions.

According to the Canberra study (2002), in order to build a classroom learning environment that supports the struggling boy, it needs to be an affirming space in which a boy belongs and feels both respected and valued as a member of that environment. With these criteria in mind, consider how the following three tools work together to establish and reinforce a nonthreatening learning environment in which a struggling boy can thrive academically and socially.

> "It is vital that we strive to build an environment which is affirming for boys. This involves promoting a culture... where leadership, success, acceptance of praise, acceptance of authority and respect for tradition are permissible within the peer culture. Boys must [also] be taught to value empathy, sharing, nurturing, and a sense of community, as well as the traditional values of strength, loyalty, and leadership" ("Canberra," 2002, p. 131).

Tool: A Climate of Safety

Just as the air around us is invisible, yet essential to our survival, the safety of the classroom climate, though intangible, is essential to a struggling boy's survival during learning. Feeling safe reduces his fear of failure and minimizes his need for

> "A safe environment in which mistakes can be made and learnt from significantly reduces students' fear of failure. When students do not fear failure they are prepared to 'have a go,' persist in the face of challenge, and are less likely to engage in self-protective behaviour that can be inimical to success" (Martin, 2002, p. 45).

self-protective behaviors. When he can drop these defensive mechanisms, he can learn better.

A climate of safety may also affect an underachieving boy's ability to pay attention to, acquire, and process what is being taught. Brain research is very clear in this regard: a stressed or frightened brain *does not learn well* (Jensen, 2005, 2008, 2009; Sousa, 2006; Wolfe, 2001). In a nutshell, a learner's brain is "emotionally hijacked" when it perceives imminent danger or distress (Caine, Caine, McClintic, & Klimek, 2008; DePorter, Reardon, & Singer-Nourie, 1999). Note that the

> "When the brain perceives threat or distress, its neural capacity to reason rationally is minimized. The brain is 'emotionally hijacked' into the fight-or-flight mode and operates at survival level. The availability of neural connections and activity actually decreases or becomes minimized in this situation, and the brain cannot [process cognitively]. This phenomenon, known as 'downshifting,' is a psycho-physiological response and can halt learning in the moment and over time" (DePorter et al., 1999, p. 22).

operative word in this description is "perceives." The question of what feels nonthreatening is complicated by the fact that a struggling boy may perceive threat when none is intended or as a result of a stimulus that others may not regard as threatening. Regardless of the source of the stimulus, however, his perception of threat triggers a fight-or-flight impulse, which in turn kicks his brain's functioning into survival mode, effectively short-circuiting cognitive thought processing. Learning stops cold in its tracks because his brain's attention shifts from the luxury of thinking to the necessity of physical preservation. This phenomenon is known as "downshifting," and it happens to underachieving boys in our classrooms every day.

Making matters worse, many struggling boys are already predisposed to feel threatened, downshifting even faster and in response to smaller stimuli. Whether in response to the Code, the reaction to a school-versus-style or teacher/student style mismatch, or the result of any number of combined factors, the more an underachieving boy has experienced threats, failure, feelings of isolation, humiliation, or other emotional pain in his past, the more likely his sensitized brain will react to it in the present. Downshifting occurs more quickly, and the resulting interference with a boy's cognitive learning capacity also lasts longer.

As educators, we cannot see downshifting happen and, even more frustrating, neither can the struggling boy who experiences it. Its detrimental effect on his learning capacity may not manifest until much later, leaving no clues as to the cause of his failure. Adding another layer of frustration, his brain has no cognitive control over when this event might occur. The shift is precipitated on an unconscious level, and no amount of wanting to stay focused will keep it from happening. Imagine, for example, a situation in which a boy is exhorted to pay attention, then threatened that he will fail if he cannot comply. His resulting anxiety triggers downshifting, which ensures that the threatened outcome will occur. Though he cognitively understands the gravity of the situation, he is powerless to control its outcome because "paying attention" is no longer a function over which he has cognitive control once his brain downshifts. We ask him to do something he cannot do and then punish him when, unsurprisingly, he is unable to do it. We may unwittingly place our most stressed learners in exactly this position on a repeated basis, not understanding the causes of their underachievement and blaming them for an outcome they cannot control.

The plain, sad truth is that many of our underachieving boys experience the paralyzing effects of downshifting on a regular basis, compounding other obstacles they may already face as learners. If we cannot and do not create environments in which these learners feel unthreatened and emotionally safe, their ability to learn effectively is continuously compromised through no fault of their own. For these boys especially, a stable and secure learning environment minimizes the likelihood that routine classroom interactions will lead to downshifting events.

Time well spent. Building the foundations for a safe climate within a classroom takes time, and like the teacher-student relationship, its development is the result of baby steps—little efforts made daily, repeated over time. The question, of course, is what do those steps look like? DePorter and colleagues give us one clue when they claim that everything in our classrooms "speaks" (1999, p. 13). Every detail says something about the teacher and the teacher's attitudes toward teaching and learning. Our classroom environments are loaded with these kinds of cues, and consciously or unconsciously, a struggling boy picks up on them, coloring his expectations about whether or not he will feel safe to learn and grow there.

Elementary school teacher Kelly Montgomery knows that students receive some of these cues the minute they walk into the classroom. She establishes a feeling of safety with an everyday routine of welcoming her students first thing each morning, by connecting with them personally in some way during the day, and by acknowledging them individually as they leave.

Hello and Goodbye

I have a simple daily practice of welcoming students to my class when they arrive and also saying goodbye when they leave. When students enter my room, I make every effort (not always easy in light of the many distractions that occur) to stand at the door and greet each one of them by name. As they leave, I say goodbye and again address them by name. I expect the same from them. I know that my students are comforted knowing that I will always, no matter what, be there to greet and make them feel welcome. This is an easy and enjoyable daily event for me.

As a parent, I see an even greater value for this practice. Mornings can be challenging for children at home. An argument with a brother or sister, waking up late, or other little things can be annoying in the morning. A teacher waiting with a calm, inviting smile and a personal greeting sets a tone for each child to feel special and wanted at school. And when students leave, a goodbye and an encouraging personal word from the teacher ensures that children are aware that their teacher knew they were present. And even though they might have been just one member of a larger group for a lot of the day, at least two times that day—at the beginning and the end—they are guaranteed a few private, personal moments with their teacher. I strongly feel that being mindful and consistent in this routine has a very positive impact on the social/emotional climate of my classroom.

Source: Kelly Montgomery, Columbus, OH. Used with permission.

A high school special education teacher shares that, for her, developing a nonthreatening learning environment starts with helping her students value their unique gifts and know that they belong.

Celebrating Differences

I teach 7th–12th grade students with special needs. At the beginning of each year, I try to establish a positive emotional climate in my classroom by celebrating these differences. I have the kids respond to the following journal prompt: "All people are different. What is one difference that makes you special?" I also give the students the option to read their response to the class. I find that this activity establishes a positive emotional climate, teaches tolerance, and helps to set an accepting tone for the school year.

Source: Dani Davis, Clio, MI. Used with permission.

These educators would very likely agree that building a nonthreatening learning environment begins the moment students walk through the classroom door and continues each day throughout the year. It relies on consistency and repetition. Teacher Elaine Duff recalls how her teacher's actions helped her feel safe again and again, perhaps in ways that her teacher was not even aware of.

Ms. Harmon

My 2nd grade teacher, Ms. Harmon, was magic. She always knew how to handle situations of potential conflict. When Keith Johnson grabbed me and kissed me on the mouth—yuck!—under the plastic mistletoe that hung over our classroom door, I slapped him and then began to cry. Ms. Harmon knew just what to say to me to make me stop crying and convince me not to do violence to my classmates, and she knew what to say to Keith so that he would stop waiting by the door to accost every female who came through. Ms. Harmon always remained calm in times of crisis. When Keith Johnson snorted a paper wad so far up his nose that he had to be taken to the emergency room, Ms. Harmon knew just what to say to keep the rest of the class calm and on task.

Now I understand that Ms. Harmon was a teacher who had mastered the art of creating a positive classroom climate. She was a teacher who took the time to know her students. Most important, Ms. Harmon was a teacher who cared.

I grew up in Beech Mountain, North Carolina, in a farming community. Because I lived in a very low wealth region of our county, once a year, donations of toys and clothing were distributed at our school. In 2nd grade, we didn't really understand that this meant we were poor, and Ms. Harmon explained it like it was a fun game, with the prize being free toys. Here's how it worked. We lined up and walked to the gym, where all the toys were laid out. As long as there wasn't a conflict over a toy, we could have any one we wanted.

So, on this particular day when we reached the gym, we ran everywhere, excitedly grabbing trucks and dolls and games. But what did I do? I stood frozen in the middle of all that chaos and excitement because I was afraid. I was an extremely shy child, and situations like this seemed to intensify my shyness. As my classmates ran everywhere and I stood in the middle of the gym trying to fight the fear rising up in me, I spotted a tiny toy grand piano over by the radiator. It was just my size and it was standing there, waiting for me. All the other girls had run for the Barbie dolls, and the boys had run for the Tonka trucks. But I wanted that piano more than anything in the world. All I had to do was walk over and pick it up. But I was too afraid.

At that moment, Ms. Harmon could have let me deal with the situation on my own. With her students running everywhere, she had so much to deal with. She could have ignored the fact that I wasn't brave enough to walk a few steps across the gym. But she didn't. Ms. Harmon noticed me standing there eyeing that piano. She came over to me and she knelt down and looked at me. She asked, "Elaine, would you like to have that piano?" I wanted to speak but no words came out, so I nodded my head almost imperceptibly. Ms. Harmon walked over, picked up the piano, and placed it in my arms. It seems like such a small thing, but it meant so much to me. I wish I had thanked her.

There isn't a dramatic ending to this piano story. I took the tiny piano home, learned to play many songs, and annoyed my mother terribly. I didn't become a music teacher, and today I can't play any musical instrument! But more important than the piano itself is the fact that Ms. Harmon helped me progress; she brought me a long way toward overcoming my shyness that year by treating me in such a gentle way. She knew what I needed. School wasn't such a scary place when she was around.

Source: Elaine Duff, Coats, NC. Used with permission.

Even the simplest of actions on the part of a teacher can have a major effect on the way a struggling child experiences school and whether he or she feels supported. Small efforts repeated over time contribute continually to the child's perception of the way a space feels, and our most insecure and challenged learners may be even more sensitive to the messages these cues convey. Although the teacher may never see the results of such efforts, a student receives and understands these messages, especially when they are given consistently over time. Just as a seed, planted long ago, may suddenly shoot up through the soil, a struggling boy may respond to his teacher's trust-building efforts at an unexpected moment. It's a moment worth waiting for.

Tool: Shared Principles

A second and equally important part of developing a nonthreatening learning environment evolves as a result of joint effort, when the students and the teacher develop the classroom's learning culture *together*. A sense of shared responsibility and enhanced feelings of safety, so critical for under-achieving boys, result when all students in the classroom are willing to support and respect one another.

Yet as important as this willingness is, the teacher cannot force students to invest in the classroom culture and each other. Consistent teacher modeling of relevant behavior is key (e.g., showing respect to students, considering their feelings, being patient, listening, supporting), but creating buy-in to the importance of a mutually respectful learning culture in ways that students understand and willingly embrace is quite another story.

First grade teacher Ann Card approaches the task of building a shared sense of purpose in several ways, and it is something to which she gives attention throughout the year. Because she knows that many of her students don't have the interpersonal skills they need when they come to her at the beginning of the year, she makes a point of teaching these skills, just as she teaches reading or math skills. Ann also communicates to her students important ideas that support the classroom learning community and govern the way they interact with one another.

Goal Setting

Learning culture is so important to me. I spend a lot of time on it throughout the school year. A supportive learning culture has to be nurtured and developed. It has to be taught, just like math and science. The classroom members have to be cognizant of individual differences, accepting of mistakes, and supportive of taking chances. In the beginning of the school year I do several projects that have to do with learning culture. The first is based on the book *Leo the Late Bloomer* by Robert Kraus. Leo is a lion who matures late and seemingly can't do anything that his friends can do. After I read the story to my students, we brainstorm things children learn to do in 1st grade. Each child thinks of something he or she can't do yet and writes a sentence to illustrate what that is. We share these and display them. As the year goes by, we stop to check in and applaud when a classmate has realized a goal. This is the first of many discussions we have about learning at one's own pace, learning styles, talents, special needs, learning English as a second language, and other things that make us unique learners.

Mistakes Are OK

Just as I have a zero-tolerance policy for bullying in any form, I also have a zero-tolerance policy for any type of humor based on mistakes, unless the person who has made the mistake laughs at himself or herself (which is a tricky distinction). I make it clear to the children that mistakes are an integral, necessary part of learning; that I make mistakes, as do all adults and children; and that those mistakes help us grow and learn. When the children get to the point where they realize mistakes are OK and accepted, they are much more willing to take chances. Putting oneself out on a limb to take an academic risk, whether in front of peers, in front of the teacher, or privately in one's own work, is where the true learning happens! I know I have achieved my goal of creating an accepting learning culture when I see risk taking.

Source: Ann Palilles Card, Groton, MA. Used with permission.

In some classrooms, students acquire a general sense of their class's shared principles without any specific labeling of these principles. The teacher consistently models the principles and communicates their value. For many children, this is enough. However, where struggling boys are involved, the potential positive impact of having an explicitly defined set of shared principles is worth considering.

Imagine for a moment an environment in which the level of distress among boys and their disenfranchisement from the educational system are so dismal that far more students end up in prison than in college, and where the dropout rate of male students has been higher than the graduation rate for many years. The boys attending inner-city Chicago's Urban Prep inhabit just such a place. Yet Urban Prep's founders, leaders, and teachers have rejected the odds stacked against their students and have created a learning culture in which community is at the core, mutual respect is demanded without exception, and both trust and self-respect are built one boy at a time, one day at a time.

Shared principles play an essential role in shaping this community of learners. They have helped to connect a school full of otherwise disenfranchised, underachieving boys to their school, their teachers, their peers, and their potential as learners, contributing to each boy's academic success as well as his growing sense of responsibility to himself and his community.

The boys of Urban Prep begin eight hours of rigorous academic study with a daily morning meeting of the entire school community, at which all members recite a school creed that infuses every action and interaction that follows. "We are exceptional—not because we say it, but because we work hard at it. We will not falter in the face of any obstacle placed before us.... We never fail because we never give up. We make no excuses" (Robinson-English, 2006, p. 1). The principles inherent in both the school's motto ("We believe") and creed—doing the necessary work, behaving with integrity, demonstrating persistence, and being responsible—form the foundation on which each boy's ensuing academic excellence is built. In concert with the support of faculty, staff, and many strong, positive role models, these principles also provide a means for building enduring skills and attitudes that ideally keep the boys at Urban Prep moving forward and into a better life. Shared

> Urban Prep Motto: "We believe."
>
> School Creed: "We believe. We are the young men of Urban Prep. We are college bound. We are exceptional—not because we say it, but because we work hard at it. We will not falter in the face of any obstacle placed before us. We are dedicated, committed and focused. We never succumb to mediocrity, uncertainty or fear. We never fail because we never give up. We make no excuses. We choose to live honestly, nonviolently and honorably. We respect ourselves and, in doing so, respect all people. We have a future for which we are accountable. We have a responsibility to our families, community and world. We are our brothers' keepers. We believe in ourselves. We believe in each other. We believe in Urban Prep. We believe" (Robinson-English, 2006, p. 1).

principles, a code of ethics, and a sense of community are reversing years of failure and giving these boys hope. The school's creed encompasses all of the advice, encouragement, and words of wisdom so often absent from these boys' lives, made explicit and then practiced again and again. The benefits that Urban Prep's boys experience as a result of embracing the school's creed help them to see that the principles underlying the creed are essential tools for success within the school community and in life. Impressive statistics illustrate the impact of these efforts. Despite the fact that only 4 percent of the boys read at grade level when they entered 9th grade, every single boy in Urban Prep's first graduating class of 2010 was accepted at an accredited four-year institution of higher education. Fully 79 percent of current students (compared with 44.4 percent of black males in the surrounding Chicago urban areas) are also on track to graduate and have outperformed minority males districtwide in all subject areas of the 2010 ACT ("Promising Practices," 2010).

Urban Prep's profound transformation in the face of immense obstacles offers a message of hope for all of us who work with struggling, underachieving boys in our classrooms. With the school's dynamic, empowering creed as inspiration, I sought to find an equally effective set of principles that could be implemented across a broad spectrum of classroom settings, adapt well to varying grade levels and subject areas, and also be used in heterogeneous classrooms. Fortunately, I found an abundance of resources well suited to the task, one of which is introduced below as the first of nine Key Resources (as I now call them) selected for this book. Although not designed solely for use in addressing the needs of struggling boys, each resource speaks directly to one or more of the essential needs of the struggling boy, and all learners (boys and girls, struggling or not) benefit from its use. Said another way, each Key Resource helps educators reach out to all learners while maintaining a focus on the needs of the struggling boy. No student has to "lose" in order for another to "win."

Key Resource: The 8 Keys of Excellence

In Figure 5.2, you will find a set of shared principles called *The 8 Keys of Excellence*, developed by Bobbi DePorter (2009). What makes these principles especially relevant to the goal of this book is not the fact that teachers' and students' lives have been transformed by using them (though they have). It's not even that they provide a foundation for the kind of supportive, trusting, mutually respectful environment in which learning is free to take place (though they do).

FIGURE 5.2
DePorter's *The 8 Keys of Excellence*

Integrity	Match behaviors with values
Failure Leads to Success	Learn from mistakes
Speak with Good Purpose	Speak honestly and kindly
This Is It!	Make the most of every moment
Commitment	Keep promises
Ownership	Take responsibility for feelings, words, and actions
Flexibility	Remain open to change
Balance	Develop mind, body, and spirit

Source: From *The 8 Keys of Excellence* (p. 3), by B. DePorter, 2009, Oceanside, CA: Learning Forum Publications. © 2009 by B. DePorter. Adapted with permission.

What makes these Keys uniquely effective for underachieving boys is that they communicate a real-world authenticity that derives from qualities and character traits of "people who...achieved great success while maintaining personal *excellence*" (DePorter, 2009, p. 2). Struggling boys can see that the strengths of character outlined by DePorter's Keys of Excellence have helped to shape the world in which we live in very real ways. Further, they characterize the actions of real people. The fact that most of these leaders in business, industry, education, and politics happened to be male provides another level on which these boys might relate. Thus, the Keys communicate not only goals for doing one's best at school but also provide authentic goals for finding success in the real world.

Practically speaking, another major benefit of using the Keys as a centerpiece for building shared principles in one's classroom is that they are so adaptable. The teachers whose ideas are presented in Figure 5.3 found creative ways to make these principles even more accessible to their students.

In Adaptation No. 1, elementary school teacher Diane Bolles integrates the Keys into her classroom culture by anchoring them to something her elementary school students already value and appreciate: their school mascot. Through her additional choice of simplified terminology and the use of "we," this variation of the Keys helps her students understand behaviors that demonstrate their responsibility to themselves as well as their role within a community of learners.

In Adaptation No. 2, middle school teacher Joy Kiedrowski adapts the language of the Keys into words and phrases that she feels might make more immediate sense to the boys in her middle school classroom. She incorporates these words and phrases into her everyday communications with students so that they become familiar and has a wall poster that lists each principle. She directs her students to the poster when a situation arises that illuminates or helps to further define the meaning of the principles as well as their purpose within their shared community.

In Adaptation No. 3, high school teacher Susan Albaugh helps her students connect with the Keys by using excerpts from films that resonate with students' own experiences. As they explore each principle in turn, students deepen their understanding by discussing how the Keys are relevant to their own lives. Throughout the year, students look for and share additional examples of the Keys from more recently released films that touch on similar themes in new ways.

Adaptation No. 4 from elementary school art teacher Erin Brandol highlights the vibrant and wonderfully unique outcome possible when students collaboratively generate their own terminology for each Key. As students engage in dialogue to define each Key's meaning and then choose words that come from their own vernacular to represent each Key, the resulting high levels of ownership increase the frequency with which students refer to and willingly embrace "their" Keys. With a high level of personal meaning, they become a natural and frequent part of everyday interactions.

FIGURE 5.3

Variations of the Keys

Adaptation No. 1

Meaning adapted for elementary school students, tied to their school mascot, the falcon.

(1) We fly high . . .
we are honest.

(2) We fly high . . .
mistakes are OK.

(3) We fly high . . .
our words are kind.

(4) We fly high . . .
we are super listeners.

(5) We fly high . . .
we do our best work.

(6) We fly high . . .
we keep our promises.

(7) We fly high . . .
we are responsible.

(8) We fly high . . .
we come to school rested and ready to learn new things.

Source: Diane Bolles, Enumclaw, WA. Used with permission.

Adaptation No. 2

Wording adapted for a group of middle schoolers.

HONESTY: Your actions and words should be true to you. Own up to your mistakes and accomplishments.

COMFORT ZONE: You may be asked to step out of your comfort zone. To succeed, you must try. You'll never know unless you take that risk.

EMPATHY: Think of others before you say or do things. Always remember the result will affect you, too.

EFFORT: Your best is always required. Your best isn't measured by someone else's best.

ENERGY: How much effort you give is a contribution to the energy of the entire room. Others see that and will use it to build a better environment.

RELIABILITY: Be dependable; let others know you are responsible for doing your job.

ACCEPTANCE: Know that your opinion is not the only one in the room. Not liking something is not a reason for not trying it.

BODY AWARENESS: Be constantly aware of what your entire body is doing: mind, physical body, and spirit.

Source: Joy Kiedrowski, Cleveland, OH. Used with permission.

Adaptation No. 3

Examples adapted for a high school English class, using films as models and specific scenes for discussion.

INTEGRITY:
Edward Scissorhands
What do you do if you find a bag full of money?

FAILURE LEADS TO SUCCESS: *Cast Away*
Tom Hanks's character makes fire after many failed attempts.

SPEAK WITH GOOD PURPOSE:
To Kill a Mockingbird
"You never really understand a person until you walk around in his shoes for a while."

THIS IS IT:
Dead Poets Society
The students' first day in Mr. Keating's class, during which he encourages them to *carpe diem* (Latin for *seize the day*).

COMMITMENT:
Rocky Balboa
Rocky tells his son, "You, me, or nobody is gonna hit as hard as life."

OWNERSHIP: *Hancock*
Hancock's publicity manager shows Hancock where he went wrong.

FLEXIBILITY: *Field of Dreams*
Kevin Costner's character plows his cornfield to build a baseball diamond.

BALANCE: *The Dark Knight*
Arthur tells Bruce to "know your limits."

Source: Susan Albaugh, New London, OH. Used with permission.

Adaptation No. 4

Language generated by students themselves.

KEEP IT REAL: Be proud of everything you do. Do the right thing even when no one is looking.

MADE IN THE SHADE: You won't always win, or always be smiling, or always feel like the top dog, but as long as you know how to do it better next time, you're already a step in the right direction.

WORD!! Say what you mean; mean what you say. Really. If you don't have anything nice to say, don't say anything.

ADDI-PADDI: Try to be the best you can. Act as if the activity you are doing right now is the only thing that matters. Give it your all.

BALL AND CHAIN: If you say you're going to do something, you have to do it. Even if you don't like it after you start, finish the job. In the end, you'll feel good about yourself for sticking with it.

NUMBER 1: Be responsible. Make sure people can count on you. If you're going to do or say it, you'd better be able to own it!

CHILL! Be willing to change if someone has a better way to get things done.

KARMA: Don't sweat the small stuff. Be grateful for the good things you have.

Source: Erin Brandol, Dublin, OH. Used with permission.

Each of these teachers adapted the Keys and created a personalized version of shared principles that could be used throughout the year to build a sense of community. Just as consistently attempting to build trust and using the leader coach model inform the behaviors, words, and choices of a teacher in a way that communicates safety to each struggling boy, so, too, do student behaviors based on shared principles gradually exemplify what a mutually respectful classroom environment *looks like* to students. The principles come to life through continued use. Ideally, as a struggling boy connects adherence to the principles with the results of his actions, he experiences both the principles' purpose and their benefit in the context of his daily life—in school and out of school. Each day that a boy without a strong positive male role model hears, understands, and practices using a set of shared principles, the ability of the Code to negatively affect that boy may diminish. The Code's narrow definition of what it means to be a man is reshaped through the words and deeds of his classmates and his teacher.

As with the development of trusting relationships, there is no quick way to build a nonthreatening classroom environment. Creating buy-in to a shared set of principles requires careful introduction; consistent clarification though the lens of daily, real-life interactions; and positive reinforcement for both successes and efforts made. It is a long-term, multifaceted effort that asks us to integrate change across time and in small increments. Lest the scope of this process seem discouraging, it is important to remember that quick fixes seldom achieve lasting results. It is by virtue of their gradual nature that the changes suggested in this book take root and continue to flourish over time. When we let go of the expectation for an easy solution, we open ourselves to a host of subtle, often simple opportunities for progress that we would have otherwise missed.

✳ **TAKE FIVE**

Do you have a set of shared principles in your classroom? If not, what might your students say the unwritten principles of your classroom are? How do they compare with the Keys? Are there any Keys you might consider adding?

Tool: Guidelines for Classroom Policies

The third tool for building a nonthreatening learning environment focuses on the development and implementation of classroom policies. I have intentionally refrained from using the word "rules" here because of the negative associations it conjures up for many people, including memories of inflexible and punitive enforcement. The purpose of developing classroom policies is to make the shared principles more tangible and "actionable." When students adhere to the principles and experience the benefits of doing so in the context of everyday classroom interactions, those principles are no longer abstract, unattainable ideals. They are, instead, practical, positive guides for everyday choices and behaviors. For the underachieving boy, they serve as both model and safety net, helping him know how to behave and providing the security of a safe place to re-engage in learning.

The process of generating classroom policies is not new, but teachers will find that the relatively new approach of actively involving students in that process yields more successful development of student ownership and, thus, compliance. Where a struggling boy is concerned, we need to be especially cognizant of several factors, namely, the way in which the policies are developed, the way they are communicated, and the way they are enforced.

The guidelines for developing classroom policies offered in Figure 5.4 (p. 90) may seem obvious, but they have more than simple common sense going for them (though they certainly have that, too). Derived from the findings of the Big Four and other experts, each guideline meets specific learning needs of underachieving boys, thereby helping them find increased success as a learner *and* as a member of the classroom community.

Guideline No. 1: Involve boys in creating the policies.

Here's why: In addition to the fact that incorporating familiar language into a policy will naturally make understanding it easier, the invitation to involve an underachieving boy in

"The social relations of school work need to be reconfigured so that students are allowed to adopt different positions of power, authority, and agency in the classroom. For boys, in particular, this may mean supporting them to learn how to operate as

setting classroom policies often generates a sense of ownership that results in an increased willingness to abide by those policies. Abiding by the policies when one has helped develop them becomes a choice rather than a restriction against which to rebel, and this, in turn, reduces defensiveness.

Additionally, the Alloway (2002) study emphasizes how important it is for boys to experience different "positions of power and agency" within the classroom (p. 9). For an underachieving boy, being consulted about the policies not only feels respectful, but it also levels the playing field, so to speak, removing the power structure from the process and making all students' views equally valuable and relevant.

learners and participants in the . . . classroom and constructing a classroom environment where students' knowledges and skills are valued and respected" (Alloway et al., 2002, p. 9).

"Teachers [should] construct . . . classrooms as democratic spaces where authority and agency are shared; where students are treated with dignity and respect; where students' knowledges, opinions and contributions are valued, and where students learn to work collaboratively and cooperatively" (Alloway et al., 2002, p. 9).

FIGURE 5.4
Guidelines for Classroom Policies

1. Involve boys in creating the policies.
2. Limit the number of policies to five or fewer.
3. State policies positively.
4. Make sure policies are fully understood before enforcing them.
5. Be consistent. Be consistent. Be consistent.
6. Enforce policies in a matter-of-fact way.
7. Forgive and forget. No grudges allowed.
8. Acknowledge effort.

(Alloway et al., 2002; "Canberra," 2002; Martin, 2002; Neall, 2002; Younger & Warrington, 2005)

Source: From *Boys and School: Challenging Underachievement, Getting It Right!* by K. Cleveland. © 2008 by TeacherOnlineEducation.com. Reprinted with permission.

Guideline No. 2: Limit the number of policies to five or fewer.

Here's why: First, five or fewer policies are usually easy for most students to remember. And for younger students, even five may be too many. One or two may be enough.

> "Providing consistent [policies] for behavior helps all students learn self-control. Set [policies] and enforce them. This is more likely to happen if you have no more than five" (James, 2007, p. 128).

Second, from a purely practical point of view, the longer the list of policies, the harder it is to enforce. Too many policies or policies that are too specific trigger the temptation for an overwhelmed underachiever to claim he "forgot" about the policy he just violated or to split hairs and use the specificity of the boundaries as a springboard for challenging them, thereby engaging you in a power struggle.

It may take a while for students to fully understand the implications of each policy, but as an underachieving boy and his teacher consistently work together to apply the policies, he learns how to recognize them in a variety of situations and is empowered as a result of his ability to understand and interpret their meaning and purpose (James, 2007). This kind of continuous, clarifying dialogue builds the teacher-student relationship along with the struggling boy's sense of belonging and competence.

Guideline No. 3: State policies positively.

Here's why: In terms of sentence structure, most policies are written as commands. Most of us are unaware that our brains ignore the word "not" in command statements. Thus, if one

> "To be effective, expectations must be stated explicitly and positively" (Neall, 2002, p. 62).

writes the policy "Do not yell," it is very likely that students' attention will be drawn to "yelling," thereby actually increasing the behavior we would like them to avoid (Terry & Churches, 2009). Many of us have experienced this frustrating outcome in our classrooms without knowing the cause.

Instead, we can state the positive behavior we wish to encourage. For example, the policy "Use quiet voices" reinforces and models the goal in a way that the brain can better process and remember. Positive phrasing also affects how the underachieving boy "hears" the words in the policy. Boys who react strongly to perceived threats, for example, may respond less defensively to a policy stated positively because positive phrasing removes punitive or negative implications.

Somewhat paradoxically, extremely specific policies may be less effective for a boy who is insecure about how to behave, so another general rule of thumb is to phrase policies at a more general, conceptual level if possible. For example, "Respect other people's property" is more effective as a policy than "Keep your hands to yourself," even though both are phrased positively. The first statement can apply to diverse situations, and although it may take a bit longer for the struggling boy to grapple with the more conceptual aspects of the policy, this approach actually avoids much of the loophole-seeking that a more specific policy such as "Keep your hands to yourself" seems to engender (e.g., "Do I have to walk with my hands glued to my side all the time?" "What if I accidentally fall and touch something?" "Can I touch something just a little?" "If I don't think it belongs to someone else, is it OK to touch it?" and so on).

Guideline No. 4: Make sure policies are fully understood before enforcing them.

Here's why: Many boys evaluate the fairness of a policy by the way it is implemented rather than by the fairness of the behavior it asks for. If an underachieving boy is prone to defensiveness and insecurity, the

> "Boys respond better to teachers who are attuned to boys' sense of justice and fairness and who are consistent in their application of [policies]" ("Canberra," 2002, p. 78).

enforcement of a policy that he doesn't yet understand may further diminish his sense of self-confidence and belonging. If he feels humiliated publicly as a result of being corrected (and recall that it is his perception rather than the reality of the situation that matters), his reaction may seem completely out of proportion, perhaps even overshadowing the original infraction. A boy who is fragile emotionally may be especially prone to overreact in such situations, and this lack of control over his emotions only serves to distance him further from other students, making him feel even more isolated. To counteract such inadvertent overreactions and support the struggling boy in learning to cope with his strong feelings at such moments, we can make sure that all students fully understand a policy before we enforce it.

We must find the right balance between creating policies so rigidly defined that they leave no questions to be asked ("Wait five seconds before raising your hand to answer") and policies so vague that they have little value in terms of guiding student interactions ("Be nice"). There is no perfect policy, but if the teacher demonstrates the ways in which policies function as boundaries for behaviors, students—especially the boys most sensitive to punitive or overzealous enforcement—learn how to manage their behaviors and choices without becoming overly defensive or inappropriately argumentative. It's a process that needs to be modeled and reinforced.

Guideline No. 5: Be consistent. Be consistent. Be consistent.

Here's why: Consistency reinforces a feeling of safety. As author Lucinda Neall says in *Bringing Out the Best in Boys*, "Boys need clear, firm boundaries; the harder they push against them, the stronger those boundaries should be. It is important to remember, however, that part of the purpose of boundaries is to give them something to push against, so don't be surprised (or angry) when they do just that!" (2002, p. 149). Although it seems counterintuitive, some boys push on a boundary because they *want* that boundary enforced. Sometimes the pushing is about checking to make sure the policy is still there. It's actually an effort to feel safe. But whatever the reason for an infraction, a swift, matter-of-fact response gives the information necessary, reinforces the feeling of safety, and maintains the boundary, all without feeling punitive.

> "Consistency is one of the keys to success.... We are successful because the teachers are incredibly consistent, to the nth degree, with these children, and that is what they have lacked in their lives—consistency" ("Canberra," 2002, p. 151).

Being consistent communicates a teacher's trustability. The same boys who push on policies to gauge their solidity may perceive inconsistent enforcement of those policies as a weakness on a teacher's part. Once a policy is set, it needs to stay set, and it also needs to be applied in the same way to everyone. A sense of security develops when there is no guessing and no wondering about how the policy will be enforced. For struggling boys, some of whom come from homes with few consistent boundaries, this is even more important. These boys need to rely on the security of the policies that govern their community without ever having to question them. Even if they push on the policies (and perhaps especially when they do), it is important that they get the same response, over and over again.

Please understand, however, that I am not advocating mindless, heartless, unflinching, and rigid adherence to these policies in the face of extenuating circumstances. Consistency is not the same thing as rigidity. Being consistent means doing one's best and making exceptions only when necessary, recognizing that there *are* times when this necessity will arise. Classroom policies are never more important than the well-being of a student. Rigid enforcement that fails to recognize the primacy of the learner actually negates many of the principles we are trying to model for our students. The bottom line in decisions of this nature is whether or not the decision is respectful to the student(s) most affected by it.

There is also a difference between making exceptions to classroom policies under extraordinary circumstances and casually making changes for no apparent reason or intentionally showing favoritism during their implementation. Whereas the first shows compassion and support, the latter two show purposeful disregard. Remember, too, that consistency is something that a teacher models on a daily basis via the routines involved in implementing classroom procedures, the timeliness of feedback, and the willingness to listen to students. Its greatest impact stems from the ongoing and predictable manner with which a teacher responds to students and to their needs as learners. Enforcing classroom policies is one part of that larger picture. If a struggling boy can count on his teacher to be consistent in this larger framework, occasional and well-founded exceptions to the policies will be understood and well tolerated.

By the same token, if there is ever a circumstance in which a policy absolutely must change—and one hopes this would be a rare occurrence—a teacher needs to share the reasoning behind the proposed change, involve the students in developing a replacement policy, and once again check for understanding before enforcing it anew.

Guideline No. 6: Enforce policies in a matter-of-fact way.

Here's why: Neall (2002) also points out that sometimes boys push on boundaries as a means of getting attention. The more attention we give in response to an infraction, the more likely the boundary will be pushed on for just that purpose. The smartest response on our part is to speak calmly and avoid shouting. Instead of dwelling on the infraction or asking questions (e.g., "Why did you do that?"), we can just restate the policy.

As we now know well, public reprimands are humiliating to boys. If a teacher responds confrontationally when an underachieving boy pushes back on or fails to follow established policies, the boy may feel he has no choice but to engage in a power struggle that he must win at all costs (including being kicked out of class or school, if necessary). No one wins in this situation. The disruption interferes with the boy's learning, the teacher's instruction, and the teacher-student relationship.

> "Young boys do not like being thought of as younger than they are and may react with disrespect to a teacher's attempt to speak gently to them, particularly when the child is upset. Boys will respond to being treated matter-of-factly and included in decision making about how to deal with a situation" (James, 2007, p. 129).
>
> "Being told off by an authority figure is almost always perceived as an attack and boys often react either by shutting down or aggressively defending themselves.... Simply describing a problem can allow boys to work out for themselves what behaviour is required" (Neall, 2002, pp. 200, 201).

However, if a teacher simply reminds the boy of the policy calmly, with clear, positive, and impersonal language, there is no need for him to be defensive or escalate the power struggle. Remember, too, that if the response requires more than a few quick words, we should make every effort to keep it private and away from other students. (Please note that I am not advocating this kind of response to life-threatening or dangerous situations, which demand immediate reactions of a very different nature.)

Guideline No. 7: Forgive and forget. No grudges allowed.

Here's why: In general, boys are more likely to actually hear what we say if we say it and then let it drop. If we can follow our comments with a firm but friendly signal that the issue is resolved and no grudge is held, all the better. In other words, many boys appreciate a cue that the student-teacher relationship is still intact, and that its strength does not depend upon being "good" or "right." The boy understands that he is liked and appreciated for who he is and not because he behaves in a specific, sanctioned manner.

When he can save face and move on, he is free to spend his energy on productive learning activities rather than on self-defense or deflection. This may be especially important for the SF/Interpersonal and NF/Self-Expressive boy, for whom the teacher-student relationship is an essential element of his ability to engage in learning. And if the boy in question comes from a home in which "being wrong" is the prelude to punishment or humiliation, knowing that the same scenario won't play out in the classroom becomes even more critical. His heightened state of apprehension can easily invoke downshifting, interfering further with his ability to function on a cognitive level and becoming yet another source of anxiety for him. To help him get back to work as quickly as possible, signal in a matter-of-fact way that bygones are just that.

> "Always give 'a way out' for the boy who has done something wrong. They must do some sort of penance but know [that] after their punishment they will again be treated fairly. I use the word 'penance' deliberately. The dictionary meaning of the word being 'a punishment agreed to, or offered to show you are sorry for doing wrong'" ("Canberra," 2002, p. 82).

> "Some teachers are concerned that they will create a bad atmosphere if they express their feelings to students; the trick is to express them and then drop them. . . . Stating clearly how [one] feels . . . clears the atmosphere and allows everyone to move on" (Neall, 2002, pp. 96–97).

Guideline No. 8: Acknowledge effort.

Here's why: If the only attention we bring to following classroom policies is negative, then it is the negative

> "Genuine praise, challenge and positive reinforcement for effort, achievement and appropriate behaviour are effective motivators for boys" ("Canberra," 2002, p. 81).

behavior we end up reinforcing. If, on the other hand, we make a point of recognizing when the class has followed the policies and then reinforce the positive behavior, we increase the likelihood that students will repeat it. Research also tells us that boys are often responsive to rewards, so it may make sense to consider offering a reward for sticking to the policies, especially at first (Alloway et al., 2002; "Canberra," 2002; Martin, 2005). Encourage further buy-in by letting the boys help you decide what that reward should be.

Remember that some of the boys who struggle most in our classrooms rarely receive affirmative feedback of any kind, and for these boys, a simple acknowledgment of success, no matter how small, can have a surprisingly positive effect. Affirmation of effort—even when it may not have been totally successful—helps a struggling boy understand that he is making progress. It's usually fine to praise students as a group, but you may find it's more effective to save individual comments for a private moment. The older a boy is, the more sensitive he may be to being singled out in front of other boys, even for a positive reason.

Everything Speaks

As Bobbi DePorter (2009) reminds us, everything we do in our classrooms speaks to our students. In following these guidelines for developing and implementing classroom policies, our actions speak volumes to our struggling boys in ways they desperately need to hear and—just as critically—in ways they actually *can* hear. Not only does this inclusive process communicate concern for our students as individuals, but it also offers a struggling boy clearly defined explanations of how to behave appropriately, how to build his personal integrity by owning his behaviors, and how to belong to a community governed by mutual respect. These skills are essential to learning and to life. They also provide an environment that supports an underachieving boy in reaching his potential as a learner.

Milepost

We've covered a great deal of territory in this first Pathway. As responses to underachieving boys' need for support, the first two Access Points—building trusting relationships and establishing a nonthreatening learning environment—offer processes by which any educator can begin to help a struggling boy want to re-engage in his learning. Teacher actions that build trust and the leader coach model work together to build strong teacher-student relationships. As a struggling boy joins his peers in understanding and embracing a set of shared principles, he not only builds his male identity in a positive way but also acquires life skills that can contribute to both his social and his academic success. And, as a result of taking part in creating guidelines for classroom policies, he experiences and practices what it means to be part of a community and builds his sense of self. In several important ways, we have begun to uncover solutions for addressing the problem of underachievement among boys by meeting each of the four goals:

- *Replace* his negative attitudes about learning with productive perspectives about the role of risk (and even failure) as a necessary and valued part of the learning process;
- *Reconnect* him with school, with learning, and with a belief in himself as a competent learner who is capable, valued, and respected;
- *Rebuild* life skills and learning skills that lead to academic success and also lay the groundwork for success in life; and
- *Reduce* his need to use unproductive and distracting behaviors as a means of self-protection.

Though neither Access Point is wholly unfamiliar to most readers, finding new ways to connect with and implement them is essential to helping our struggling boys stretch enough to be able to learn. Subtle changes in the things we do and say can have a major effect on whether a struggling boy sees us as supportive and sees our classrooms as safe places in which to risk learning. Simple daily efforts over time can make a difference. Together, building trusting relationships and establishing a nonthreatening learning environment pave the way for success in the Support Pathway. No other Access Points are more essential, and the ultimate success of each subsequent Pathway and Access Point builds on the foundation of these first two.

A Long-Term, Integrated, Multifaceted Approach

Hopefully, as you explored the Support Pathway, you also began to see with increased clarity why re-engaging underachieving boys is necessarily a long-term, integrated, multifaceted process.

Long-term. The process of building trust is not simple, nor can it be hurried. It requires efforts on multiple levels to make it strong: relational, emotional, and instructional. A supportive teacher-student relationship leads to a nonthreatening classroom climate in which all students, but especially our struggling boys, can find the support they need to stretch and embrace the risks of deep, engaged learning in a community in which they belong and are valued. To build their sense of self as capable learners, struggling boys need to see school as something not done *to* them but rather *with* them and *for* them.

Integrated. A trusting teacher-student relationship models what respectful interactions look like. A nonthreatening classroom environment builds trust between students and their teacher. Clear policies help the teacher and students establish that environment and give the teacher and students an opportunity to practice both the policies and the principles on which they are based. How these ideas and strategies are introduced and implemented depends on the teacher, the needs of his or her students, the issues that need to be addressed, and the context of the situation. There is no foolproof recipe, and each teacher's decision-making process, choices, and solutions will be different. This approach is necessarily flexible and nonprescriptive, a means by which we, as educators, can take what we know about the struggling boys in our classrooms and the research on boys in general and use it in ways specific to our classrooms and our students.

Multifaceted. Everything we do "speaks" to our students. When our behavior, classroom climate, and classroom policies consistently convey the principles we want students to comprehend, their meaning and relevance resonate more deeply. By living them every day, students see these principles in action, define them on a personal level, and then own them.

BUILDING A REPERTOIRE OF RESPONSES

Before you move on to the next chapter, pause to note any "aha!" moments you've had thus far.

1. What do you now understand about how struggling boys learn best that you didn't know before?

2. Of the strategies you are currently using, which could be tweaked or used more intentionally for an even greater positive outcome?

3. Which ideas or strategies caught your attention the most?

4. Choose one idea or strategy related to this Pathway that you could implement right now.

What's Next?

In Pathway No. 2: Guide, we will expand on the notion of involving boys in building their own success. Three new Access Points (Clear Directions, Informational Feedback, and Positive Reinforcement) give us the means to further set the stage for learning success and help our struggling boys begin to take responsibility for managing many of the most distracting behaviors that interfere with their own learning and our teaching.

CHAPTER 6

Pathway No. 2: Guide

....

Things which matter most must never be at the mercy of things which matter least.

—Johann Wolfgang von Goethe

....

Pathway No. 2: Guide emphasizes providing clear communication in the form of expectations, feedback, and reinforcement as a means of empowering a struggling boy to help himself. With a strong teacher-student relationship and a nonthreatening learning environment as a foundation, the next three Access Points offer educators the specific means by which we can support an underachieving boy academically while also nudging him toward greater responsibility for his own behavior and his own learning. Fear of failure diminishes as his self-confidence and competence grow.

Tool: Basic Requests About Communicating

Written in boys' own language, the requests about communication laid out in Figure 6.1 (p. 103) help us understand the connection between what we say and how our struggling

> "Boys do not know what is in our hearts, but draw conclusions from what they see and hear" (Neall, 2002, p. 38).

boys hear us. Just as a teacher's actions and attitudes speak volumes to an underachieving boy, so, too, do the words a teacher chooses and the ways in which those words are expressed. Imagine that in addition to masculine identity building and school-versus-style dynamics, the requests in Figure 6.1 are now peppered throughout the Pathways to Re-Engagement model. Keep these requests in mind as you continue through the Pathways.

Several requests may seem quite familiar. You encountered them in a previous Access Point, and I have carried them forward because they work so well as general guidelines for all kinds of communication. The other requests may, at first glance, seem to have little to do with communication, but a closer look reveals that that is absolutely not the case. A teacher's willingness to laugh appropriately at himself or herself and infuse humor into the classroom can have a strong positive effect on the teacher-student relationship, the classroom environment, and an underachieving boy's attentiveness. Inspired, enthusiastic teachers make even the most difficult content easier to focus on and absorb, and connecting what is being taught to its value in the real world helps a reluctant learner to envision the role it plays, grasp why it is important, and understand in a concrete way why it is worthwhile to invest time and energy in learning the content. Lastly, when we can let a struggling boy in on the secret of why he has done well and what he needs to do to be more successful, he can begin to understand who he is as a learner and how to harness his skills.

Each request helps to clarify that *how* a teacher communicates is as important as *what* a teacher communicates. An awareness of these 10 basic requests when we choose our words and decide how best to express them can positively affect the manner in which they are received, regarded, and understood by the underachieving boys who need to hear them most.

Access Point: Clear Expectations

How a teacher communicates with his or her students has enormous potential to either reinforce or derail a struggling boy's willingness to engage fully in learning and take the risks that will ultimately lead to his academic success. If one of our chief goals is to keep his fear of failure at bay, we need to

FIGURE 6.1
Basic Requests for Communicating

1.	Give me a way out.	Sometimes I screw up, but that doesn't mean I'll always act that way. I need a way to move on without being too embarrassed about how stupidly I just behaved. Tell me how I can be better. I want to know.
2.	Help me know my strengths.	Help me understand what skills I have or am improving in, both academically and socially. I don't always know what they are or how to make the most of them.
3.	Help me relax into learning.	Laugh sometimes, even at yourself. If I know you make mistakes, it makes it easier to accept when I do.
4.	Help me "save face."	Don't humiliate or make fun of me in front of others. It does not make me want to work harder. I will hate you for it and be forced to get back at you.
5.	Inspire me.	Share your passion about what you are teaching with me. Help me to feel excited about what I'm learning. Your enthusiasm rubs off.
6.	Keep it private.	If I make a mistake, be matter-of-fact in telling me why, and do it as privately as possible.
7.	Let me know I matter.	Greet me as though you care and are glad I'm there.
8.	Make it real.	Help me understand why things are important in the real world. It helps me want to learn more.
9.	Notice when I try.	Let me know somehow when I do things well. I like to hear that. It's OK if you tell my parents.
10.	Speak to me with respect.	Treat me with respect and show me what that looks like. Sometimes I don't know, and if I mess up, a kind response speaks loudest to me.

Source: From *Boys, Literacy and Schooling: Expanding the Repertoires of Practice*, by N. Alloway et al., 2002, Canberra, Australia: Commonwealth Department of Education, Science & Training. © 2002 by Alloway, Freebody, Gilbert and Muspratt; *Boys: Getting It Right. Report on the Inquiry into the Education of Boys*, by the House of Representatives Standing Committee on Education and Training, 2002, Canberra, Australia: Australian Government Publishing Service. © 2002 by the AGPS; *Teaching the Male Brain: How Boys Think, Feel, and Learn in School*, by A. N. James, 2007, Thousand Oaks, CA: Corwin Press. © 2007 by A. N. James; *Improving the Educational Outcomes of Boys: Final Report to ACT Department of Education, Youth and Family Services*, by A. J. Martin, 2002, Tuggeranong, Australian Capital Territory: Department of Education, Youth and Family Services. © 2002 by A. J. Martin; *Bringing Out the Best in Boys: Communication Strategies for Teachers*, by L. Neall, 2002, Stroud, UK: Hawthorne Press. © 2002 by L. Neall; and *Raising Boys' Achievement* (Research Report No. 636), by M. Younger and M. Warrington, 2005, Cambridge, UK: Department for Education and Skills. © 2005 by Younger and Warrington. Adapted with permission.

create learning scenarios that set him up for success each step of the way. Clear expectations are essential to this outcome.

> "The boys had to have very short-term, very achievable goals. They had to know what they were going to achieve immediately, not in a week's time, not in two days' time, but straight there and then.... I find it is very important, with boys in particular, to really explain the sequence of activities that they're going to be involved in, the purpose of them, why they're doing them and how they are going to be assessed on part of it" ("Canberra," 2002, p. 81).

From the first moment a learning activity begins, the manner in which a teacher gives directions and outlines steps for completing tasks affects an underachieving boy's ability to complete a learning task successfully. Explicit guidelines about how to achieve success provide an antidote to his frequently unarticulated fear of failure, strengthening his "safety net" in a proactive way that lowers his apprehension and reduces defensiveness or the need to distract and divert attention.

There is also a physiological, brain-based reason for providing clear, explicit directions. Research indicates that boys, in general, have somewhat less acute hearing than girls ("Canberra," 2002; Eliot, 2009). Given that most directions in American classrooms are given verbally, teachers must make certain that boys—especially struggling boys, who are less likely to ask for help—hear each step of the directions *right from the start*, before they make unnecessary mistakes and shut down in embarrassment.

Tool: Effective Directions in a Nutshell

In Figure 6.2, you will find a simple set of steps designed to maximize teacher-student communication. This direction-giving sequence supports a struggling boy's ability to perform successfully in three ways: first, by meeting the requests for effective communication (see Figure 6.1); second, by optimizing his brain's engagement; and third, by continually reinforcing the boy's ability to perform as a competent and capable learner.

Of the many tools you will encounter in this book, this sequence for giving directions is among the most practical means by which we can help a struggling boy to build his confidence as a learner, develop life skills, and interact with others confidently. The more the sequence is used, the greater its positive effect. We will examine each step, looking at its specific purpose, its relevance to the learning process, how it might look in action, and why it supports a struggling boy's ability to be more successful as a learner.

FIGURE 6.2
Effective Directions in a Nutshell

Step 1	Change state.
Step 2	Explain relevance.
Step 3	Be crystal clear.
Step 4	Engage multiple modalities.
Step 5	Check for understanding.
Step 6	Announce duration.
Step 7	Pair verbal commands with auditory start/stop signals .
Step 8	Provide backup.
Step 9	Give fair warning.
Step 10	Acknowledge effort.

Source: From *Boys and School: Challenging Underachievement, Getting It Right!* by K. Cleveland. © 2008 by TeacherOnlineEducation.com. Reprinted with permission.

Step 1: Change state. Have you ever started to give directions to your class and then had to start over because you realized one or more students weren't listening? One practical and effective way to prevent this scenario is by making a "state change" before explaining directions. A successful state change brings closure to the previous mental or physical activity and readies the learner to focus on what's ahead.

Data about brain-based learning help us understand why the state change is such an important step for the underachieving boy during learning. In short, our brains typically follow a very specific path during a learning experience:

Phase 1, Initial Sensory Awareness: Information enters the "sensory register" and is noticed on a sensory level.

Phase 2, Initial Cognitive Awareness: Information enters "immediate" memory; the brain "wakes up" and notices its arrival.

Phase 3, Processing: Information moves into "working" memory; the brain consciously endeavors to make sense of and find meaning in it.

Phase 4, Remembering: Information moves into long-term memory; the brain has developed enough connections between old and new learning to store it for future retrieval (Sousa, 2006).

The most salient aspect of this cycle for any learner, but especially for underachieving boys, is that each successive phase of the learning process relies on the completion of the prior one. If the brain isn't engaged in the first phase, there won't be a successful second, third, or fourth phase. Thus, gaining an underachieving boy's initial attention is hugely important where direction giving is concerned. He will benefit most if he is fully attentive to and able to recall the directions we give in Phases 1 and 2 so that he can use those directions to find meaning in and complete the task at hand (Phase 3) and, most importantly, remember what was learned (Phase 4). For boys who are unfocused, highly social, inattentive, or easily distracted, staying fully present for this entire process can be especially challenging.

What does this look like?

Many teachers already use simple state changers and don't recognize them as such. Flashing the lights, call-and-response clapping, or even a raised hand are all state changers. If you're already using these effectively, keep right on doing so! If not, you can try any of the techniques just stated or some of the ones explained below.

Listen and Clap

• Say: *If you can hear my voice, clap once.* Then clap. Students will join in.
• Say: *If you can hear my voice, clap twice.* Then clap twice. More students will join in.
• Soften your voice and say: *If you can hear my voice, look this way.* By this time, all students (even those who didn't clap) should be focused and ready to listen.

Why does this work? By softening his or her voice while simultaneously giving a command, the teacher interrupts extraneous activity and conversations and prepares students to listen to the teacher's natural speaking volume. If a student has not brought his or her attention to the teacher by the time this step is reached, the ensuing quietness of the room will naturally bring that student to attention without the need to say or do anything else.

Variation: Older students may find clapping unappealing because they view it as childish, but using just the third step—softening one's voice and then quietly waiting—is still highly effective.

Whistle Stop

• Find a wooden whistle that sounds like a train (or another similarly recognizable and pleasant sound signal) when blown.
• Establish the signal. When you blow one time, students will raise their hands to indicate they are ready to listen. When hands go up, mouths are shut.
• Practice this signal-and-response exercise several times, especially when it's least expected, and challenge the class to reduce the time it takes for all students to raise their hands. Make practice into a game. When students are accomplished in responding to the signal, begin using this strategy before giving directions.

Why does this work? As with the earlier Listen and Clap strategy, the more the routine is used, the more quickly it works to effect subsequent state changes. Here, however, instead of a verbal signal, only a sound signal is used. This works only if the command to come to attention is initially taught along with the sound signal. Gradually, as students associate the sound with the procedure of coming to attention, the teacher will no longer need to give the associated verbal cues to effect this change because the brain has, in essence, collapsed two signals into one: when the learner hears the whistle, his brain also recalls the verbal instructions to come to attention.

Variation: Adding an element of fun and novelty to this state changer can have real learning benefits for students. That's because associating positive emotions with the sounds used as the signal will enhance students' abilities to focus as well as to recall the learning that follows. You can encourage these positive associations by picking unusual sounds to use and by periodically asking students to bring in new sounds. Consider assigning groups to be in charge of picking a new sound for the month, or sponsor a contest and let students vote on the sound to be used next.

Brain Boosters

• Lead students in one-minute, cross-lateral exercises (movements during which one or both extremities—hands or feet—cross the midline of the body) or engage students in simple repeated "pretend you are . . ." movements (e.g., swinging arms like a windmill, washing windows, or catching butterflies).
• Remember that this strategy requires that you use a signal to end the activity, at which time students know that they are to sit down and focus their attention on you.
• Before you try to use this strategy during direction giving, practice the entire sequence.
• When you judge that students are comfortable with the sequence—both the exercises and coming to attention afterward—begin using this strategy before giving directions.

Why does this work? Physical movement energizes the brain by increasing blood flow and oxygen. Cross-laterals add another level of cognitive stimulation because our limbs are controlled by the opposing side of the brain. That is, the right side of the body is controlled by the left side of the brain and vice versa. When we engage in such movements, we make our brain work harder (Hannaford, 2005). For boys who enjoy the challenge of this kind of physical activity, leading the class in new cross-laterals can be fun as well as help build self-esteem.

Variation: Older students respond well when the teacher gives a more general directive. This can be done by saying something like, "Let's all stand up, stretch, roll our heads, stomp our feet, and walk around a bit."

Step 2: Explain relevance. The Big Four repeatedly mention establishing relevance as an effective means of engaging a boy's attention (Alloway et al., 2002; "Canberra," 2002; Martin, 2002; Younger & Warrington, 2005). The Canberra study, for example, explains that "[b]oys like to be able to see how what they are learning relates to life outside or beyond school and may find it difficult to engage with what appears to be irrelevant subject matter" (2002, p. 72). Explaining the relevance of a task creates a context for what we are about to teach and helps a boy connect with it immediately. And when he connects with the material, attentiveness naturally follows.

What does this look like?

After changing students' states, set the stage for what is to come by explaining how the lesson relates to what they already know and by *inviting them to continue learning.* Your introduction to this new material might sound like the following introductory statements:

• Say: *Thank you for coming to attention so quickly. We have some important work to do today! I am confident that you will do well. Students just like you have been successful in completing this task.*

• Say: *In the last lesson, we did* _____ *as a way of gaining expertise in* _____ .

• Say: *Today, we will continue that process by doing* _____ . (Give a general overview only.)

• Say: *This is going to help you become more skilled at* _____ .

• Say: *So, to review, the goal for this lesson is* _____ .

• Say: *Let's get started!* (DePorter et al., 1999)

Why does it work? First, note how many of the basic requests from Figure 6.1 are met in this step alone: (2) help me know my strengths; (3) help me relax into learning; (5) inspire me; (7) let me know I matter; (8) make it real; and (10) speak to me with respect. Second, this kind of routine connection to the big picture and to previous "chunks" of learning helps boys with the NT/Thinker-Knower and NF/Self-Expressive styles stay engaged and gives them a sense of what's to come. They need to see the big picture to make sense of the details. Third, for boys with the ST/Practical/Doer style, the clarity about how to achieve mastery provides an additional hook into the lesson.

Step 3: Be crystal clear. Many students get frustrated when the teacher says one thing but means another, leaves out important steps, or simply leaves it up to the students to figure out what to do. There is a time and a place for this last approach—called problem-based learning—but in most other situations, directions need to be as clear as possible, right from the beginning. Where struggling boys are concerned, three golden rules apply when giving directions: (1) use fewer words, (2) use familiar words, and (3) number steps in a sequence if it's important that directions be followed in a specific order ("Canberra," 2002; Neall, 2002).

What does this look like?

When you have students' attention and have established the relevance of the task at hand, give specific instructions about how to complete the task. For example, the teacher in the preceding example might continue by saying something like this:

• Say: *There are three steps you will need to complete in order.*
• Say: *Step 1: First, you will _____.*
• Say: *Step 2: Second, you will _____.*
• Say: *Step 3: Third, you will _____.*

Why does it work?

• *Fewer words.* If a teacher drones on and on with verbal directions, a struggling boy may tune out. Keeping directions short helps his brain stay focused.
• *Familiar words.* If a boy doesn't understand what his teacher means, he may guess rather than risk the possible embarrassment of asking for clarification. Neither the teacher nor the boy may catch the problem until it's too late to fix it.
• *Numbering steps in a sequence.* For a learner who has difficulty pulling discrete steps from directions written in paragraph form (often SF/Interpersonal and NF/Self-Expressive learners), the use of numbering clarifies visually where one step ends and another begins. For a boy who may not process spoken or written language quickly, the numbers also help him keep the sequence organized, and when giving him feedback, his teacher can more readily call his attention to "Step 2" than by saying, "Look at paragraph one of the directions. See what the second sentence tells you to do?"

Step 4: Engage multiple modalities. Engaging multiple modalities, also called dual coding, simply means that a teacher stimulates two or more of the learner's senses (modalities) during Phase 1 of the learning process (in this case, giving directions). For a struggling boy, this dual engagement increases his initial attentiveness and optimizes his ability to process and retain information provided during the ensuing phases because he receives the initial jolt of information on two or more "channels."

For example, if your habit is to deliver directions visually (e.g., via an overhead projector, whiteboard, or worksheets), then read them aloud, too. Conversely, if your practice is to deliver directions verbally, consider giving students a written handout or, better still, use a visual aid such as PowerPoint or a chart so that a boy who doesn't recall auditory directives easily can also follow along visually.

When using visual aids that offer the opportunity to add written comments to the existing text (e.g., a transparency for an overhead projector or a chart), you can further enhance an underachieving boy's attention by underlining important words as you read them aloud, using multiple colors to distinguish one step from another. (Do remember, however, to establish a consistent pattern when doing this. If the most important words are usually underlined in orange, a sudden switch to purple would be disorienting.) If you also ask students to underline or highlight parts of the written directions along with you, you will activate the kinesthetic modality as well.

What does this look like?

Lab Report Sleuths

Rather than hand the lab worksheets out the day before and ask that students read through them, I first put the lab on the overhead (visual modality) with key words and phrases missing, including the title. I then ask students to sort through the chemicals and apparatus they'll be using for the lab (kinesthetic modality), and we go through the lab worksheet line by line, trying to figure out what the missing words and phrases might be. As soon as possible, the students come up with a title for the lab, having read through the procedures and having become familiar with the task and the materials involved *before* actually starting the lab (visual, kinesthetic, and auditory modalities).

Source: Lou Kristopson, Stow, OH. Used with permission.

Why does this work? As students see the lab report on the overhead, touch and verbally identify the materials they will be using, and discuss potential titles for the forthcoming lab, they acquire the necessary preparatory information using three modalities (verbal, auditory, and kinesthetic). Compare the strength of this kind of sensory involvement to an individual student passively reading of a set of directions, and its value for the underachieving boy is apparent. Lou approaches direction giving by involving his students in active construction of their understanding of what the next day's lab will be about. The struggling boy is able to make sense of the task in a variety of ways. His brain builds understanding of the steps required to complete the task, in this case a lab, rather than passively observing them with no real engagement, and as a result, he owns the outcome of his efforts (which, of course, helps him recall and be able to use the information long term). For the underachieving SF/ Interpersonal boy, the opportunity to verbalize his understanding and engage in acquisition of that understanding by interacting with other students is an invaluable means of helping him digest and recall the pertinent information.

Step 5: Check for understanding. You may recall from the earlier discussion of the Boy Code that many boys avoid doing anything that could be regarded as feminine. Asking for clarification is, to many boys, an admission of weakness, which by association makes the action "feminine" and, thus, to be avoided at all costs. One of the simplest ways to avoid this situation is to make sure students understand what you expect before you begin a task. And though this process adds a few minutes to the lesson's duration, it is an investment with a big payoff when precious minutes are no longer consumed in the correction of unnecessary mistakes later on.

What does this look like?

Pairs Check

After explaining directions, ask students to quickly form pairs and review what you have explained. A teacher might follow the "pairs check" with the random selection of one pair to share its review with the class. The pair's explanation might also include questions about any steps that are still unclear.

Why does it work? All students potentially benefit from the process of putting what they have heard into their own words and getting feedback on that preliminary understanding from a peer, but this interim review is especially helpful to the SF/Interpersonal or NF/Self-Expressive boy, who often has difficulty recalling sequenced steps within procedures. First, he has the opportunity to process information through verbal interactions with another student. Second, as he listens to his partner's response and compares it to his own understanding, he has the opportunity to review the sequence of steps he needs to follow, identify any errors, and fill in the gaps. When it's time for him to start work on his own, he has a better idea of what steps will lead him to a successful outcome.

Show Me

When directions have multiple steps, the "Show Me" strategy offers teachers a way to quickly gauge students' understanding after each step is explained. Students use prepared indicators to respond nonverbally about whether or not they understand each step. Prepared indicators are such things as sticks with smiley or frowny faces on them (for younger students), hand movements (e.g., thumbs up or thumbs down), or response cards with various one- or two-word phrases such as "Got it!" "Not yet" or "Almost" printed or written on them. If you are fortunate enough to have access to individual whiteboards, these can also be used for quick classwide "Show Me" surveys.

The teacher pauses for the students' response after explaining each step (or two), scanning the raised indicators for a sense of whether students are ready to proceed. If the teacher sees a mixed response—or even if just one student indicates a lack of understanding—the teacher immediately knows clarification is needed and for whom that clarification is intended. The teacher could easily insert a quick "Pairs Check" as a means of actively engaging all students in a review if the misunderstanding is widespread.

Why does it work? By checking for understanding frequently and routinely during direction giving, the teacher communicates three important messages about his or her expectations: first, that it is normal for all students to sometimes need clarification about directions; second, that it is important as well as acceptable to ask for clarification; and third, that it is each student's responsibility to indicate when there is a need for it.

Because all students respond at the same time and direct their indicators toward the teacher's attention, the "Show Me" strategy feels safe to a struggling boy because he can respond to the teacher's check for understanding and ask for clarification without being singled out. The more a teacher establishes this process as a classroom norm and the more this strategy is routinely used and practiced, the greater the likelihood that a struggling learner will feel safe to use it. Recognize that in a classroom characterized by a nonthreatening learning environment and shared principles, this strategy will become effective more rapidly than in a classroom characterized by a highly competitive atmosphere.

Step 6: Indicate duration. Brain-based learning expert Eric Jensen recommends following the general announcement of an activity's duration with a simple and reassuring statement to the effect that students will have plenty of time to accomplish the task within the time allowed.

What does this look like?

Say: *I have set aside approximately* _____ *(minutes, hours, days) for you to complete your work. You will have enough time to finish this task in the allotted time.*

Why does it work? The first sentence provides a boy who responds to having clear temporal boundaries with information that can help him use his time more wisely. For boys with ADD or ADHD, this is not only helpful, it's essential. At the same time, the second sentence allays any rising apprehension a struggling learner may feel when given a time limit. As we know from earlier discussions about the effects of stress on the brain, sometimes a boy becomes so anxious about getting his work done that the anxiety actually paralyzes his cognitive functions. The more he watches the clock, the greater his anxiety. The greater the anxiety, the less able he is to complete the work at hand. Once panic and frustration take root, learning takes flight. It's a vicious cycle, and while we certainly want boys who have difficulty managing their time to acquire the skills necessary to work more effectively, rigidly enforced time limits don't teach those skills. They just reinforce a boy's awareness of his shortcomings without giving him any alternatives to address them. Remember that the goal of this direction-giving sequence is to support the struggling boy so that he can be more successful academically, not to increase his anxiety in a way that derails a positive outcome before it has a chance to get under way.

Step 7: Pair verbal commands with auditory start/stop signals. If you've ever had students begin an activity before you've finished giving the directions or given the go-ahead to begin, you will immediately appreciate the utility of this step. Prior to giving the go-ahead to begin a task, teachers can maintain students' attention by pairing verbal commands with auditory signals to start and stop. For example, educator and author Rick Smith uses a chime with two tones as the signal: a single tone to begin and a double tone for closure. The verbal command always precedes the initial auditory signal to start, and the verbal command follows the chime when it's time to stop.

What does this look like?

To start the activity,

• Say: *When I give the signal, then you will* _____.
• Give the auditory start signal.

To close the activity,

• Give the auditory stop signal.
• Say: *Please stop.*

Why does it work? The preparatory statement sends two important messages at once: (1) it cues students that they need to wait to begin the activity and (2) it provides a directive that summarizes what students should do first. For a struggling boy, using this procedure consistently provides the kind of repetition that leads to a feeling of safety; it is one more thing about the classroom structure he knows he can count on. For boys with ADD or ADHD—who tend to be impulsive as well as inattentive—this step is especially effective. The only caveat in regard to the use of the auditory signals for this step is that once established, a start or stop signal needs to remain constant (unlike auditory state-change signals, which benefit from frequent variation).

Step 8: Provide backup. In the same way that an underachieving boy may hesitate to clarify directions before the activity starts, he may also hesitate to do so once it actually begins, and no matter how well or carefully his teacher explains the directions, some boys may still need clarification after the activity begins. This is especially true if the activity has multiple steps or the steps are unfamiliar.

The same potential stigma of being singled out or publicly embarrassed holds sway during this step just as it did in Step 7, with the added difficulty that there is no way for the learner to avoid "being seen" asking for help. Thus, it is incumbent upon the teacher to set the stage for this step and make it safe for struggling students to get the help they need, reiterating for all students the same three messages about asking for clarification: first, that it is normal for all students to sometimes need clarification about directions; second, that it is important as well as acceptable to ask for clarification; and third, that it is each student's responsibility to indicate when there is a need for clarification. As was true in Step 7, these messages are more likely to be received in a classroom with a nonthreatening learning climate and a well-developed sense of community in which students support rather than compete with one another. Given repeated practice and opportunity, even the most hesitant boy may feel safe enough to risk asking for help.

Other than the timing of the request for help, the difference between Step 7 and Step 8 is in the way help is requested. In the two strategies that follow, notice that the student initiates the request and it is his responsibility to act upon it and access the available support.

What does this look like?

Several ideas for resolving this problem come from the world of differentiated instruction, particularly the work of Carol Ann Tomlinson (1999).

Record It!

Using any one of the many audio or video recording devices readily available in most classrooms, a teacher can record activity directions ahead of time or even while giving them in class, making recorded directions available to students so that they can easily listen to or view them again, as needed. This strategy is especially helpful for a struggling boy who is highly auditory, who processes language slowly, or who speaks English as a second language. In all of these cases, one exposure may be insufficient. Although auditory learners prefer to gather information using the auditory modality, this does not necessarily mean that they will automatically "get it" on the first hearing. If an auditory learner does not rely on written directions or note taking, he may need to hear directions several times, especially when multiple steps are involved.

Student Experts

Establishing a student role such as "Homework Helper" or even "Subject Matter Expert" (which comes from the world of educational technology and appeals to older students) normalizes the act of one student consulting another for help during learning. This strategy works as a means of clarifying directions once students have begun an activity. In addition to availing himself of help from another student, the struggling boy also has the opportunity to become the Homework Helper or Subject Matter Expert himself, which can be very empowering. Of course, in order for this to work, these positions must be rotated among all students and not saved for those who get the best grades.

To ensure the success of a less secure boy, a teacher might provide the directions for which he is to be responsible ahead of time and let him either take them home to review with a parent or an older sibling or practice with the teacher before the activity commences. A struggling boy might also be paired with another student, allowing them to work together as "consultants."

Why do these strategies work? If we establish for students the normalcy of having to ask for clarification or recheck that they are following the directions correctly once they begin working, the stigma attached to this action begins to fade. A boy who might otherwise feel singled out or shamed by asking for help is freed to do so without compunction. The more we characterize this as a normal and expected activity, the more easily a struggling boy may take advantage of his peers' support as a resource and, thus, have this real-world skill reinforced.

Step 9: Give fair warning. The two-minute, time-is-almost-up reminder is a state change, similar to that employed in Step 1 but used here for a different purpose. This signal can help students prepare for the impending transition to a new activity in a timely manner, minimizing the disruptive frustration of not being quite finished in time.

What does this look like?

Say: *Fair warning, everyone. You have two minutes to finish up what you're doing. At the next signal, please stop work and give me your attention.*

Why does it work? For younger boys, whose emotional immaturity can make it hard to stop doing an activity they are enjoying, this signal is an important boundary. For the first few times, a teacher may want to follow the signal with a quiet verbal reminder to a boy who remains unaware, perhaps casually tapping on his shoulder to make sure he registers what is happening.

A boy with ADD or ADHD often "hyperfocuses," and it may be especially difficult for him to change state once he is finally engaged. The signal can heighten his awareness about the passage of time and reorient him in the here and now.

For a boy who is an NT/Thinker-Knower or an NF/Self-Expressive, both of whom dislike time limits when they are engaged in creative or cerebral activities they feel are important, the reminder may bring him back to reality in a way that is less abrupt.

For an ST/Practical/Doer boy, who may want to keep working because he hasn't gotten his work quite the way he wants it, this signal lets him choose how to make the best use of his remaining time.

Whatever his reason or need, this signal offers a boy the opportunity to self-manage successfully, affirming his competence as a learner and helping him develop the life skill of self-regulation.

Step 10: Acknowledge effort. For some boys, starting and stopping an activity on time and following directions takes a lot of effort. A simple verbal recognition of this fact communicates appreciation for the boy's effort as well as recognition of the difficulty of the task.

What does this look like?

Say: *Thank you for finishing up on time* [or for whatever it is students have done in a timely manner].

Why does this work? For boys who have not done especially well at bringing their work to closure in the past, it's important to acknowledge both the effort to do so and the achievement when they succeed. A simple blanket statement made to the entire class will be heard as recognition of that effort. If you would like to recognize the efforts of a specific student, remember that individual praise should be given carefully. If the student in question shines when given public acknowledgment, then a public statement like "Good effort, John" will be fine. For other students, a moment of eye contact or a subtle thumbs-up will suffice.

The power of this sequence. Each step in this sequence addresses in one or more ways the requests for effective communication in Figure 6.1. These steps are most effective if used frequently, consistently, and in sequence. When boys make simple mistakes or hand in incomplete work because they missed a part of the directions for that activity, the resulting grades can indicate a lack of proficiency that may, in fact, be inaccurate. These are unnecessary and preventable forms of failure.

If we can maximize a struggling boy's ability to attend, listen, understand, self-monitor, and complete classroom tasks without the need to distract us or other students, we also help him to build his competence as a learner. By following the guidelines for providing effective directions, we empower an underachieving boy to demonstrate what he knows in the manner expected, from beginning to end.

Figure 6.3 (p. 120) shows how easy it is to put all the steps together in order. Although this sequence may appear time-consuming at first glance, in reality, the steps are quickly accomplished. And where helping struggling boys is concerned, an initial investment in learning and using these steps on our part can pay major dividends, both for us and our students.

TAKE FIVE

Take a moment to think about the ways you typically give directions to your students. As you review the steps of effective directions in Figure 6.3, think about which step(s) you could easily add to those you're already using. Which boy(s) might benefit as a result?

Access Point: Informational Feedback

Feedback is the most powerful single moderator that enhances achievement.

—John Hattie, professor of education,
University of Auckland, New Zealand

Teacher feedback during learning is an invaluable tool on multiple levels, and it is encouraging to know that something we can easily do on a daily basis has the potential to profoundly affect a struggling boy's academic success (Assessment Reform Group, 2002b; Black & Wiliam, 1998a, 1998b; Boston, 2002). In concert with providing clear directions, the practice of giving informational feedback is another useful way we can address a struggling boy's fear of failure as we help him to move forward in his learning.

Whereas clear directions help an underachieving boy to complete the procedural elements of learning activities more accurately and effectively, the use of high-quality, informational feedback sustains and directs his

FIGURE 6.3
Effective Directions in Sequence

Step 1	Change state.	• *If you can hear my voice, clap once.* (Clap. Students will join in.) • *If you can hear my voice, clap twice.* (Clap twice. More students will join in.) • Soften your voice and say: *If you can hear my voice, look this way.* (By this time, all students—even those who didn't clap—should be focused and ready to listen.)
Step 2	Explain relevance.	• *Thank you for coming to attention so quickly. We have some important work to do today! I am confident that you will do well. Students just like you have been successful in completing this task.* • *In the last lesson we did _____ as a way of gaining expertise in _____.* • *Today, we will continue that process by doing _____.* (Give a general overview only.) • *This is going to help you become more skilled at _____.* • *So, to review, the goal for this lesson is _____.* • *Let's get started!*
Step 3	Be crystal clear.	• *There are three steps to complete in order.* • *Step 1: First, we will _____.* • *Step 2: Second, we will _____.* • *Step 3: Third, we will _____.*
Step 4	Engage multiple modalities.	• *As you read the directions along with me, I will highlight the important words on the overhead.*
Step 5	Check for understanding.	• *Turn to your neighbor and make sure you understand each step.* (Allow several seconds.) • *Group Two, please explain the directions in your own words.*
Step 6	Announce duration.	• *I have set aside approximately _____ (minutes, hours, days) for you to complete your work.* • *You will have plenty of time to finish.*
Step 7	Pair verbal commands with auditory start/stop signals.	• *When I give the signal, you will _____.* (State first step of task.) • Give signal.
Step 8	Provide backup.	• Leave visible the overhead showing written directions.
Step 9	Give fair warning.	• *Students, you have two minutes to finish your work.* • When time is up, give the auditory stop signal. • *Please stop.*
Step 10	Acknowledge effort.	• *Thank you for completing your task and coming to attention.*

Source: From *Boys and School: Challenging Underachievement, Getting It Right!* by K. Cleveland. © 2008 by TeacherOnlineEducation.com. Adapted with permission.

engagement during learning. In addition to reinforcing the trusting relationship between teacher and student, informational feedback helps to replace the underachieving boy's gnawing fear of failure with feelings of self-confidence, because he knows what he is doing well and how to address his shortcomings.

Feedback enhances achievement. Research is unequivocal about feedback as the great enhancer of achievement (Black, Harrison, Lee, Marshall, & Wiliam, 2004; Black & Wiliam, 1998a, 1998b), yet teachers' use of effective feedback is quite limited. To make matters worse, when they do use feedback, many teachers use the wrong kind. Martin suggests, in fact, that ineffective feedback has probably done more to convince struggling boys of their *inability* to succeed than it has ever encouraged them (2002).

We know feedback can help students succeed. The question is how do we offer it in a productive, effective manner?

What makes feedback effective? In Figure 6.4 (pp. 122–123), you will find a comparison between the two types of feedback teachers typically use: judgmental or informational. As you compare the characteristics and examples for each type of feedback, take note of the way that informational feedback always supports a struggling boy in some way, reducing his defensiveness, promoting self-awareness and responsibility, encouraging forward momentum, and inviting him to enter into the learning process actively. We can identify four essential differences between judgmental and informational feedback that account for these positive outcomes.

A difference in timing. The point at which the feedback occurs in relation to the learning experience makes a difference in the underachieving boy's ability to use the feedback productively. Judgmental feedback, as its name suggests, is often given *after* the learning experience ends, at which point an underachieving boy can no longer use it to improve the outcome

> "Feedback . . . helps learners become aware of any gaps that exist between their desired goal and their current knowledge. . . . This type of feedback may be particularly helpful to the lower achieving students because it emphasizes that students can improve as a result of effort rather than be doomed to low achievement due to some presumed lack of ability" (Boston, 2002, p. 2).

of his efforts. A judgmental, though well-meant, "Good job!" doesn't help him know what he did well any more than its opposite—"Needs work"—explains

FIGURE 6.4
Judgmental vs. Informational Feedback

Judgmental Feedback	Informational Feedback
• Focuses on judging • Often interpreted as judging learner (labels) vs. learning • Nonspecific (even if well-meaning) • Summative (no opportunity to revise and improve) • Learner cannot discern what has been done well or poorly • Levied against student with no invitation to participate • Characterizes success as "winning" over others	• Focuses on learning • Central to classroom processes (natural) • Sensitive and constructive • Promotes understanding of goals and criteria • Helps learner know how to improve • Invitational; develops the capacity for self-assessment • Recognizes achievement measured against a standard

Examples	*Characteristics*		*Examples*
Nothing is finished yet? When are you going to get with it?	**Judgmental** ←1→	**Descriptive** (what, where, when, how)	I see each part of the assignment is partially completed. The second step needs two additional sentences.
Nice sentence. See if you can write a few more. Good work.	**Generalized** ←2→	**Specific**	This sentence could be a strong model to use for the others. It's got all of the necessary parts in the correct order.
You really need to work on your coloring.	**About student or student's ability** ←3→	**About a task or behavior** (performance)	Notice how you were able to keep the colors inside the lines that outline this shape? See if you can do that again in this one.
If you had tried harder to get the lab report in on time, you might have gotten a better score.	**Does not benefit the learner** (change is not possible) ←4→	**Benefits the learner** (change is possible)	You consistently do an excellent job following the lab procedures successfully. Think about what might help you to recall what you learned so that you can write about it on the lab report.
Write four more sentences to practice.	**Managerial** ←5→	**Enhances understanding and transfer**	I noticed that you were able to write this sentence more easily after you talked with your study buddy. What do you think helped you?

FIGURE 6.4
Judgmental vs. Informational Feedback (*continued*)

"–2" (numerical score with no additional information) What is wrong with you? You should be able to get these words spelled correctly if you practice that much.	**Focuses on results**	←6→	**Recognizes growth and progress**	You've worked hard on practicing your spelling words with Jimmy. The three-syllable words used to be so hard, but now you are spelling them with ease.
You just don't get it, do you?	**Concludes**	←7→	**Guides**	I know you are trying hard to remember the steps for this problem. Let's look at the ones you've remembered and see what to work on next.

Source: From *Assessment for Learning: 10 Principles* (pamphlet), by the Assessment Reform Group, 2002, Cambridge, UK: University of Cambridge Faculty of Education. © 2002 by the ARG; "Assessment as Feedback," by G. Wiggins, 2004, in *New Horizons for Learning.* Available: www.newhorizons.org/strategies/assess/wiggins.htm. © 2004 by New Horizons for Learning. Adapted with permission.

how to fix the problems he is having. Informational feedback, on the other hand, is typically given *during* the learning experience (e.g., "Notice how you were able to keep the colors inside the lines that outline this shape. See if you can do that again in this one.").

A difference in purpose. The perceived purpose of the feedback makes a difference in the way a learner understands it. Judgmental feedback quantifies the results of a boy's efforts, and many students interpret it as a judgment of who they are as a person or their overall ability to learn (i.e., "Stupid mistake" is perceived as "You are stupid"). Because the student sees

> "Pupils who encounter difficulties are led to believe that they lack ability, and this belief leads them to attribute their difficulties to a defect in themselves about which they cannot do a great deal. Thus they avoid investing in learning that can only lead to disappointment, and they try to build up their self-esteem in other ways" (Black & Wiliam, 1998b, p. 142).

no way to change the judgment, even if he subsequently acquires the proficiency he previously lacked, he may also feel a sense of hopelessness or react with a "why bother?" attitude, thereby intensifying the negative effect of the feedback.

Conversely, the purpose of informational feedback is to enhance the possibility of a boy's success by helping him to catch his errors and misconceptions *before* they are assessed, while he can still shore up any weak spots and clarify misperceptions and misunderstandings. This kind of feedback continually empowers a struggling boy because it shows him how to rectify problem areas (e.g., "I see each part of the assignment is partially completed, so you have a good start. The second step needs two additional sentences.").

A difference in focus. Judgmental feedback usually compares students with one another to determine who is "best." A struggling boy rarely comes out on top in this contest, and his

> "Learners' beliefs about their own capacity as learners can affect their achievement" (Black & Wiliam, 1998a, p. 24).

view of himself as both incompetent and stupid may be reinforced again and again, even though he might be making enormous strides personally. Informational feedback, by contrast, compares a boy's work with his past progress on specific proficiencies. The focus is on helping him improve (e.g., "You consistently do an excellent job in following the lab procedures. Think about what might help you recall what you learned so that you can write about it on the lab report."). He is able to see his progress, noting each incremental step forward and building his sense of competence as a result. This is key to getting an underachieving boy to re-engage with learning, because a sense of personal competence as a learner is often central to his ability or desire to persist (Black & Wiliam, 1998a; Gardner, Harlen, Hayward, & Stobart, 2008).

A difference in language. The language used when giving judgmental feedback differs vastly from that used when giving informational feedback. Judgmental feedback often takes the form of a quantitative or comparative

> "Feedback should be private, must be linked to opportunities for improvement, and should encourage the view that mistakes are part of learning" (Black & Wiliam, 1998a, p. 24).

label, for example, a score, a letter grade, or a comment such as "Nice!" or "Needs work." As such, it offers a struggling boy no help in terms of better understanding how he is or is not proficient and what he did well or still needs to work on. It is meaningless feedback in terms of helping him *learn* and do better. Informational feedback, on the other hand, actually identifies a boy's strengths and shortcomings, focusing on how the boy can use his knowledge of both to move forward, for example, "I know you are trying hard to remember the steps for this problem. Let's look at the ones you've completed and see what to work on next." These types of comments affirm him as a learner and show him how to continue improving. They focus on his progress. Notice that the examples of informational feedback in Figure 6.4 demonstrate these qualities of affirmation and providing concrete suggestions for improvement, whereas the examples of judgmental feedback do just the opposite.

In virtually every respect, informational feedback does precisely what a struggling boy most needs it to do: it provides initial encouragement as well as ongoing support that continually build his sense of competence. Assessment experts remind us that feedback (which is, after all, a form of assessment) has an emotional component that is linked to a learner's motivation (Black & Wiliam, 1998a, 1998b). Recall also that the boys most at risk in our classrooms are SF/Interpersonal and NF/Self-Expressive in style, and their style, coupled with their sensitivity to prior failure, may make them even more attuned to the emotional valence of our feedback, especially when it is corrective in nature. If we genuinely want our feedback to support student growth, we must pay attention to these sensitivities and, thus, to what we say and how we say it.

An invaluable tool for supporting struggling boys. Although many of us recognize and appreciate the differences between informational and judgmental feedback, we tend to use judgmental feedback anyway because that is what we received as students. In

> "It yields particularly good results with low achievers by concentrating on specific problems with their work and giving them a clear understanding of what is wrong and how to put it right" (Black & Wiliam, 1998b, p. 143).

a pinch, we revert to what was done to us. Unfortunately, even as we acknowledge the folly of this practice, few of us realize that by using judgmental feedback, we also forfeit one of the most powerful tools at our disposal.

Informational feedback is among the most effective means for supporting the academic achievement of those who struggle most to learn. Multiple studies confirm that the performance and motivation of low achievers, in particular, benefit from informational feedback (Assessment Reform Group, 1999; Black & Wiliam, 1998a, 1998b; Black et al., 2004). The list of positive outcomes that result from the use of informational feedback includes increased interest, effort, persistence, self-esteem, self-belief, and emotional investment; learned resourcefulness; and an attitude of hope, belonging, and willingness (Petty, n.d.).

Key Resource: Geoff Petty's Medals & Missions

Geoff Petty's "medals and missions" formula for providing informational feedback (n.d.) offers educators a concrete, easy-to-use approach for giving struggling boys the feedback they need in a way that lowers defensiveness and also makes real-world sense. It builds on success rather than focusing on failure, addressing the task without levying any judgment against the boy himself.

Figure 6.5 illustrates the simplicity of the medals and missions formula. Step One requires us to stop and think before offering verbal feedback to the student. In Step Two—before we say anything corrective—we affirm the boy by describing something he has done successfully (the medal). Only then do we complete Step Three, delivering informational feedback that can be characterized as a goal or a "mission."

The idea behind medals and missions is that the best way to motivate a struggling boy, in terms of the feedback we give him, is to combine information about what he has done well (the medal), followed by information about what he still needs to fix, stating the latter in the context of meeting

---

FIGURE 6.5
The Medals & Missions Feedback Formula

Step One	Step Two	Step Three
Before you say a word, stop and think.	Describe what's right or what has been done well (the *medal*).	Describe what needs to be done (the *mission*).

Source: From "Assessment and Classroom Learning," by P. Black and D. Wiliam, 1998, *Assessment in Education,* 5(1). © 1998 by Black and Wiliam. Adapted by G. Petty for *Black and Wiliam 1998,* n.d., p. 3. Available: www.geoffpetty.com/downloads/WORD/BlackandWiliam.doc. Adapted with permission.

a goal (the mission). One of the greatest assets of this simple strategy is the frequency with which it can be used to reinforce and support a struggling boy on a daily basis. Each use meets many of the basic requests for effective communication mentioned earlier in this chapter (see Figure 6.1): the medal allows the boy to save face (Request No. 4) and acknowledges his efforts (Request No. 9); the mission explains clearly what the boy needs to do next (Request No. 1); the effort taken to explain what is meeting expectations and what needs improvement communicates that the boy matters (Request No. 7); and the interchange itself feels respectful (Request No. 10). Thus, using the medals and missions approach helps an underachieving boy (especially one who may be defensive as a result of prior failure) to hear and process what he needs to know in order to improve.

Research clearly indicates that boys who believe they can achieve are often able to do just that, and the converse, sadly, is equally true (Black & Wiliam, 1998b). If we take a closer look at the "medal" and the "mission," we can see why they are so effective at instilling the former in struggling learners. When we offer the underachieving boy a medal—that is, we take the time to pause and begin our feedback with something affirming—the boy interprets this as: "My teacher doesn't think I'm a complete failure. That's a good thing. My teacher thinks I have done things well before, so that means I can do things well again." In other words, offering the medal acknowledges the boy as competent, and then proceeds to offer him a way to increase that competence, all the while communicating both support and an expectation that he *can* achieve the goal.

The mission portion of the process frames the need for change using language that resonates well with many boys because of its real-world conno-tations. The term "mission" refocuses the boy's attention on moving forward rather than feeling sensitive or defensive about why this is necessary. It takes the sting out of making a mistake or "not getting it" by focusing on what to do next instead of focusing on what is lacking. Because we have already engaged the boy by affirming him, he is now able to actually hear what needs to be done next. And when we phrase our feedback as a mission to be undertaken rather than as a correction, he is also more able to take the risk required to move forward.

In Figure 6.6 you'll find several examples of how medals and missions feedback might sound in practical use.

FIGURE 6.6
Examples of Medals & Missions Feedback

Step One: Pause & Think	Step Two: The "Medal"	Step Three: The "Mission"
Instead of saying something like this…	*Describe what's right or what has been done well (the medal).*	*Describe what needs to be done (the mission).*
Oh, for goodness' sake. Don't tell me you forgot to add the heading to your paper again. Are you ever going to get it right?	You've got the first and second pages of this report finished. I see that you have the date correct.	Before you turn in the finished report, check the format for the heading. An example of it is on the board.
This is the third time this quarter that you have turned in a lab report late. Can't you read the schedule? Do you know how to read a calendar?	You consistently do an excellent job in following the lab procedures successfully.	Think about what might help you to recall what you learned so that you can write about it on the lab report.
You'd think you'd understand this by now. We've been over it time and time again.	I see that you are trying hard to remember the steps for this problem. It looks like the first two steps are in the right order.	Let's look at just the next step for a moment and see if you can find a way to remember it as well.
You can't write a story with just one fact listed after another. Can't you see that it's boring? There's no description, no interesting words, and you don't even have a conclusion.	I see that you know many facts about dinosaurs. You must be very interested in this topic.	To turn your ideas into a story, you can use this organizer. You can begin by putting one fact in each of these boxes labeled "main idea."

Source: From *Boys and School: Challenging Underachievement, Getting It Right!* by K. Cleveland. © 2008 by TeacherOnlineEducation.com. Adapted with permission.

> ✿ **TAKE FIVE**
>
> Take a moment to think about the ways you typically offer corrective feedback to your underachieving boys during learning activities. Do you typically preface the mission with a medal, or do you tend to skip right to the mission? And how do you phrase the mission? Is it in the form of informational or judgmental feedback? Can you think of any boys who might hear and process your corrective feedback better if you took just a moment to insert a medal first? What would that sound like?

Access Point: Positive Reinforcement

As we continue to think about the connections between feedback and motivation (e.g., giving the medal before the mission when providing feedback), it is worth noting that many of the participating teachers in the Alloway study (2002) shared a common observation that their boys' underachievement had much to do with low self-concept. When a boy is

> "Through their project reports and at interview, teachers made frequent comment about the importance of focusing on boys' self-esteem. However, the term was more often directly equated with boys' confidence in themselves as learners at school and literacy learners in particular than with a globalised valuing of themselves as human beings" (Alloway et al., 2002, p. 140).

unable to see himself as capable, he is prone to give up rather than to persist when the going gets rough. If that same boy also feels unworthy of getting the help he needs, he is unlikely to ask for it, perhaps convinced that he will be ignored even if he does ask. In other words, a boy's perception of himself as capable or worthy can affect his academic achievement in ways that are less obvious than lack of skill or diminished readiness, but equally detrimental.

Thus, the potential importance of positive reinforcement becomes clear. As with informational feedback, this kind of feedback supports a struggling boy's academic achievement, but the process and the results are slightly different. With positive reinforcement, achievement increases because a boy's perception of himself as a learner shifts.

Key Resource: John F. Taylor's Super Strokes

In his book *From Defiance to Cooperation: Real Solutions for Transforming the Angry, Defiant, Discouraged Child* (2001a), John F. Taylor offers simple affirming statements—what he calls "super strokes"—that we can use to reinforce struggling boys verbally (see Figure 6.7, pp. 132–133). As Taylor explains, these "super strokes are statements that tend to develop, maintain, or enhance the child's experiencing of self-worth, social impact, self-direction, or self-confidence" (p. 79). In other words, they focus on the boy, not on his learning. As such, they are trust builders, similar to the leader coach strategy, supporting the boy in a way that builds the trust that ultimately frees him to undertake the risks of learning.

I have included this resource because many teachers reach a point of real exasperation in dealing with some of their struggling boys, a state that can be difficult to "undo." When there has been little in the way of positive communication between a teacher and a student, a boy, rightly or wrongly, may perceive that his teacher thinks he is "bad," no matter what he tries to do. And his perception may become a self-fulfilling prophecy if the pattern of negative communication and behavior continues its downward spiral. In light of what we already know about how important the relationship between boy and teacher is, a teacher's ready access to simple statements such as Taylor's super strokes can help to break the cycle of negativity and rebuild the damaged relationship.

In fact, you may have noticed that many of these statements could also work as the medal in medals and missions feedback. These brief affirmations are also helpful in moments when we just can't think of anything to say, yet we know that even a few words need to be said. They recognize something good and valuable in a struggling boy, words many of these boys *never* hear. Their "being" is rarely noticed, let alone affirmed. Using these statements purposefully and intentionally can be a simple yet powerful gift.

I offer them with a word of caution, however, especially for readers who have a tendency toward sarcasm. All kids, but especially our most vulnerable ones, are highly attuned to the real intent behind our words. If you are unable to say these phrases with sincerity, it may be best not to say them at all. Students will know if your words are not heartfelt and, if such is the case, these statements communicate not support but rather the opposite.

> ✳ **TAKE FIVE**
>
> Take a moment to think about the ways you communicate verbally with the boys who either struggle the most in your classroom or with whom you seem to have difficulty forming a trusting relationship. How often do you give these students positive feedback or reinforcement that is not strictly related to work or performance? What might happen if you did? Which of the 13 affirming statements from Figure 6.7 could you adapt to use at times like this?

Milepost

Pathway No. 2: Guide is about communicating with a struggling boy in ways that will help him to do his best. Whether during academic work or during informal teacher-student interactions, our heightened awareness about both the words we use and the way we deliver them can make a difference in what a struggling boy hears and how he responds. We can enhance the likelihood of successful academic outcomes by using care in the *ways we give directions*, and we may help to keep the fear of failure at bay using *informational feedback* along with *positive reinforcement*, building the underachieving boy's sense of self along with his feelings of capability.

> **BUILDING A REPERTOIRE OF RESPONSES**
>
> Before you move on to the next chapter, pause to note any "aha!" moments you've had along the way.
>
> 1. What do you now understand about how struggling boys learn best that you didn't know before?
>
> 2. Of the strategies you are currently using, which could be tweaked or used more intentionally for an even greater positive outcome?
>
> 3. Which ideas or strategies caught your attention the most?
>
> 4. Choose one idea or strategy related to this Pathway that you could implement right now.

FIGURE 6.7
Affirming Statements for Struggling Boys

Purpose of Statement	Examples
Acknowledge Effort	• You remembered not to speak again until everyone else had had a turn. • I noticed that you (got here earlier, completed more practice problems, worked on your margins).
Affirm Growth	• You definitely finished this task more quickly today. • I can see that this is getting easier for you now. • Look at how many of the words you spelled correctly! • Do you remember how hard it used to be for you to (sit still, talk in class, volunteer an answer, turn in your work on time, get to class on time, work in groups, wait to raise your hand)?
Clarify Positive Self-Impact	• Your soccer practices are helping you build stamina and muscle strength. • Choosing the topic you want may make your research more fun. • Trying PowerPoint might be a great way to incorporate the graphics you like to use. • With your new notebook system, you'll be able to track your homework.
Describe the Act	• You cleaned off your desk. • You brought back your book order form. • You got in line quickly and quietly. • You kept your hands to yourself when you were waiting.
Empathize	• It seemed like you really enjoyed (doing something, seeing something, talking with someone, going somewhere, trying something). • That sounded like it was (scary, fun, awful, hilarious, embarrassing).
Identify Positive Consequences	• If you can make sure your parents sign the form, I'll be able to include you in the field trip next week. • Because you helped John find his lost pencil yesterday, he wants to help you when it's your job to empty the trash. • Asking the Student Helper for clarification helped you finish each step in order.
Notice a Skill	• You really seem to know your way around your (computer, software, engine, book). • You used some very interesting (words, drawings, graphics, ideas) here.
Show Gratitude	• Thanks! • I appreciated it when you/that you (helped, tried, came back on time, finished on time, paid attention, hung up your coat, brought back the note).

FIGURE 6.7

Affirming Statements for Struggling Boys (*continued*)

Notice Something Personal	• You have such a great smile! Always nice to see it. • New (haircut, jeans, top, cell phone, book)?
Point Out Positive Social Impact	• When you were honest about what you thought, others were encouraged to speak up, too. • Taking the time to finish your chart helped your whole group's grade go up.
Reframe Behaviors with a Positive "Spin"	• Doodling can help you organize your thoughts. • Talking things out with a friend can help you figure out what's important. • Taking time to answer gives you more time to think about what you want to say.
Reinforce Self-Determination	• You get to make this choice. • If that's what you decide, then plan where to start first.
Show Interest	• How were you able to (make that work, fix that problem, find that answer)? • Tell me more about (your ideas, what this means, this picture, what happened, what you enjoyed).

Source: From *From Defiance to Cooperation: Real Solutions for Transforming the Angry, Defiant, Discouraged Child* (p. 79), by J. F. Taylor, 2001, New York: Three Rivers Press. © 2001 by J. F. Taylor. Adapted with permission.

What's Next?

In Pathway No. 3: Reinforce, we will explore two skill sets that many underachieving boys have not developed—communication and collaboration. Their lack of proficiency in these two areas frequently interferes with their academic success due to their inability to negotiate the social and interpersonal aspects of classroom learning. By connecting communication and collaboration skills to their value as real-world tools, we help underachieving boys learn to be more successful in school and beyond.

CHAPTER 7

Pathway No. 3: Reinforce

Must possess strong verbal and written communication skills, interpersonal skills, a positive attitude, and the ability to thrive in a collaborative agency environment.

—Job description, March 2010

Business and industry leaders are crying out for better-prepared graduates, and as the job description above illustrates, among the most desired skills in new hires are the abilities to communicate and work collaboratively. It will likely come as no surprise that these same skills are cited as distinguishing characteristics of boys who are most successful in our schools and, conversely, that they are among those least developed in our unsuccessful boys (Partnership for 21st Century Skills, 2009). Universally applicable to any content area or grade level and critical to both the social and the academic aspects of the learning process, communication and collaboration skills act as skeleton keys to a variety of doorways to academic success. Individually, each skill set is highly beneficial to the underachieving boy; when both are in place, their value increases exponentially.

Yet if these skills are so important in the real world and recognized as essential to a boy's success while in school, perhaps the larger question is why so many boys have not developed them. To be sure, the Code's influence, combined with the widespread absence of positive male role models who might offer real-life examples of such skills, aggravates the situation. But there is more at work here. Somewhere along the line, we stopped teaching these skills explicitly; communication and collaboration have unceremoniously been added to what Smith and Wilhelm call the ever-growing "list of secret things that accomplished [learners] know, yet never talk about" (2006, pp. 21–22), a considerable handicap for those boys who have no way to acquire or practice these skills elsewhere. Smith and Wilhelm go on to say that where boys are concerned, we must teach these skills explicitly, and that includes finding ways to help boys acquire, practice, apply, and make sense of them. This, then, is the focus of Pathway No. 3: Reinforce and its two Access Points: Communication Skill Building and Collaboration Skill Building.

When it comes to motivating boys to acquire and master communication and collaboration skills, we are fortunate to have a boy-friendly tool in our toolbox: real-world relevance. As the Big Four repeatedly point out, connecting learning to the real world is one of the most effective ways we can engage boys in any kind of learning. Many boys crave this connection, and we can use this natural preference as a way to help boys develop skills that may be difficult to learn or understand.

> "Maximising the relevance and meaning of school requires educators to: Link what is taught with world events, students' lives or interests, [and] what they may do when they leave school... [and] show how school not only teaches students facts but also teaches them how to think and analyse and that these help them in many walks of life including their social and personal lives, in the workplace, and on the sporting field" (Martin, 2002, p. 96).

Emphasizing real-world relevance opens up two avenues for approaching the daunting task of cultivating communication and collaboration skills in our underachieving boys. First, it helps underachieving boys understand the practical value of these skills, and second, it has very few application limitations, that is, there is no shortage of authentic settings in which students can practice these skills. It's "real-world" times three: a real-world skill with a real-world purpose practiced in a setting with real-world authenticity. Approaching the introduction and reinforcement of communication and collaboration in this manner, perhaps more than any other strategies discussed in this book, offers underachieving boys with the SF/Interpersonal or NF/Self-Expressive profile a unique opportunity to hone their natural skills and receive affirmation for their inherent abilities.

Access Point: Tools for Communicating

If we are to live and work together, we have to talk to each other.

—Eleanor Roosevelt

Though boys crave opportunities to interact with their peers—a need that intensifies when they reach middle school—the degree of success experienced during these exchanges relies on a boy's possession of skills commonly lumped together under the title "communication skills" (i.e., the ability to speak to, listen to, and "read" other people). When a boy, for any number of reasons, does not possess such skills, his unsuccessful attempts to interact with others may push him toward the world of "electronica"—video games, chat rooms, instant messaging—where he can easily escape the awkwardness and difficulty of face-to-face interactions (Cox, 2006a). The further a boy retreats from genuine social interaction, the harder it may be for him to reenter the process. Author Adam Cox goes so far as to suggest that "many boys are on the verge of social bankruptcy" (2006a, p. 53), with communication skills being the main "currency" lost as a result of their retreat.

The Role of Emotional Literacy

Prison educator Robert Pleasants supports Cox's sense of urgency in addressing boys' widespread problems with communication, a skill set Pleasants sees not just as the foundation of social interaction but also of emotional literacy and self-awareness (2007). Wise choices about how to respond to others' words and actions

> "Adolescent males can build their emotional literacy by learning how to identify others' emotions as well as their own. In order to deal with their emotions, they must first be able to recognize them. They also need to understand the situation or reactions that produce their emotional states, especially if those feelings may

depend on a boy's self-awareness and empathy, both of which are rooted in his emotional literacy or his ability to recognize, describe, interpret, and respond appropriately to emotional states of being, in oneself and in others.

eventually lead to violence. Becoming aware of their own emotions and developing empathy for others may help prevent male offenders from committing other crimes" (Pleasants, 2007, p. 6).

Unfortunately, thanks to the Code's demands for emotional stoicism and a shortage of either real-world or classroom opportunities to practice, many boys never get the chance to develop emotional literacy, and its absence affects the productivity of their interpersonal verbal communication as well as behavioral self-regulation (i.e., interpreting the actions of others and reacting appropriately). The restrictions placed on emotional growth by the Code are especially detrimental for the underachieving boy who may already experience lack of academic or social success.

For the at-risk SF/Interpersonal or NF/Self-Expressive boy, the Code's condemnation of emotional awareness and the ability to express oneself is especially ironic because interpersonal communication and emotional literacy are actually two of his distinctive strengths as a learner. Like boys of all learning styles, however, they are often prevented from developing these abilities in our schools, cut short in one of two ways: by their peers as a result of the Code's influence, which labels the SF/NF boy's natural desire to connect and support others as feminine and, thus, to be avoided at all costs; and second, by their teachers, as a result of our own (albeit unintentional) short-sightedness when it comes to recognizing the ways in which connecting with and supporting others can play a valuable role in academic learning.

In the end, all boys suffer at the hands of the Code's pernicious influence. The boys most able to communicate with others are restricted from doing so just as much as the boys least gifted in this skill set. When we reframe communication as an essential real-world skill and provide opportunities for boys to learn and practice communicating in authentic settings, we reactivate the use of these gifts in our SF/Interpersonal and NF/Self-Expressive boys and expand these capacities within our ST/Practical Doer and NT/Thinker-Knower boys, making their use and practice acceptably masculine and elevating their value as tools in the real world. Rather than marking a "feeling" boy as "different from," the ability to communicate now marks him as capable, giving him permission to use the skills that will help him achieve academically. And rather than further handicap our "thinker" boys by failing to support the development of a skill they lack, we bolster their efforts to achieve proficiency.

An exhaustive examination of the topic of communication skills and the acquisition thereof lies outside the scope of this book, but with this Access Point, we can at least look at the strategies for building communication skills that are most likely to benefit underachieving boys, as well as how we can help boys learn those skills in our classrooms.

Key Resource: Adam Cox's Pragmatic Communication Skills

By teasing out many of the "sub-skills" associated with communication competence, Adam Cox's list of pragmatic communication skills helps clarify why achieving competence is so daunting for the many boys who struggle to communicate effectively and why it is equally challenging for us to teach them how (see Figure 7.1). Communication isn't just about finding which words to say; teaching boys to communicate involves helping them understand the emotional subtext of words and body language in order to receive and respond to others appropriately (2006b, pp. 2–3). Learning to "read" others informs a boy's thinking, his emotions, his language, and his behaviors. As Figure 7.1 demonstrates, the process of communicating effectively involves physical, verbal, and cognitive skills.

> "Expressive communication paves the way for greater social and academic success in childhood, as well as greater personal and professional opportunities in adulthood. Boys who fail to understand the nuances of social interaction, and who aren't given the tools they need to define and express their feelings and wishes, are at a disadvantage in most aspects of contemporary life" (Cox, 2006b, p. 1).

As you examine this list of communication skills, doubtless an array of boys' faces comes to mind, each missing a combination of skills, each suffering in some way from a disconnect between what he says or does and how it affects others. The missing link is often his inability to understand and respond to subtleties of human expression, both in himself and in others.

FIGURE 7.1
Cox's Pragmatic Communication Skills

Domain	Skill	
Physical	(1)	Maintaining appropriate conversational distance
	(2)	Maintaining eye contact
	(3)	Linking gestures with ideas or emotions
	(4)	Using facial expression effectively
Verbal	(5)	Attending to time and place
	(6)	Turn taking
	(7)	Voice modulation
	(8)	Giving compliments
	(9)	Greetings and farewells
Cognitive	(10)	Detecting emotions in others
	(11)	Perceiving and expressing humor
	(12)	Knowing how to make conversational transitions
	(13)	Anticipating other people's reactions

Source: From *Teaching Boys Pragmatic Communication* by A. J. Cox, 2006. Available: www.dradamcox.com/pdf/ PragmaticCommunication.pdf. Adapted with permission.

• Jake stands too close when he talks, speaks with his head down, and sometimes just walks away without explanation while someone is talking to him. *Communication skills missing: (1) maintaining appropriate conversational distance, (2) maintaining eye contact, and (9) greetings and farewells.*

• Mikey hears the other kids laugh at an "inside joke." Even though he doesn't get the joke, he tries to repeat it, thinking the group will like him better as a result and not understanding when they ignore or disdain him further. *Communication skills missing: (11) perceiving and expressing humor and (13) anticipating other people's reactions.*

• Eli has a hard time during group work because he interrupts others constantly and doesn't seem to notice how irritated this makes his peers. Once Eli starts talking, he is usually oblivious to nonverbal signals of others and doesn't sense when they are bored with his endless, meandering language. *Communication skills missing: (5) attending to time and place, (6) turn taking, (10) detecting emotions in others, and (13) anticipating other people's reactions.*

- Colin doesn't realize that when someone smiles at him, he should smile back. He is confused when he tries to talk to the person who smiled earlier and is met with hostile silence in return. *Communication skills missing: (3) linking gestures with ideas or emotions and (4) using facial expression effectively.*

- Finn wants so badly to belong that he laughs loudly at others' jokes, thinking that the volume of his response communicates the degree of his interest. *Communication skills missing: (7) voice modulation and (13) anticipating other people's reactions.*

- Though he is trying to be helpful, Alex comes across as conceited when he tells other students what they could have done better. *Communication skills missing: (8) giving compliments and (13) anticipating other people's reactions.*

- Talking with Braden sometimes feels like talking to a brick wall. Even though he may be interested in the conversation, it's almost impossible to tell. He rarely picks up the thread of a conversation, so if the speaker stops talking, there is silence. *Communication skills missing: (4) using facial expression effectively and (12) knowing how to make conversational transitions.*

Cox argues persuasively that the most effective way to help boys develop missing communication skills is to offer explicit instruction along with practice sessions embedded within everyday academic learning activities, thereby adding real-world relevance to both the skill development and the learning.

In the following three scenarios, you will see all 13 of Cox's pragmatic communication skills addressed, sometimes singly and at other times combined in a role-playing exercise or integrated into an activity that requires their use in order to achieve a positive outcome. These three scenarios demonstrate different ways to approach teaching boys the same set of communication skills: by providing explicit instruction and guided practice, by modeling the skills, or by embedding their use in a real-world activity. All three offer a real-world connection along with an opportunity for boys to practice and own the skills, making sense of them by experiencing their value in an authentic context. And though each scenario is ostensibly tied to a specific grade-level grouping, the approaches in each scenario are easily applied to all levels.

Scenario A: Jan Deets, Grade 4

Social Skills Instruction

Marcus came to my classroom shortly after school started. I gradually found out that he was the youngest of five children and that his father had left the family the year before. It wasn't long before the other kids started to complain about his behavior. It wasn't that he was malicious so much as oblivious to how his behavior was affecting others. He wanted to make friends, but would butt into established conversations or stand way too close and make the other students uncomfortable. No one knew quite what to say, but it was obvious that things were getting worse. The harder Marcus tried, the less kids liked him or wanted to give him any leeway for being new.

I decided to see if I could help Marcus develop some of the skills he seemed to be missing without singling him out. After we'd done some initial class-building activities, I started putting the kids in teams. You can imagine the response from the kids who had Marcus in their groups. So I backed off from group work for a while and focused on teaching some general social skills first, ones that I hoped, in time, would help Marcus function better in a team setting.

Every few weeks or so, I'd introduce a new communication skill. I'd give an idea of what the skill looked like in context by demonstrating it, and then I'd ask the students to create a "Looks like/Sounds like" chart on which they recorded examples of language and behaviors that might exemplify this skill. We posted the chart on a special area of the bulletin board at the front of the classroom, where it remained throughout the week. Students referred to the information on the chart during practice sessions, when they would role-play situations that required the use of the new communication skill.

Whenever we started on a new skill, we'd create a new "Looks like/Sounds like" chart and move the old one to a spot on the classroom wall near the bulletin board so that we could continue to practice it, too. By the end of the year, we had quite an impressive collection!

We started off with really basic things like how far apart one should stand when talking, how to make appropriate eye contact, and how loudly to talk in different situations. For the first skill, we even got out rulers and made our own determination of what a good distance was. Because we couldn't decide at first, we taped three distances on the floor (12, 18, and 24 inches apart). For two days, the kids took turns trying out these distances during conversations and judging which one they thought was best. When we voted, the general consensus was that 18 inches was just about right for a regular conversation, but that 12 inches was sometimes necessary during classwork so that kids could keep their voices down and still be heard.

Every month, we'd have a "scavenger hunt." I'd announce the communication skill(s) the students were to look for that day (they could be any of the ones we had learned and practiced thus far), and their job was to keep a record of any time they "found" someone who was using the skill. They'd watch me, each other, other kids in the school, other teachers, the school staff, and even the principal to see if they could glimpse anyone using that skill. At day's end, we'd gather all of our examples and write them on sticky notes. Each student got to share at least one example and then add his or her sticky note(s) to the "Looks like/Sounds like" chart with the name of the skill on it. As weeks passed, we added some additional challenges to the hunt, such as only having a certain number of hours to make observations or only getting examples from students (not teachers or staff).

What made it especially fun as the year went on is that the students got really good at looking for the skills in action. They talked about them, compared their observations, and took pride in knowing the skills. Gradually, the skills made their way into students' interactions, too.

As for Marcus, we couldn't quite believe the change in him. For whatever reason, he became the expert at standing exactly 18 inches away from other kids. He realized that he didn't have to speak loudly to be heard, and that if he wanted someone's attention, he could get it without butting in. It wasn't a perfect solution, but my goodness, what a difference it made! In time, he was able to understand so much more about relating to others that he finally made a few close friends. One boy in particular, who was having lots of problems with writing, became Marcus's project. Marcus started to help him with ideas, and before long, they were best buddies. Marcus left our class before the school year was up, but I'd like to think that he took some of these newfound skills with him to the next classroom he entered.

Scenario B: Andy Merrill, Grade 7

Visiting Mentor

I noticed that many of the boys in my classroom were oblivious to their general lack of communication skills, and though it was clear that they had increasing interest in social interaction with girls, few boys even attempted it. The girls, by comparison, seemed light years ahead in their ability to talk with one another and to express what they were thinking and feeling.

After listening to a business friend complain about the poor communication skills he saw in job applicants, I thought of a way that I could get at some of the skills many of my boys (and girls) lacked without actually announcing the deficit. Our next language arts lesson was on summarizing information to determine main points, and I invited my friend, John, to be a guest speaker in our class. It helped that he had grown up in our neighborhood and was familiar to many of my students, so the kids were pretty interested that he was coming. Their assigned task was to interact with John, asking him questions about what he looks for in the student interns he hires each spring. The goal was to gather as much information as they could, then work in small groups to identify the key points of John's presentation. The groups would then share their lists, and the class would come to a consensus on the key points. At that point, we would invite John back and see if we had successfully summarized his main ideas.

What my students didn't know was that I'd asked John to talk specifically about communication problems he saw in the prospective interns he met with. John and I singled out three of the biggest problems, all of which were common to the boys in my classroom: maintaining appropriate conversational distance, making eye contact, and using body language to demonstrate interest and attentiveness.

As John talked, he made a point of emphasizing how important these three skills were. He involved the students by pulling "volunteers" from the audience and demonstrating what was appropriate and inappropriate. He shared relevant stories of his experiences and explained why he looked for applicants with strong communication skills.

After he left, the students did a great job of summarizing his talk, which just happened to be about communication skills. We eventually agreed on four main points and invited John back to see how well we'd summarized what he wanted to say. He returned not just once but many times during the year. Each time, he would find ways to affirm students for their communication skills, and they would find ways to demonstrate them. During John's visits, he often made a point of talking with the girls, too, always modeling additional communication skills whenever he had a chance. Of course, these gradually made their way into several boys' repertoires, too.

Scenario C: Patrick McNeeley, Grade 11

Buying a Car

I run a school-to-work program for several area high schools. Transportation to the job site is required for work-study students, and many of my seniors are at a stage where they are looking to purchase their own car for this purpose. Knowing that most of my students had never taken part in any kind of formal business transaction, I wanted to help them prepare for this major life task by building up their communication skills.

In the classroom, we started out by discussing what kinds of cars students wanted to purchase. By asking a series of questions, I got them to think about practical issues regarding the purchase of an automobile.

We examined a listing of vehicles up for auction, and as we discussed the pros and cons of the automobiles listed, students generated selection criteria based on affordability and reliability. The more they talked, the more precise their language became. Eventually, the students selected three vehicles that met the established criteria.

Next, we took a field trip to a car auction, where they viewed the automobiles they'd discussed. They walked through the process of obtaining an auction number and learned about the auction process. I explained how much money is required to make a bid and what one says when making a bid. Their job was to follow the three vehicles as they moved through the actual auction process. When the students returned to the classroom, they discussed the auction and used the NADA (National Automobile Dealers Association) used car guide to look up the value of one of the vehicles and determine if the purchaser got a "good buy."

Each student chose one of the three cars he or she had seen at the auction and filled out a loan application form to purchase that vehicle. We generated questions to ask the loan officer from the credit union, and before we actually visited the loan officer, we also did some role-playing so students could get a sense of what they would be asked and how to respond. We talked about eye contact and handshakes and standing up straight. During the role-plays, I intentionally did all kinds of things wrong and asked the students to critique me (which they *loved*).

When we visited the credit union, the students presented the loan officer with the questions they had prepared. After getting answers as a group, the kids split up and each got a chance to go through the loan application process. I looked across the room and could see each one sitting up tall, making eye contact, asking questions, and responding clearly.

Clearly, each of these scenarios offers boys who struggle to communicate the opportunity to acquire and practice essential skills in authentic settings. Let's also stop and examine how these three examples fit into the larger picture of helping underachieving boys succeed.

Reliance on a trusting teacher-student relationship. For starters, each of these scenarios reinforces the necessity of a strong and trusting teacher-student relationship and a nonthreatening learning community. Each of these teachers succeeded in reaching their students because these foundations were already in place.

Access and relevance. Each scenario also offers two invaluable points of access that make these communication-building activities both practical and purposeful. First, each can be accomplished in heterogeneous classroom settings as an integral part of daily academic learning activities. In other words, we don't have to separate boys from girls in order to help boys build these skills. Second, the skill building occurs within the context of student-to-student interaction. Thus, it has immediate social relevance to the underachiever and, over time, academic relevance as well, because the communication skills eventually become an integral part of academic learning. Success in one realm leads to success in the other.

In each scenario, communication skills instruction is an integral part of daily classroom operations. In addition, the choice of what skill to focus on during any given lesson is frequently an organic decision, arising out of the teacher's awareness of specific issues with which his or her boys are wrestling, thereby ensuring the relevance of the skill being taught. Because the skills are interwoven into the everyday "goings-on" of the class, no one boy's deficits are singled out. Every student owns and practices the skill in a succession of activities, and the emphasis is on that skill's benefit to all students, rather than on pointing a finger at any one boy as if to say, "We have to work on this because *you* and you alone are so incompetent."

Distributed practice. The opportunity to practice each communication skill repeatedly and in context over time helps the struggling boy internalize and "own" the embedded communication skill as well as the language associated with it. One would be hard pressed to find better or more effective "on-the-job training." Additionally, the interaction among students during these activities automatically provides the opportunity for boys to model the skills for one another. Sometimes, seeing and hearing another student use the specific skill is the best teacher. When boys learn from one another, they also understand one another better, which leads to better communication. And good communication strengthens the learning climate.

Experience first. You may have noticed that in each of the three scenarios, boys' skills improved as they had the chance to see the skills modeled for them and then also had a chance to practice the skills themselves. In many instances, a boy's personal involvement in learning the skill is the catalyst that generates the language he needs to continue effectively using that skill. In other words, the authenticity of the learning experience and its real-world relevance help a boy to not only understand the kinds of language he needs to master but also to recall and generate that language on his own when necessary. We will touch on this process again in Pathway No. 6: Empower when discussing many boys' challenges with written language.

A final word. Last, but certainly not least, if you find yourself dismissing the idea of explicitly teaching basic communication skills in a class not specifically centered around such skills, please reconsider. For boys who have never had the chance to understand and practice these skills, their explicit instruction has a value that most of us—who grew up seeing them modeled and used them as a matter of course—cannot fully appreciate. More than any physical attribute, the possession of strong communication skills is a mark of competence and social status. When we open our mouths to speak, we share who we are and where we come from.

For this very reason, schools that seek to improve the academic achievement of severely underprivileged children offer explicit instruction of communication skills. Things as seemingly obvious—but with which many students struggle nonetheless—as what to do when someone asks a question, which words to use when expressing gratitude, how to politely express disagreement, how loud to clap, or even how to answer the telephone are taught and modeled, repeatedly and explicitly, right along with academic content and other procedural skills (Clark, 2004). To paraphrase the words of award-winning educator Ron Clark, this kind of instruction leads directly to self-respect, respect for others, and a positive environment in which to succeed. These skills don't just improve grades; they change lives.

> ✿ **TAKE FIVE**
>
> Take a moment to think about the ways in which you see the boys in your classroom struggle with communication. Can you think of one way that you could begin to help those same boys develop any of the pragmatic communication skills they are missing? How might this look in your classroom? Which boys might be more successful academically as a result of having opportunities to learn and practice these communication skills?

Access Point: Tools for Collaborating

What the child can do in cooperation today, he can do alone tomorrow. Therefore the only good kind of instruction is that which marches ahead of development and leads it; it must be aimed not so much at the ripe as the ripening action.

—Lev Vygotsky, psychologist

Although many boys crave interaction with their peers (regardless of their learning-style profile), they don't always know how to navigate the opportunities for interaction that arise during group learning activities. Just as many boys don't have experience in communicating skillfully, neither do they know how to function effectively in group learning situations. Many teachers dislike group work because the frequent result is off-task behavior, unfinished work, acting out, and frustration on almost everyone's part. In response, teachers eliminate one of the activities that most endears the experience of school to boys, only to become painfully aware that the then-unmet need for social interaction finds other, far less productive ways to assert itself into classroom life. This Access Point seeks to help boys develop collaboration skills, capitalizing on the benefits of peer-to-peer interaction within the framework of a group-learning situation.

Key Resource: Kagan's Roles, Gambits, and Structures

Efforts that help underachieving boys acquire and practice Cox's pragmatic communication skills lay the groundwork for the acquisition of many of the specific skills that turn the unproductive "group work" discussed at the beginning of this Access Point into true collaboration. Successful collaborative learning settings create a direct connection between effective communication and academic achievement.

> "Improving students' skills in asking for and giving help has direct positive effects on achievement" (Black & Wiliam, 1998a, p. 52).

Cooperative learning and styles. When it comes to teaching and learning to collaborate as a means of supporting learning, there is no more effective approach for both teachers and their students than cooperative learning. Readers already familiar with the principles of cooperative learning may not, however, be aware of the specific ways in which cooperative learning offers boys with the learning style most often at risk in our classrooms—the SF/Interpersonal style—an opportunity to learn in the format most likely to help them achieve academic success. Such activities also allow the SF/Interpersonal's unique abilities to shine. His natural inclination to support both the collaborative process and communication among members enriches both his own and others' learning.

Although cooperative learning is particularly well suited to SF/Interpersonal learners, struggling boys of all styles can benefit from learning the many communication and collaboration skills embedded in cooperative learning. As boys work collaboratively in their groups, they begin to understand that two, or three, or four heads are often better than one. And along with that understanding comes the realization that learning and communicating aren't just about getting and keeping knowledge. As their own academic skills and abilities grow, they begin to appreciate the value of the collaborative process. Collaboration—giving and supporting in addition to receiving—allows the group to achieve what the individual cannot.

In the following vignette, a middle school history teacher uses a variety of cooperative learning experiences to re-engage his students in learning. And as this particular class's experience shows, repeated opportunities for group collaboration actually lead students toward higher levels of individual academic achievement. If you are unfamiliar with cooperative learning structures, it may be helpful to explore the explanations of Expert Group Jigsaw, Numbered Heads Together, Turn-4-Learning, and ThinkDOTS in Figures 7.2–7.5 before you read the vignette.

FIGURE 7.2
Expert Group Jigsaw

Collaborative task: The acquisition and comprehension of large segments of new information.

Overview: The teacher divides the reading assignment into roughly equal portions, as many portions as there are members in each group. Each home group receives one set of the divided reading materials.

Suggested roles: Task Master, Gate Keeper, Summarizer, Recorder

Each home group member is assigned a role that will help to orchestrate the interchange and contributions during sharing.

Step 1: Each group member selects one portion of the reading assignment and reads it.

Step 2: After all the group members read their assigned segments, they leave their original groups and join with like members of other groups as "experts." Each expert group discusses its assigned segment and comes to a consensus on what key information to share.

Step 3: Experts return to their home groups and share, using the roles to facilitate the interchange.

Source: From *Cooperative Learning,* by S. Kagan, 1992, San Juan Capistrano, CA, Resources for Teachers. © by S. Kagan. Adapted with permission.

FIGURE 7.3
Numbered Heads Together

Collaborative task: The review or sharing of information in which all students are simultaneously involved in discussion. Useful before, during, or after a lesson or unit.

Overview: Students are organized in groups of four. Within each group, each student has a number: 1, 2, 3, or 4 (which is where the term "numbered heads" comes from).

Optional roles: Task Master, Checker, Summarizer, Praiser

Step 1: The teacher poses a question, and each group of four students (the "numbered heads") discusses its answer to the question.

Step 2: When the time is up, the teacher spins a spinner to identify which "numbered head" within each group will be responsible for answering. For example, a spin landing on "1" would indicate that the "1" in each group would stand and prepare to share his or her group's answer with the class.

Step 3: The teacher randomly calls on the standing "1s" to share their answers. This three-step cycle repeats with each question posed and answered.

Source: From *Kagan Cooperative Learning,* by S. Kagan and M. Kagan, San Clemente, CA: Kagan Publishing. © 2009 by Kagan and Kagan. Adapted with permission.

FIGURE 7.4
Turn-4-Learning

Collaborative task: The review or sharing of information. Useful before, during, or after a lesson or unit of study.

Overview: Students are organized into groups of four. The teacher provides each group with a set of questions in an envelope. Each question is written on a separate card. Students rotate through the same sequence of steps to answer each question, each group member taking responsibility for one role during each round of question-answering.

Embedded roles: Roles are embedded in the sequence of steps completed in answering each question: Question Reader, Question Answerer, Extender, and Summarizer.

Step 1: Question Reader selects and reads a question card.

Step 2: Question Answerer (the person to the Reader's left) answers the question.

Step 3: Extender (the person to the Answerer's left) extends the answer just given.

Step 4: Summarizer (the fourth and final person in the group) summarizes key points.

The four-step cycle repeats, the responsibility for starting the sequence rotating to the left by one person for each successive question.

Source: From *Cooperative Learning,* by S. Kagan, 1992, San Juan Capistrano, CA, Resources for Teachers. © 1992 by S. Kagan. Adapted with permission.

FIGURE 7.5
ThinkDOTS

Collaborative task: The review or sharing of information in which all students are simultaneously involved in discussion. Useful before, during, or after a lesson or unit.

Overview: Students are organized into groups of three or six. Students take turns throwing a die to choose which question from a set of six questions they will answer. The six questions correspond to the six levels in Bloom's Taxonomy. The level of Bloom's Taxonomy is indicated by the number of "dots." Thus, a question at Level 1 (Remember) of the taxonomy would have one "dot" on it. A question at Level 2 (Understand) would have two "dots," and so forth.

Often, each card will have more than one question to accommodate the likelihood that a level may be selected several times during the random throwing of the die. If the die indicates a level for which all questions have already been answered, the thrower of the die may throw again, extend the previous answer to one of the existing questions, or create a question of his or her own to answer.

Optional roles: Task Master, Checker, Summarizer, Praiser

To use this strategy as a cooperative learning structure, roles may be added to enhance the quality of sharing. Roles may remain constant as the responsibility for choosing and answering a question rotates around the group, or roles may rotate along with the responsibility for choosing and answering the question (e.g., the person to the right of the die roller is always the Praiser, the person across from the die roller is always the Summarizer, and so forth).

Source: From *Differentiation at Work, K–5: Principles, Lessons, and Strategies,* by M. L. Narvaez and K. Brimijoin, Thousand Oaks, CA: Corwin Press. © 2010 by Narvaez and Brimijoin. Adapted with permission.

Cooperative Learning in Middle School History

Mike Downs teaches middle school history. His class is in the midst of a unit on the California gold rush of 1849. Mike is concerned because his students' interest has deteriorated markedly as the unit progresses. They don't seem engaged, and he knows that even if some of them memorize information for the test, they'll quickly forget it.

Earlier in the week, the language arts teacher for his students had been talking about teaching the kids to use questions from Bloom's taxonomy to stimulate their understanding. Mike wondered if there was a way to incorporate these questions into some kind of game that he could use to jump-start his students' interest again. His class was already comfortable with working in small groups. Building on this level of experience, he came up with several new ways to help the kids acquire and process the information they were learning using four different cooperative learning strategies.

• He implemented Expert Group Jigsaws when reading assignments were lengthy. This lightened the reading load, and kids got more because they processed information frequently and with friends.

• In lieu of quizzes, he used Numbered Heads Together for quick reviews. Because kids in each group were all involved in answering each question, he noticed a high level of engagement from the students who didn't ordinarily raise their hands as volunteers. As the "Numbered Head" in their group, they loved the attention of being able to give the "right" answer. The class liked it when Mike used the spinner and groaned in mock dismay when it was their turn to respond twice in a row.

• When the end of the unit was near, Mike used the Turn-4-Learning structure to consolidate their learning. Students worked in their groups to generate questions about what they had learned. Their previous experiences during the Expert Group Jigsaw and Numbered Heads Together activities had helped them develop fluency with concepts and ideas within the unit, and they took pleasure in discussing the key points they had learned as they generated their own sets of questions about them (and, of course, the answers, too). After several delightedly raucous rounds of the new game in which groups exchanged their sets of questions with one another, students reflected on the topic areas in which their greatest confusion still remained.

• Each group took one of these topics and generated a set of six ThinkDOTS questions, one question for each level of Bloom's taxonomy. Kids puzzled over the process of generating questions for each level, and it was fun for them to grapple with ways to ask about the same topic in six different ways. During the final review, the groups exchanged their questions with one another to play several rounds of the ThinkDOTS game.

The kids were excited about how well they felt they were going to do on the unit test, and their scores were indeed higher than they'd ever been. In their groups and as a result of using the four cooperative learning strategies, students had continually clarified their understanding, improved their ability to articulate essential knowledge from the unit, and dramatically increased their confidence as learners. Working collaboratively gave all of Mike's students practice in improving their communication skills, and the boys in his class who had frequently failed to excel within the regular classroom format gained new confidence, along with practical experience and increased understanding.

The format of cooperative learning that I have found most accessible over the years is an approach developed by Spencer Kagan (1992; Kagan & Kagan, 2009), which includes (among others) the following three essential elements: *roles, gambits,* and *structures.*

Roles and gambits. Collaborative *roles* and *gambits* reinforce the cooperative learning principles of positive interdependence and individual accountability, orchestrating the interaction during group work and enhancing it by building a collaborative mentality.

Developing roles and gambits for any particular collaboration skill and then helping students learn to use them follow the same basic process, as illustrated in Figure 7.6 (p. 154). The teacher identifies a collaboration skill that students lack or with which they need additional practice and encodes the skill into a "role," the title of which becomes a sort of shorthand for the skill. For example, the Task Master keeps the group on task, the Gate Keeper makes sure all group members have the opportunity to participate and give input, and the Checker stops the group to check that everyone understands the information discussed before the group moves on.

The teacher (often with student input) develops appropriate gambits for each role. Gambits are the verbal components of the role, and these statements are similar to the "Sounds like" part of the "Looks like/Sounds like" charts students developed to learn communication skills. For example, the Task Master might keep the group moving ahead by saying, "We need to move on to the next question."

The teacher models using the role and its gambits, and students practice using them in context, often during role-playing scenarios, until they are comfortable with them. The teacher then employs the role during cooperative group work, during which the role helps them work more effectively in a collaborative manner. Students critique their performance of each role and set goals for improvement. New roles are added and practiced in continual fashion, and eventually, each student will have a different role during any group interaction. For example, in a group of four students, one might be the Task Master (to help the group stay on task and refrain from talking about personal things instead of the lesson); the second member might be the Gate Keeper (to equalize participation and prevent any one member from either

FIGURE 7.6
A Sequence for Teaching Roles and Gambits

1 Pick a specific PROBLEM during group work	2 Identify the COLLABORATION SKILL needed	3 Develop a ROLE
1. Talking about personal things instead of the lesson 2. Taking over conversation and unwillingness to give others a turn 3. Not listening with the intent to understand 4. Has ideas but won't share them 5. Jumps to conclusions 6. No way to gather or record group's decisions or ideas	1. Staying on task, using time wisely 2. Equalizing participation, recognizing the rights of others 3. Summarizing, paraphrasing, reflecting group progress 4. Coaching, helping 5. Checking for understanding 6. Recording key information	1. Task Master 2. Gate Keeper 3. Summarizer or Paraphraser 4. Coach 5. Checker 6. Recorder

4 Develop GAMBITS for the role	5 MODEL, DEMONSTRATE, & PRACTICE the skill's role and gambits without content	6 APPLY multiple skills (roles and gambits) in context using STRUCTURES
1. **Task Master:** "Let's move on to the next question." "We still need to decide which book we want to read." 2. **Gate Keeper:** "Mark, that's a good point. Sally, what do you think?" 3. **Summarizer:** "This is what I hear you say: _____." (Explains) "In other words, you mean that _____ ." (Explains) 4. **Coach:** "You had an interesting point earlier, John. Can you explain more about your thinking?" 5. **Checker:** "Before we make a decision, can anyone summarize this for us?" 6. **Recorder:** "Here are the main ideas we have identified."	**Skill of the Week** PARAPHRASING Role: PARAPHRASER **Looks like:** · Leaning forward · Listening carefully · Making notes of words or phrases that are important **Sounds like:** · So if I understand, you meant that _____. (Explains) · Let me see if I have this right, Eli. (Explains) · Let me try to put this in my own words. (Explains)	· Expert Group Jigsaw · Numbered Heads Together · Turn-4-Learning · ThinkDOTS (adapted for cooperative learning)

Source: From *Kagan Cooperative Learning* by S. Kagan and M. Kagan, 2009, San Clemente, CA: Kagan Publishing. © 2009 by Kagan and Kagan. Adapted with permission.

controlling the group or not taking part); the third member might be the Checker (to check for understanding and prevent the group from jumping to conclusions); and the fourth member might be the Recorder (to keep a record of the group's decisions so that they can refer to them, report them accurately to the class, or use them to complete an assignment). For the underachieving boy, this approach offers instant access to success by providing both clear guidelines about how to "do" each collaborative skill and the opportunity to practice using each skill in a context that makes sense, feels safe, and helps him to learn.

It may have already occurred to you that this aspect of cooperative learning could be extremely useful for helping boys acquire Cox's pragmatic communication skills. Indeed, Figure 7.7 (p. 156) shows the correspondence between the two. In essence, when boys practice these cooperative learning roles and gambits, they are also building essential communication skills. Collaboration and communication skills grow together, one role at a time. This is part of the beauty of cooperative learning: its singular approach yields multiple positive outcomes.

Structures. *Structures* is Kagan's word for strategies. Although roles and gambits have value in their own right, it is their use within the *structures* (or strategies) of the cooperative learning process that provides boys who struggle to communicate and collaborate the greatest opportunities for authentic, contextualized practice. Think of structures as a framework for orchestrating interaction. They are, themselves, content-free. As such, they can accommodate content from virtually any subject area because the content gets "plugged into" the structure's framework. Each structure contains the essential principles of cooperative learning with a focus on collaboration, integrating roles purposefully into a sequenced activity that supports a group of learners' joint abilities to learn together. Boys learn by doing, and the structures orchestrate their success. Further, boredom is unlikely, given that teachers have dozens of established structures from which to choose, and many structures can be implemented in such a way that they feel game-like to students.

Among my favorite structures are those that Mike Downs used to engage his students throughout the unit on the gold rush of 1849: Expert Group

FIGURE 7.7

Similarities Between Pragmatic Communication Skills and Cooperative Learning Roles

Pragmatic Communication Skill	COMMUNICATION SKILL	Cooperative Learning Roles	
(3) Linking gestures with ideas or emotions	→ LISTENING ←	Checker	Checks for understanding
(4) Using facial expression effectively		Reflector	Reflects on group progress
(13) Anticipating other people's reactions			
(6) Turn taking	→ TURN TAKING ←	Gate Keeper	Equalizes participation
(10) Detecting emotions in others	→ HELPING ←	Encourager	Encourages contributions
		Coach	Helps others express themselves
		Question Commander	Asks for help
		Task Master	Helps group stay on task
(8) Giving compliments	→ PRAISING ←	Praiser	Praises group members' efforts
		Cheerleader	Celebrates group's accomplishments
(5) Attending to time and place	→ POLITE WAITING ←	Quiet Captain	Monitors speaking volume and unnecessary conversation
(12) Knowing how to make conversational transitions			

Source: From *Cooperative Learning* (p. 146), by S. Kagan, 1992, San Clemente, CA: Kagan Publishing. © 1992 by S. Kagan; and *Teaching Boys Pragmatic Communication* by A. J. Cox, 2006b. Available: www.dradamcox.com/pdf/PragmaticCommunication.pdf. Adapted with permission.

Jigsaw, Turn-4-Learning, and Numbered Heads Together. In addition to dozens of other similarly effective cooperative learning structures, teachers can adapt other strategies to the cooperative learning format, as Mike did with ThinkDOTS by adding roles to enhance interaction.

I recommend that anyone who wants to learn more about these cooperative learning structures find a copy of Kagan's *Cooperative Learning* (1992) or the more recently revised version, *Kagan Cooperative Learning* (Kagan & Kagan, 2009). Either book is an invaluable resource for learning about all things related to cooperative learning.

By now, I hope you see the tremendous potential that cooperative learning roles, gambits, and structures have for building both communication and collaboration skills. Boys of all learning styles benefit from their use, and few approaches can rival their ability to integrate critical real-world skills into everyday classroom interactions.

TAKE FIVE

Were you aware of the unique capacity of cooperative learning to develop two of the most essential real-world skills that underachieving boys lack—communication and collaboration? Are you using any type of cooperative learning now? If so, how could you build on that foundation to help the boys in your classroom develop collaboration skills? If not, which of the collaboration skills might be a good first choice for use in your classroom? How would you get started?

Milepost

In Pathway No. 3, we examined two essential real-world skills that our struggling boys need in order to succeed during their school careers and beyond. The skills of communication and collaboration reach into all areas

> "Students value school more and see its relevance to them and to the world more generally when school and what they learn are seen in the context of other processes, agents, and systems outside the school" (Martin, 2002, p. 57).

of academic learning as well as social interaction. Mastery of the two strengthens the social fabric of the learning environment along with a boy's sense of competence, allowing him to see himself as a capable learner in and out of school, now and in the future.

BUILDING A REPERTOIRE OF RESPONSES

Before you move on to the next chapter, pause to note any "aha!" moments you've had along the way.

1. What do you now understand about how struggling boys learn best that you didn't know before?

2. Of the strategies you are currently using, which could be tweaked or used more intentionally for an even greater positive outcome?

3. Which ideas or strategies caught your attention the most?

4. Choose one idea or strategy related to this Pathway that you could implement right now.

What's Next?

In Pathway No. 4: Adjust, we will take a look at ways to reconfigure our classrooms as spaces for active and engaged learning, using the physical arrangement of the classroom itself to help easily distracted and high-energy boys learn to self-regulate.

CHAPTER 8

Pathway No. 4: Adjust

As educators, each of us works within certain constraints over which we have little or no control—classroom size and location, for example. Although some of us are fortunate enough to have large, brightly lit rooms with windows that open for fresh air and lots of space in which to move around, others of us may teach each day in small, windowless interior rooms with inadequate heating and lighting. In many of our schools, recess time has also been cut short or eliminated, curtailing opportunities for physical movement and for informal social interaction. Under these conditions, even when a nonthreatening learning climate and strong teacher-student and peer-to-peer relationships are in place, shortcomings in the physical arrangement of the classroom can work to undermine the learning success of struggling boys.

As a first step in exploring this connection, let's revisit some of the negative behaviors often associated with underachieving boys—acting out, off-task behavior, and inattentiveness—and ask the following questions:

• Is it possible that some of these behaviors are the result of a boy's inability to function well within the physical environment itself?

• Are there ways we can organize our classroom spaces that might minimize some of these behaviors?

• Might some of these adjustments also help boys to learn self-regulation, building a stronger sense of self along with reducing the need for constant policing?

Depending on the needs of our students, we can potentially answer "yes" to all of these questions. When we examine the points at which physical aspects of the classroom intersect with what a boy needs in order to function successfully as a learner there, the importance of the physical arrangement of the spaces in which we teach becomes clear.

Intersection No. 1: A need for increased physical activity. A higher need for physical activity is most apparent among boys in grades 3 and lower. Physical maturation gradually helps many boys control this initial need, but it remains present to some degree among boys of all ages. In addition to the release of tension, both physical and emotional, that physical activity provides, there are also boys who need to move their bodies before and while they are learning so that they can learn.

The degree to which this need interferes with a boy's ability to learn has much to do with the options for purposeful activity at his disposal in the classroom, how well he understands when to take advantage of those options, and whether or not he chooses to do so at moments of strategic importance (i.e., when it actually aids in his learning).

Intersection No. 2: A need for social interaction. The desire for social interaction at school typically increases as a boy grows older, peaking in middle school, precisely at a time when his opportunities for natural social interaction with other boys (and girls) are eroded by reductions in free time before and after school, at lunch, and at recess. Considering that peer interaction is one of the factors that boys most enjoy about the experience of school, it behooves us to find ways to orchestrate it in our classrooms. For the SF/Interpersonal boy, in particular, social interaction isn't just a pleasant social experience; it's an essential condition for his learning. Regardless of the impetus, however, in the absence of teacher-orchestrated opportunities, many boys find their own ways to interact with one another, with or without permission (e.g., misbehavior and disrupted lessons).

Intersection No. 3: A need for a reduction of visual and auditory distractions. There is a strong argument that many boys are mislabeled as having ADD or ADHD because they have difficulty paying attention, are easily distracted, and have poor impulse control (Sciutto & Eisenberg, 2007). Some believe that the physical arrangement of classrooms provokes many behaviors commonly associated with ADD or ADHD and that by making simple adjustments to the classroom layout (and the positioning of students within that layout), many of these behaviors can be minimized. It's not easy to know which is the proverbial "chicken" and which the "egg" in this argument, but whatever the root cause, there are ways to minimize the negative impact of sensory overload, helping both the "distractors" and the "distractees" find ways to function within the same space.

Intersection No. 4: A need for physical comfort. A less obvious but equally important aspect of the classroom's physical arrangement relates to a boy's physical comfort while learning. When students feel physically comfortable, feelings of emotional safety increase, discipline problems dramatically decline, and learning improves. Not surprisingly, if an underachieving boy doesn't expect to be comfortable, he may not even be aware that his discomfort is interfering with his ability to pay attention or remain focused. His discovery that there might actually be another option is a little like the "aha!" most of us experienced the first time we put on a garment with some extra stretch in it. We didn't know how uncomfortable we'd been until that extra wiggle room suddenly made everything a little better, a little easier.

Because comfort comes in as many sizes and shapes as we and our underachieving boys do, we can address this need by providing opportunities for a boy to try out a variety of strategies for becoming more at ease during learning. This experimentation builds self-awareness and gives each boy his own set of personalized and portable learning tools to carry with him into future classrooms or learning situations. And, as we will explore in greater depth later, these options to exercise choice and control are powerful motivators, contributing to a positive learning climate as well as to a boy's sense of efficacy therein.

Access Point: Zones of Comfort prods us to reconfigure our classrooms as active places in which academic success is enhanced by judicious management of physical space and functional design. Teachers can use the tools offered in this Access Point to make space, literally and figuratively, for increased mobility, interaction among students, the development of self-awareness about how one learns, and opportunities for boys to practice self-regulation. The ideas presented address underachievement by helping a boy keep his mental and physical energy trained on learning rather than on the obstacles in his way. In other words, for a struggling boy, adjustments to the physical learning environment can simultaneously be both solution for and prevention of behaviors that interrupt the learning process.

Access Point: Zones of Comfort

Educational practices should be gauged not only by the skills and knowledge they impart for present use but also by what they do to children's beliefs about their capabilities, which affects how they approach the future. Students who develop a strong sense of self-efficacy are well equipped to educate themselves when they have to rely on their own initiative.

—Albert Bandura

Zones of Comfort encompasses a set of strategies designed to help our underachieving boys maximize their potential as learners by accommodating their needs for physical activity, social interaction, reduced sensory distractions (primarily visual and auditory), and comfort within the classroom. Within the more obvious and observable outcomes of implementing these strategies lies an auxiliary yet equally valuable opportunity for the underachieving boy to develop personal competence through self-regulation. In addition, several strategies offer an SF/Interpersonal or NF/Self-Expressive boy opportunities to facilitate group decision making or to exercise his creativity and problem-solving skills. These strategies allow SF and NF learners—who often do not understand or value their talents—to develop their natural gifts and, as a result of using those gifts, receive peer validation for the tangible contributions they make to the well-being of the class.

Another benefit of these strategies is their ability to address multiple needs at once. For example, a strategy that meets the need for physical activity may also provide for social interaction; one designed to reduce distraction may simultaneously provide physical comfort; one that accommodates student interaction may also minimize auditory or visual distractions. Thus, even though the strategies below are organized in groups according to need, their use is not limited to that need alone.

To extract optimal benefit from these strategies, please suspend any initial judgments about what aspects seem either too childish or too adult for your particular group of students. Look instead for *possibilities*. The examples provided vary by grade level and content area, and I encourage you to read each strategy and pause before you move ahead to ask yourself how you might possibly adapt each new idea to your own needs. I hope you are surprised many times over by the creativity of these suggestions, as well as by the adaptations that you are able to come up with in response.

Strategies to Increase Physical Movement

Moving Time

Create distinct seating and desk arrangements for daily learning scenarios that are frequently repeated: for example, direct instruction (when all desks or bodies typically face in one direction); individual work, paired or small-group work, whole-class or small-group discussions, and structured small-group activities such as Socratic seminars or fishbowls (when desks are reorganized into groupings of varying numbers); or the use of centers or stations (around which desks are moved to accommodate access).

Teach the students how to quickly and quietly move desks, necessary materials, and their bodies from one configuration to another. Practice these shifts until students can accomplish them quickly and easily. The more skilled students become at accomplishing these reconfigurations, the more frequently you can change the classroom arrangement without disrupting learning or wasting time. Consider making the practice sessions into a game, with the class members competing against their own or another class's record.

Why does this help? Simple as these physical shifts seem, the purposeful opportunities for physical movement they provide can have a substantial effect on students. Aside from the obvious stimulation of muscle movement and increased blood flow, they also work as "state changers." Much as an adult might feel refreshed by rearranging the living room furniture from time to time, the rearrangement of the classroom furniture energizes a struggling boy's brain by giving him a new perspective.

Some boys may also discover that each configuration serves as a mental anchor for the kind of work that happens there. The combination of patterned movement and spatial awareness stimulates his episodic memory ("I am now going to sit in my reading group"), which may help him remember what to bring and what to do once he arrives in the new physical space ("I need my story draft and red pencil because we always help each other edit when in this grouping").

Standing Time

To help boys with a high need for physical movement improve their concentration and focus, establish the option of walking to the back or side of the room, where a boy may stand as needed during presentations or move during self-directed activities in which long periods of sitting in one place are required (Armstrong, 1999; Taylor, 2001b). Designate a specific area to which he may go, and establish a clear agreement about how and when this option may be exercised, how long the option may be used (so that others may also take advantage of it), whether or not permission is required first, how to obtain permission, and any limitations on how many times a day the option may be used. For boys in grades 2 and lower, when self-regulation and immaturity may make both waiting and "timing" a challenge, as well as for older boys (all the way up through high school age), consider letting a boy stand whenever he finds it necessary. It may be useful to place the desks of boys who use this option more frequently in rows along either side of the classroom, thereby making it easier for them to exercise this option without disturbing others.

Why does this help? If a boy's need to stand is accepted as ordinary and no stigma is attached to it, the boy is able to meet this need without the discomfort of having to justify or explain himself, which, in addition to being embarrassing, may be beyond the limits of his self-awareness or self-expression. When the option is presented in a straightforward manner, it becomes just another way to "do school," no different from lining up or turning in homework.

In subtle but important ways, the mere presence of this option demonstrates both acceptance of and value for multiple ways of learning and being. Once established, this kind of routine teaches each class member how to functionally meet one's own needs without disrupting the needs of others. It's an active lesson in the principles of building a supportive community.

Errands

Prearrange with several other teachers or school personnel (e.g., librarian, janitor, or office staff) that when you send a boy with a note asking for an item (e.g., "The book you were saving for me"), each person on the "route" will send the boy along to another "station" or back to his own classroom, according to a prearranged plan. For example, when Mark arrives at Mrs. James's classroom with a note from his teacher, Mrs. James knows to give him a book to return to Mr. Smith in the media center. Mr. Smith gives Mark a book to take to Ms. Pearce, the office secretary. When Mark gives her the book from Mr. Smith, she knows to send Mark back to his classroom and gives him another note to give to his teacher, who thanks Mark for his help.

Why does this help? The most obvious purpose of sending a boy on an errand is to provide him with physical exercise, during with he can expend some of his excess energy constructively. The secondary purpose speaks to a boy's emotional fitness. The responsibility implied by being asked to run an errand and the success experienced at its completion contribute to the struggling boy's often tenuous sense of competence and self-respect. The student understands that he has been trusted to complete a task, and therefore feels special. This trust-building outcome is a gift in and of itself.

Energizer Monitor

For a struggling boy with a high need for physical movement, the job of monitoring the energy levels of the classroom may also be a perfect fit. Up to a certain number of times daily (and under agreed-upon conditions), the boy can give a prearranged signal that it's time for a one-minute energizer. He may also enjoy taking responsibility for learning and leading these energizers.

Why does this help? Combining face-saving permission to do what he needs most (i.e., move) with equal measures of confidence boosting and trust building, this option helps the boy who can't sit still become the boy who has responsibility within the learning community, the respect of a leadership role, the power of decision making, and the chance to be physically active without resorting to disruption and acting out.

Strategies to Increase Social Interaction

Study Buddies

Assign each student a "study buddy" with whom he has permission to consult on learning matters (Taylor, 2007). Place study buddies in different locations in the classroom, and give buddies tacit permission to quietly get up and move to each other's desks a certain number of times each day. The need for social interaction is bolstered by the side benefits of physical movement and a deeper understanding of the course material through discussion with the study buddy.

If a boy has a diagnosis of ADD or ADHD, the interaction may need to be more carefully orchestrated, with movement limited rather than increased. It may be wise to seat him in the very front in the row closest to the right side of the classroom (facing forward) with his study buddy sitting at his immediate left (at the front of the row second closest to the right side of the classroom). This seating pattern eliminates as much distraction from the ADD or ADHD boy's right field of vision as possible and keeps the majority of visual and auditory distractions from other students behind him. Proximity and permission combine to offer this boy a chance for prized social interaction without the resultant overstimulation of unregulated movement.

Why does this help? The Study Buddy strategy is to the boy who needs to interact with peers what the Energizer Monitor strategy is to the boy with excess energy. This strategy offers boys purposeful opportunities for physical movement (similar to Moving Time or Standing Time), along with the social interaction so many boys crave. For the SF/Interpersonal boy, who needs to process information with another person, this strategy is an especially effective antidote to the Code's prohibition against asking for help. It provides both the impetus and the justification for doing precisely what the SF/Interpersonal boy needs to do. The Study Buddy strategy also offers struggling boys of all styles the opportunity to practice three key elements of self-regulation on a daily basis: self-awareness, choice, and control. Knowing when one needs to move and when one needs to ask for help requires self-awareness, while having choices about when to do these things not only strengthens a boy's ability to self-regulate but also gives him a sense of control over his environment.

Strategies to Reduce Distractions

One of Four

Make sure that the front of the room is visually calm by placing only consistent design configurations in this visual field (e.g., a whiteboard with daily assignments, a bulletin board with the social skills strategy of the week, a monthly calendar, or a set of hanging pockets with daily small-group assignments). Though the information provided by or associated with each of these elements may change, their visual configuration remains constant. As much as possible, save the brightest colors, images, and designs for the other three walls. Remember to stand in front of this "calm" wall when you present important information, for example, when you introduce new topics or make announcements about important events.

Why does this help? Ironically, boys may be visually distracted by many of the very things we intentionally use to enliven and add warmth and interest to our classrooms: bright colors, eye-catching designs, and interesting images or patterns. Without realizing it, we are sometimes our own worst enemies in this regard. One of Four offers us a way to include visually energizing elements in our classrooms while minimizing their ability to distract a struggling boy's attention. During critical moments when a boy's attention and focus are most necessary to his success as a learner, the visual "boredom" of the one-in-four wall does not compete for his attention. He may also maintain a better focus on his work when his desk routinely faces this wall during seated and group work. Boys with ADHD and ADD, who are distracted by most sensory input, may respond positively to the visual consistency that One in Four provides, as may highly visual-spatial boys and boys with a strong need for stability and routine (often ST/Practical Doers).

Traffic Lanes

Configure the classroom so that there are always several "traffic lanes" for students to use when moving to and from different parts of the room.

Why does this help? Traffic Lanes are especially productive when used in conjunction with almost all of the other strategies shared in this chapter. They accommodate frequent movement while minimizing distraction. For example, you could combine the Study Buddy strategy and Do-It-Yourself Modality Zones (covered under Strategies to Increase Comfort) with Traffic Lanes so that the majority of movement taking place in the classroom falls out of the visual range of the highly distractible boy (e.g., behind him). The amount of movement is minimized in general because students take the most direct route to and from different areas of the classroom.

As students learn to physically negotiate the classroom using these "lanes," they get to practice self-directed decision making and experience the benefits of mutually respectful interaction. If you happen to have a pacer (someone who likes or needs to walk while thinking), consider creating a "pacing lane" at the back of the classroom and set up rules and regulations for how and when he may use it.

Testing Circle

Move desks into a circle facing *outwards* as a means of reducing distraction during high-stakes testing or similarly stressful situations in which an under-achieving boy most needs to focus (Taylor, 2007). Combine this configuration with the option for a boy to wear noise-reduction headphones if he is easily distracted auditorily, and remember to orient the desks of those boys who are most easily distracted so that they face the most visually calm classroom wall (i.e., One of Four).

Why does this help? This simple configuration minimizes the disruptive influ-ence of unintentional visual distractions by pushing the potential distractions to a boy's peripheral field of vision. If we want underachieving boys to func-tion at their best during stressful academic experiences, when even minimal distractions are magnified by the anxiety of the situation, simple efforts such as these can make all the difference. The larger the circle, the less interference a boy will experience from his nearest neighbors. Moving his desk farther out of the circle reduces the potential for distraction.

Strategies to Increase Comfort

Niggle Busters

Many boys with ADD or ADHD respond to multiple external distractions or a too-high demand for their limited attention with an internal feeling of agitation, a constant "niggle" that won't go away. There is a natural tendency to soothe this discomfort in one or more of the following three ways: fidgeting, rocking, and applying pressure to the skin. The following strategies are especially helpful in accommodating these often irritating behaviors in a manner that is respectful to the boy and to his classmates (Taylor, 2007).

Fidget Grabbers. For a boy who unconsciously drums his fingers or taps a pencil repeatedly on his desktop, give him permission to hold and manipulate any of the following items, each of which is easy to acquire, make, or replace and, just as important, quiet when dropped, as they will be at some point: small beanbags; a stress ball that returns to its original shape each time it is compressed; squares of textured cloth (felt, velvet, tapestry); a heavy-duty balloon (or maybe two together) filled with sand, salt, flour, malleable clay or Silly Putty, or even small smooth stones; lengths of yarn or ribbon; or worry beads strung with fishing line or elastic cord.

Kick Stopper. For a boy who can't seem to stop kicking the desk in front of him or jiggling his legs or feet while thinking or working, wrap something stretchy (e.g., bungee cords, a knotted ring of heavy-duty sewing elastic, or exercise bands) around the front two legs of the boy's desk or chair. This provides him with resistance against which to constantly (and quietly) bounce his legs.

Rocking Chair. For a boy who rocks back and forth at his desk, place a rocking chair at the back of the room for him to use when he needs to calm himself. Alternatively, consider letting him fold his jacket or coat underneath him and "rock" quietly on that. If his motion is visually distracting for others, you may want to place his desk on the left side of the room. If he needs to work while he rocks, he may find it helpful to use a clipboard as a portable desk (see Flex Zone).

Calm-Down Vest. A surprisingly effective "niggle buster" that most boys won't realize they like until they "feel" it is a calm-down vest. Create one from an old down vest by cutting small openings at the top of each "channel" and replacing the down filling with dried beans or wooden or plastic beads. Then sew the slits shut tightly. The resulting vest will feel very heavy, and to many agitated boys with ADD or ADHD, it may also feel amazingly comforting.

Why does this help? Just as the boy sensitized to anxiety and stress cannot control downshifting, the ADD or ADHD boy cannot control his response to the sensory overstimulation he experiences. The "niggle" he feels is his body's way of prompting him to soothe his unnamed, yet palpable, discomfort.

Niggles come in all varieties, and tacit permission to use any of these solutions can help a struggling boy bring his attention back to learning. Whether from ADD or ADHD, stress, or just the culmination of events on a bad day, all learners can use these simple solutions to soothe jumbled thoughts and feelings by calming their bodies' agitation.

Do-It-Yourself Modality Zones

It's challenging to accommodate multiple modalities in one classroom, especially if just one or two students have a strong preference for any one modality. A workable solution is to create "modality zones." Frame their use as valuable tools that an underachieving boy can use to create a personal zone of comfort in which to do his work any time he needs to. Allow all students to experience each zone, and model using them yourself from time to time.

Earphone Zone. For a boy who especially needs quiet in order to concentrate, keep a supply of earphone headsets (minus the cords) for him and other students to put on when noises around them are distracting them from their work.

Nonglare Zone. Some students find the bright lights of the classroom so distracting that they have difficulty paying attention or reading for any length of time, especially if the light source is fluorescent. Keep a supply of sun visors on hand, and give students permission to put them on whenever too-bright lights cause eye fatigue or difficulties in focusing.

Flex Zone. For a boy who benefits from changing his position physically while working, a supply of ready-to-use clipboards may help him stay on task even when he sits sideways, walks to another area of the classroom, stands up, or slouches down in order to be more comfortable.

Lamp Zone. If you prefer to keep your classroom less brightly lit than some boys need or like, give them permission to bring a battery operated lamp for their desks. Alternatively, invite students to bring battery operated mini-lights that clip onto whatever they are reading or working on. With a light attached to a clipboard, the student has a portable, well-lit mini-desk ready to accompany him wherever he needs to work.

Why does this help? As a struggling boy develops his self-awareness, he experiences how simple adjustments to his personal learning environment can optimize his ability to focus and concentrate in any learning situation, now and in the future. The ability to control the quality of his learning experience is especially empowering for a struggling boy, who may often feel at the mercy of conditions over which he has no control or input. Further, by virtue of the opportunity for all members of the classroom community to try out the various "zones," this set of options helps all learners understand more about how they—and others—learn best.

Design-a-Room

Early in the school year, determine which students belong to each of the four style groups: ST/Practical Doers, NT/Thinker-Knowers, SF/Interpersonals, or NF/Self-Expressives. Allow each group to design a room configuration that its members feel is ideal for their learning profile. Let each group put its plan into action for at least a week, then collect feedback from all class members about the aspects of each arrangement they liked best. After each group has had its week to shine, ask one representative from each group to form a team that will create a "best-of-all-worlds" design—a configuration with something for each style that everyone can live with.

Why does this help? As the most sophisticated idea among those offered here, Design-a-Room combines a boy's self-awareness with his creativity and problem-solving abilities on a grander scale than Do-It-Yourself Modality Zones. Students orchestrate the planning and decisions involved in creating and implementing these designs. The necessity for collaborative group work is an ideal vehicle for the SF/Interpersonal and NF/Self-Expressive learners to join forces, taking on leadership and supportive roles not only during the design of their own room but also in helping the other two styles develop theirs. While keeping in mind the everyday functionality of the classroom, this challenge offers all learners the opportunity to work collaboratively, stretching their understanding of other styles (and their learning needs) and, finally, experiencing the benefits of "giving a little to get a little."

As you think about these strategies and the ways in which each offers an underachieving boy a chance to negotiate the demands of learning within the physical constraints of the classroom, remember how important the comfort of the learning environment is to his ability to succeed academically. Without judging a boy's needs or explaining them away as "boys being boys," these strategies help the boy who struggles academically as a result of the physical constraints of the classroom to build a sense of competence and confidence in his ability to self-regulate. He comes to understand how he can function effectively within limitations over which he might otherwise feel he has no control, as well as how to make optimal, responsible use of available options that meet his needs.

�֎ **TAKE FIVE**

Take a moment to think about your current classroom configuration. How flexible is it? Have you noticed any boys who seem to struggle consistently in your classroom but do not in others? What would help you be comfortable as a learner in your classroom? How might the very elements that you find pleasing be the source of irritation for others?

Milepost

In Pathway No. 4, we looked at ways to bolster struggling boys' sense of competence by helping them to help themselves—becoming better learners through self-awareness, self-regulation, and opportunities to practice being a respectful member of a diverse community. Of the many ideas shared in this book, these tools may be among the simplest and most accessible. Implementation of any one has the potential to reinforce the teacher-student bond and tangibly enhance the positive nature of the classroom climate.

What's Next?

In Pathway No. 5: Ignite, we will explore ways to enliven our teaching, focusing on how to motivate and engage an underachieving boy and draw him into learning by meeting his needs for meaning, relevance, and social interaction and providing access to the support that will help him to persist.

BUILDING A REPERTOIRE OF RESPONSES

Before you move on to the next chapter, pause to note any "aha!" moments you've had along the way.

1. What do you now understand about how struggling boys learn best that you didn't know before?

2. Of the strategies you are currently using, which could be tweaked or used more intentionally for an even greater positive outcome?

3. Which ideas or strategies caught your attention the most?

4. Choose one idea or strategy related to this Pathway that you could implement right now.

CHAPTER 9

Pathway No. 5: Ignite

....

Teaching is an instinctual act, mindful of potential, craving of realizations, a pausing, seamless process, where one rehearses constantly while acting, sits as a spectator at a play one directs, engages every part in order to keep the choices open and the shape alive for the student, so that the student may enter in and begin to do what the teacher has done: make choices.

—A. Bartlett Giamatti, former Yale University president

....

At some point, nearly every educator who has thought about the problem of boys' underachievement suggests that we need to integrate more "active learning" into our classrooms. "Boys need more physical activity," they may say, or "Hands-on learning is the ticket."

Well, yes... and no. What I discovered early on is that "active learning" is frequently interpreted, especially in mass media materials, as the need to add physical movement to boys' learning, usually in one of two ways: by incorporating activities like races and games that provide a release of energy and freedom from desk work or by adding hands-on learning activities that stimulate the kinesthetic modality. And although both of these elements are related to what I eventually came to understand as active learning, they are only a small part of the story where struggling boys are concerned.

As I thought about what puts many boys at risk for underachievement in our classrooms, it seemed that "active learning" should be less about physical activity and more about *engaging* boys as learners, finding new ways to help them become active builders of their understanding and owners of the processes in which they are involved.

My emerging thoughts about active learning coalesced when I discovered a tremendous resource called the InTime project (Integrating New Technologies into the Methods of Education), a series of 300 teacher-created video demonstrations made possible by a multimillion-dollar grant to the University of Northern Iowa (University of Northern Iowa College of Education, n.d.). Each video models one or more of the research-based principles of active learning.

Scope and volume aside, the most impressive aspect of the InTime project—and the most relevant to our discussion—is the broader definitions of active learning developed as the foundation for the best practices demonstrated in the videos. These criteria provide a means for generating learning activities with the potential to bring a boy who lingers on the fringes of his potential for academic achievement into an active pursuit of it.

Access Point: Active Learning

All genuine learning is active, not passive. It involves the use of the mind, not just the memory. It is the process of discovery, in which the student is the main agent, not the teacher.

—Mortimer J. Adler, philosopher, educator, and author

Key Resource: InTime Principles of Active Learning

Have you ever had the experience of running into a former coworker who has a new job? It's hard to envision that person in a different setting because you are so used to associating him or her with the prior one. In much the same way, it can be a challenge to see the eight principles of active learning in Figure 9.1 on page 176 (column one) in a new light. Doubtless, you will be familiar with most of them, yet you may be surprised to discover that the terms you think you understand are actually quite different than you imagined, especially in regard to how they help us meet the needs of underachieving boys.

FIGURE 9.1
Active Learning's Positive Outcomes for the Underachieving Boy

Active Learning Principles		Positive Outcomes
1. Active involvement	→	*Active construction of understanding*
2. Compelling situations	→	*Added relevance and personal meaning*
3. Direct experience	→	*Increased attention and memory*
4. Enjoyable setting	→	*Reduced anxiety*
5. Frequent feedback	→	*Belief in the possibility of success*
6. Informal learning	→	*Elaboration*
7. Patterns and connections	→	*Consolidation of learning*
8. Reflection	→	*Insight*

Source: Active Learning Principles adapted from University of Northern Iowa College of Education, InTime Project Videos, http://www.intime.uni.edu/model/learning. Adapted with permission.

1. Active involvement helps a struggling boy create a personal connection to the knowledge or skill at hand, adding both sense and meaning to its acquisition along with increasing his ability to retrieve and apply it in new situations. The "activity" of active involvement is more mental than physical, and its benefit is something like the difference between hearing about someone else's vacation plans and making your own. When we get to be part of the action, we take ownership of its outcome. *The struggling boy's outcome from active involvement is **active construction of his understanding**.*

2. Compelling situations stimulate an underachieving boy's desire to be engaged in learning with real-world circumstances that feel both relevant and worthy of his time and attention. Responding to challenging, complex, real-life situations involves his emotions as well as his problem-solving abilities.

The learner's initial drive to take part is a bit like the feeling of excited anticipation when we open the newspaper and discover an ad for a concert we would like to attend. The effort we must expend to figure out how to obtain tickets, juggle finances to pay for them, get time off work, and travel to and from a nearby city are worth it because the outcome of our efforts is something that interests us in a very personal way. *The struggling boy's outcome from compelling situations is* **added relevance and personal meaning.**

   3. Direct experience engages an underachieving boy by activating his senses during learning, heightening the quality of the experience as well as helping him to recall it afterward. It's a little like the surprising level of detail we can remember about tasks we've completed, even though we weren't consciously aware of them. Thinking about the brownies we made yesterday, for example, we might remember the way the batter looked when we swirled the chocolate and the flour together, the sound of the mixer going from slow to high speed, and the whoosh of heat when we opened the oven door to put the pan in to bake. The "doing" aids the "remembering." *The struggling boy's outcome from direct experience is* **increased attention and memory.**

   4. Enjoyable setting invites an underachieving boy to engage in learning that often involves social interaction in a companionable and relaxed setting. It's a bit like the sense of pleasure we have when we spy one of those big, comfy armchairs hidden among the shelves at the bookstore. We can plop down and just enjoy the moment, relaxing while we decide which book we will buy. *The struggling boy's outcome from an enjoyable setting is* **reduced anxiety.**

   5. Frequent feedback (specifically informational feedback) helps an underachieving boy feel safe while he is learning new things. It lets him know what he needs to do and what is coming next. It's a little like the comforting sense of orientation we get when taking a trip with a GPS at our fingertips. We know where to go at every step of the way and don't expend energy on worrying about getting lost. If we get turned around, we can still find the way. No matter where we are at any given point, we feel secure in the knowledge that we'll get where we want to go. *The struggling boy's outcome from frequent feedback is* **belief in the possibility of success.**

   6. Informal learning is the happy by-product of a learning activity. It is an underachieving boy's unique reactions, observations, and perceptions that result from a learning experience. These enhance his participation much the way that quirky and unexpected events enliven a trip. When we get back home, the main events show up in our vacation pictures, but the funny stories we tell add the context that gives them extra meaning. *The struggling boy's outcome from informal learning is **elaboration.***

7. **Patterns and connections** support an underachieving boy's comprehension and memory in two ways: first, by helping him to merge prior learning with new learning and second, by helping him combine disparate ideas into configurations that are useful and make sense to him. It's a little like buying a new wardrobe and organizing it so you know what you have, where to find each kind of clothing, and what goes with what. *The struggling boy's outcome from patterns and connections is **consolidation of learning.***

8. **Reflection** builds a boy's self-awareness as a learner. He comes to understand how his choices affect outcomes, how he learns best, and how to gauge his progress and optimize it. It's a little like the "aha!" moment we experience when we look back on a past event with the benefit of hindsight. Looking back helps us to recall the most important moments of our past experiences and savor their impact. *The struggling boy's outcome from reflection is **insight.***

Notice that none of the principles focus on adding movement to learning simply for the sake of generating physical activity. Although an observable increase in physical animation may result when these principles are implemented, their purpose is to engage the learner in learning rather than to distract him from it. More significantly, through the deep engagement that comes from participating in activities that employ these principles, the underachieving boy truly owns the positive outcome of his efforts, which affirms him and motivates him to continue. It is in this respect that active learning contributes to both his short-term and long-term potential as a learner, helping him succeed in the moment as well as motivating him to continue.

Upon closer inspection, we also realize that these eight principles of active learning actually target many of the unmet needs of the at-risk SF/Interpersonal or NF/Self-Expressive learner: his desire for a harmonious setting, the need to learn interactively with others, his need to find an engaging and meaningful purpose to the learning, the opportunity to connect disparate facts and details with the larger picture, and the time for him to reflect on his personal growth and self-awareness. In other words, the principles of active learning are especially valuable in helping us reach the boys we most need to support.

Active learning leads to powerful positive outcomes for underachieving boys. Perhaps the best way to demonstrate their tremendous positive effect is to show you how outcomes shift for the underachieving learner when one or more active learning principles are intentionally implemented in a planned learning activity. The following two lessons start with an unadulterated "before" version, which is followed by an "after" version that has been invigorated with the principles of active learning. We will examine the problems presented to the struggling boy in the "before" version and the positive outcomes available to him in the "after" version.

Coordinate Planes (Algebra, Grade 8)

Before

Usually, the first 10 minutes of class are spent on a homework quiz of the previous day's material while I take care of attendance and other routine tasks. Then we go over the quiz, and by this time, a good 15–20 minutes of class have passed. I usually teach the main part of my lesson during the middle portion of the class. I use some lecture combined with small-group discussions and guided practice activities. Then I give the last minutes of class for students to practice what I just taught them or to begin their homework.

Problems for the struggling boy: A struggling boy in this classroom starts off in a position of weakness and instability as a learner. He has no way to know if he understands prior learning before he is quizzed on it, and taking the quiz will not help him learn what he has missed. Lecture is equally problematic as a means for his acquisition of new learning because his underdeveloped literacy skills make note taking difficult. His attention is divided between writing and listening, and he may miss important information. The string of disorganized notes he manages to record may have little meaning for him later unless he can confirm and expand their meaning by discussing them immediately with other students. The small-group discussions may be the saving grace of his learning experience, yet if he is asked to return to solitary seat work before his understanding is fully developed, he may end up practicing an unformed or ill-conceived understanding, which does little to prepare him to complete his homework successfully. When he is quizzed on this knowledge yet again the following day, the cycle repeats itself. He will again be at a loss to know the source of his misunderstanding or how to fix it. New knowledge is added to the same shaky foundation, but little in the way of genuine understanding is built as a result.

After

As students walk into the classroom, they will notice that all the desks have been pushed to the side and there is a giant coordinate plane made out of masking tape on the classroom floor. I will give each student an index card with either a word (origin, x-axis, y-axis, quadrant I, quadrant II, quadrant III, or quadrant IV) or a pair of numbers (e.g., [1, –3]). I will instruct the students where to stand on the coordinate grid as they enter the classroom. The same coordinate grid will be drawn on the board with the same words and pairs of numbers labeled to reinforce where they are standing. I'm hoping that, during this first part of the class, using the physical activity of moving around the giant coordinate plane will help cement the learning of these new words.

Once everyone is standing in their assigned spot, we will go around the coordinate plane and say each word or number pair out loud. After each word or number pair is stated out loud, I will tell the students what each word or number pair means. Then we will go around the coordinate plane again and each student will say their word or number pair again, and this time, they will explain to everyone what it means. (For example, "The origin is where the x-axis and y-axis intersect.") If there is time, we will go around once more and each student will not only state his or her word and its meaning but also those of other students.

Students will then put their desks into groups of four to create one large table, on which I will place graph paper. As a team, they are to label each term and about 10–15 number pairs (ordered pairs) on a coordinate plane that they will draw on the graph paper. During this time, I will take attendance, pass out papers, and take care of other routine tasks that need my attention.

During the final 10–12 minutes of class, teams will be randomly given three or four words or number pairs and will be asked to demonstrate to the class where each is located on the coordinate plane and what it means. During this time, I will be able to indirectly assess whether or not the lesson was successful in general. At the end of this activity, just before the end of class, students will be given a homework assignment that practices working with the coordinate plane.

Source: Karen Washer Everly, Columbus, OH. Used with permission.

Positive outcomes: The minute boys enter the room, their attention is drawn to the changes they see and the coordinate plane Karen has put on the floor (*added relevance and personal meaning, increased attention and memory*). When Karen gives a struggling boy his index card, he begins to engage in solving the problem at hand (*active construction of understanding, increased attention and memory*). As he experiences the concept bodily and visual-spatially, his brain encodes the experience in multiple ways (*increased attention and memory*). When Karen associates each abstract term with an enactment of its definition, she helps him connect the new words with per-sonal experiences (*active construction of understanding, added relevance and personal meaning, consolidation of learning*). When the boy restates his position using these terms, he further confirms his understanding, and Karen is able to check for accuracy (*frequent feedback, consolidation of learning*). In his team, he and the other group members talk about what they've expe-rienced (*reduced anxiety*) and practice applying what they have learned in a new situation (*consolidation of learning*). During the final moments of class, students again practice "being" points on the coordinate plane (*increased attention and memory, consolidation of learning*). As the boy observes others, he gains additional experience (*elaboration*), and Karen's supportive feed-back to all groups clarifies misunderstandings before the students are given a homework assignment (*belief in the possibility of success*).

Notice that a struggling boy in this classroom has the opportunity to acquire the information he needs in multiple ways, the chance to talk about it with oth-ers so that he can clarify his thinking, another opportunity to apply his newly developed understanding, and continuous feedback to dispel any lingering confusion before he is asked to apply what he has learned individually. The homework assignment becomes a reinforcement of his learning, and when he takes the quiz at the beginning of the next day, both his understanding and his confidence are confirmed.

Civil Rights Lesson (Social Studies, Grade 3)

Before

For several years, I have been using picture books to begin a unit of study on the civil rights movement. I believe giving students the opportunity to walk (even slightly) in another person's shoes can begin to help them understand the injustices that African Americans struggled against during this time.

I read *Rosa*, a picture book by Nikki Giovanni, out loud to my students. I explain to them that today I need them to use their imaginations to go back in time to December 1, 1955. I then begin to read the book. Once the book is finished, we have "think time," where the class quietly sits for a few moments and thinks about what we have just experienced together. I then ask students to turn and talk to the peer next to them for 40 seconds. As a class, we discuss their thoughts. Students then open their Writer's Notebooks and record their feelings, thoughts, and ideas.

Problems for the struggling boy: If a boy has no prior experience or understanding of the concept of segregation, he will have difficulty imagining what a world from more than 50 years ago might have been like. Even if his teacher is a wonderful and engaging reader, the passivity of the listening experience may give him the chance to tune out and think of other things instead. Because he often has difficulty finding the words he wants to use to describe what he's thinking about, he will likely simply listen to his partner during the 40-second interchange and will be equally silent during the following class discussion. When he is asked to write on his own, he may recall a few things that his partner or other students mentioned, but the thoughts are not his own, and, as usual, he writes little. The word "segregation" is perhaps now slightly less mysterious, but he has not yet formed any genuine understanding of what it means.

After

I will explain to my students that today I need them to use their imaginations to go back in time to December 1, 1955. I tell them that that is the only place we will be going today. We will walk to the front of the school where a school bus will be parked, and I will hand them the fare for the bus. Students will hand their fare to the driver and then get off the bus and reenter the bus from the rear, just like Rosa Parks did.

As students sit in the back of the bus, I will stand and read the book *Rosa*. Once I finish reading, we will have "think time" for a few moments and ponder what we have just experienced together. I will ask students to turn and share their thoughts with the peer next to them. As a class, we will discuss students' shared insights, feelings, and responses to the experience of hearing a story about segregation and a seminal moment in the civil rights movement while sitting at the back of the bus. Students will then open their Writer's Notebooks and write about their feelings, thoughts, and ideas.

Source: Christi Caronis-Pomeroy, Galena, OH. Used with permission.

Positive outcomes: As a boy leaves the classroom and heads toward the school bus, his attention is activated and his curiosity is piqued (*added relevance and personal meaning, increased attention and memory*). When his teacher asks him to pay the bus driver and then exit the bus, he finds it jarring that he must exit after paying, reenter the bus at the rear (where he usually exits), and sit only in the seats at the back (*active construction of understanding, added relevance and personal meaning, increased attention and memory*). When his teacher asks him to imagine that the year is 1955, he is able to get a sense of time and place as he experiences the significance of how segregation affected Rosa Parks's access to public services and her freedom of choice (*added relevance and personal meaning, consolidation of learning*). When his teacher reads the story *Rosa* to the class, he imagines what it might have been like for a child close to his age to be as brave as Rosa was and how scary it must have been for her (*active construction of understanding*). When he has a chance to talk with the boy next to him about his reactions to the story, he has enough time to talk about the parts of the story that he remembers most (*active construction of understanding, added relevance and personal meaning, reduced anxiety*). And even though he may focus on the action sequence of the story, he begins to understand the emotional ramifications of living with segregation as he recounts the event (*added relevance and personal meaning, consolidation of learning*). When other students talk about some of their feelings, he can relate to them because he may have felt that way, too. Their words help him to understand how to express those kinds of inner thoughts (*reduced anxiety, elaboration*). When his teacher asks him to write in his journal, he is able to use his own insights to talk about the story and the concept of segregation (*insight*). That evening, he asks his parents if they have heard this word (*consolidation of learning*).

A struggling boy in this classroom has the opportunity to begin to develop a personalized understanding of the concept of segregation because he is able to experience it, albeit in a limited capacity, and then he uses his experience as a link to make sense of the story. This connection helps him understand and remember the word and the information associated with it (i.e., the sequence of events). Because he feels somehow connected to the story through this experience, he pays closer attention to the story and to his reactions. As he discusses what he remembers, he consolidates his understanding by putting it into his own words. The ideas shared by others make sense because he has a framework in which to place them. Their comments elaborate his own understanding. As he writes about his impressions of the activity, he has experiences and feelings on which to draw.

Even a cursory read of the previous two lessons leaves little doubt that the "after" versions are superior as vehicles for helping an underachieving boy engage deeply in the learning activity. By looking at these before-and-after scenarios with the outcomes of the eight principles of active learning in mind, we can begin to understand more fully why the "before" and "after" differences are so profound. The "after" versions of the lessons allow the learner to build his understanding, his ability to express himself, and his feelings of competence as a learner. These multilayered outcomes become the fuel for his increasing motivation to persist. This, then, is the critical difference between a "learning activity" and an activity that embodies the principles of "active learning." Whereas the former may momentarily be stimulating and fun, the latter also achieves the long-term benefit of helping a struggling boy become more successful as a learner, and this is a gift he carries with him from that day forward into all other classrooms and subject areas.

The previous two scenarios demonstrated how the principles of active learning can enliven existing lessons. Keeping the learning needs of an underachieving boy in mind, we can also use the principles of active learning to plan new lessons, as in the following three lesson examples.

Three-Dimensional Shapes

Heather West helps her 2nd graders learn about three-dimensional shapes by first connecting the abstract shapes to a series of real-world objects (*consolidation of learning*). Students practice describing the ways in which each abstract shape is like a familiar concrete object during a mock competition in which everyone can contribute and the whole class wins by virtue of the shared insights that come out of the activity (*active construction of understanding, added relevance and personal meaning, increased attention and memory, reduced anxiety*). Heather then has students pick a three-dimensional object from home that they will share with the rest of the class. In preparation, students draw their object (as a means of confirming the presence of the abstract shape in their object) and use the drawing during a practice session with a family member to explain the correspondence between their three-dimensional object and the abstract shape (*added relevance and personal meaning, reduced anxiety, belief in the possibility of success, consolidation of learning*). In class, students take turns sharing their drawings and rehearsed explanations.

Source: Heather West, Los Angeles, CA. Used with permission.

Pasta Punctuation

Sarah Scott helps her middle schoolers learn grammar and punctuation with something she calls "Pasta Punctuation." As students learn each successive punctuation rule, they practice applying it in groups, using "Pasta Envelopes," in which students find an assortment of pasta shapes and a set of sentence strips that need correction. Each pasta shape corresponds to a specific punctuation mark (e.g., elbow macaroni are commas, small shells are quotation marks, orzo are periods, penne become dashes, rotini become parentheses, and so on). As students learn new rules of grammar that require additional forms of punctuation, Sarah introduces new pasta shapes to the Pasta Envelopes, along with new sets of sentence strips.

During a practice activity using the Pasta Envelopes, students work in groups of four. Each group has its own Pasta Envelope, and the challenge for each group is to correct the errors in each of the sentence strips in the Pasta Envelope by using the pasta shapes available. Students must also be able to explain to the teacher (or the rest of the class or another group, depending on the situation) the errors in each strip, the correct punctuation for each error, and the rule of grammar that guided each correction made (*active construction of understanding, increased attention and memory, reduced anxiety, belief in the possibility of success, elaboration*). In time, students move from using

Sarah's prepared sentence strips to writing their own sentences for other groups to correct, which requires that they know what the corrections should be based on the rules involved. After groups exchange their sentences, they take turns as the experts checking one another's work and deciding if the exchanged sentences have been punctuated correctly by the other group (*active construction of understanding, added relevance and personal meaning, increased attention and memory, elaboration, consolidation of learning, insight*).

Source: Sarah Scott, Maryville, OH. Used with permission.

Save the Egg!

In Andy Sovchik's high school physics classroom, students learn the story of a remote island where eggs grow on trees and the islands' inhabitants are in an uproar because the eggs keep falling and breaking (*added relevance and personal meaning*). Students must find a way to protect the eggs during their 20-foot drop, using only cardboard, string, tape, and paper clips (*active construction of understanding, added relevance and personal meaning, increased attention and memory*). As students wrestle with the task, they develop a timeline, create rubrics for the finished device, produce mechanical drawings, and then build their device to scale (*active construction of understanding, increased attention and memory, reduced anxiety, belief in the possibility of success*). Testing each device's success in protecting an egg's 20-foot drop creates a fun, jovial atmosphere (*reduced anxiety*) in which students become aware of the infinite variety of possible solutions to the problem at hand (*consolidation of learning*); their abilities as problem solvers (*active construction of understanding, consolidation of learning*); the real-world application of the principles they have studied (*added relevance and personal meaning, elaboration*); and the fact that failure is an opportunity to improve (*elaboration, insight*).

Source: Andy Sovchik, Akron, OH. Used with permission.

In the end, active learning comprises a set of principles that we can use to engage an underachieving boy in his learning no matter what the activity. Although activities like those you've just read about enrich learning for boys of all styles, they are especially valuable as tools for helping the boys most disenfranchised from their potential to achieve academic success, giving them the opportunity to enter into the learning process in ways that are most natural, comfortable, and productive for them. The more we intentionally look for ways to implement these principles, the more our struggling boys—especially those least connected to a belief in their competence as learners—can find ways to make sense of, own, and enjoy what they are learning. What truly makes active learning such a valuable tool is its ability to ignite the whole boy: his mind, his body, his enthusiasm, his curiosity, his love of social interaction, his problem-solving capabilities, and his need for real-world experience.

> ✤ **TAKE FIVE**
>
> How have your definitions of the eight principles of active learning changed since you started reading this chapter? Which of the principles do you use most often and successfully? If you were to pick just one that you could work on implementing immediately, what would it be? How might you use it, and who might benefit most as a result?

Milepost

The principles laid out in Pathway No. 5: Ignite connect to virtually everything discussed in this book thus far. Each time we intentionally build a lesson around one or more principles of active learning, we might also imagine every element in the Pathways to Re-Engagement model lighting up in response: each Pathway, each Access Point, each Tool, and each goal. The more we use these principles, the greater their potential to re-engage the boys who can benefit most from their use and the outcomes they offer. In Pathway No. 5, we glimpse yet again the multifaceted, integrated nature of the ideas expressed in this book. At some level, everything works together in support of everything else.

BUILDING REPERTOIRES OF RESPONSES

Before you move on to the next chapter, pause to note any "aha!" moments you've had along the way.

1. What do you now understand about how struggling boys learn best that you didn't know before?

2. Of the strategies you are currently using, which could be tweaked or used more intentionally for an even greater positive outcome?

3. Which ideas or strategies caught your attention the most?

4. Choose one idea or strategy related to this Pathway that you could implement right now.

What's Next?

Pathway No. 6: Empower draws the principles of active learning into the arena of literacy, approaching the monumental task of engaging boys in literacy by using what we know about them from prior Pathways and applying that knowledge to the single skill set that filters into every content area and grade level.

CHAPTER 10

Pathway No. 6: Empower

> To this end, teachers sought to improve boys' literacy learning through all that they knew about boys—through engagement of their bodies, their interests, their preferences, their opinions, their cultures, their emotions and their sense of self as learners.
>
> —The Alloway study, p. 133

Pathway No. 6: Empower addresses one of the most knotty and compelling challenges involved in meeting the needs of underachieving boys: support for literacy.

Framing the problem. Regardless of the content area, literacy skills are a universal key to academic success (Salomone, 2003). There is simply nowhere to hide or "get by" if a boy cannot read, and if he cannot or will

> "Reading is crucial for all learning, so this gap [in reading proficiency] likely contributes to the lower grades that boys earn throughout high school and college in all subjects, even math and science" (Eliot, 2009, p. 177).

not read, his ability to write is also diminished in nearly equal proportion. It is through reading that he grasps the information and directions that guide his written demonstrations of knowledge and skill. Reading is also his point of access to the vocabulary, grammar, syntax, organizational models, and editing skills of the writing process itself. He must read in order to learn to write.

Experts tell us that after grade 4, shortcomings in reading and writing become increasingly debilitating because the skill of reading is no longer taught explicitly. Instead of "learning to read," a boy must instead "read in order to learn." If he is not yet proficient as a reader, this added burden may jeopardize his continued academic progress. As the difficulty and scope of written materials increase, a struggling boy's ability to acquire and integrate knowledge and skills may not be sufficient to the task. The more he misses, the less he subsequently understands, because the connections his brain needs in order to store and then retrieve newly added information are unavailable. It's a bit like trying to build on a foundation made of Jell-O. No matter how hard he tries, it's an impossible task.

More often than not, the demonstration of a boy's proficiency also relies on his facility to read well and express himself in writing. A diminished facility in reading and writing may unfairly label him as either unintelligent or incapable. A smart boy who cannot demonstrate what he knows and understands via the written word is not seen as "smart," and this lack of recognition further undermines his willingness to persist.

> "Lower achieving pupils are doubly disadvantaged by tests. Being labeled as failures has an impact on how they feel about their ability to learn. It also lowers further their already low self-esteem and reduces the chance of future effort and success" (Assessment Reform Group, 2002b, p. 5).

Style. Again. The manner in which a boy's style predisposes him to use the symbolic elements of spoken or written language affects his acquisition and subsequent development of literacy skills. From the get-go, some boys have a more difficult time learning to read and write, and thus, by extension, with reading in order to learn. This may be especially the case for an SF/Interpersonal boy.

In the 2009 movie *The Blind Side*, Michael Oher exemplifies the challenges of a boy who struggles to function in school without ever having developed proficiencies in reading or writing. Michael is the quintessential SF/Interpersonal learner, and the story of how he turned the tables on his history of literacy underachievement is all the more compelling because it is true.

Michael grew up in the housing projects of Memphis, Tennessee, and was passed from grade to grade thanks to his athletic ability. By a strange turn of events, he finds himself in an upscale suburban private high school, completely adrift as a learner and wholly unable to adequately express himself verbally or in written form. His teachers initially view him as either mentally challenged or lazy, and his standardized test scores confirm these perceptions. When one of his teachers realizes that Michael understands what she is teaching but is unable to express his understanding in writing, she takes a risk and begins to assess him verbally instead. During their ensuing interchanges, and as a trusting relationship develops between teacher and student, Michael's intelligence emerges. As his confidence as a learner steadily grows, so too do his abilities to express what he has read and learned, verbally and in written form. And as a result of the bond he forms with his tutor (the strength of which sustains him through college), Michael continues to develop the quality of his written work by verbalizing his understanding, discussing areas of confusion, and making personal sense of what he is learning.

While I'm not suggesting that all SF/Interpersonal or NF/Self-Expressive learners need personal tutors in order to achieve literacy, I *am* saying that we often don't know how much or how well a boy can learn when the primary means by which

> "Learners whose styles are accommodated more frequently in school achieve more immediate success. Students who struggle to adapt to an uncomfortable way of learning often underachieve" (Guild, 2001).

knowledge or skill is measured is through written assessments. There are four issues to keep in mind when considering how and why a boy may have difficulty developing and demonstrating his literacy skills, and I've used Michael's story as a point of reference:

1. *We don't see what we're not looking for.* Michael Oher was "smart" all along, but his teachers didn't see his intelligence because he was unable to express or develop his "smartness" in a manner they recognized or supported.

2. *Once a label is given, we seldom question the decisions behind it.* Michael's label of having below average intelligence, along with a folder full of report cards with abysmal grades, marked him as not worthy of any extra effort. His teachers gave up on him without knowing what his potential was. The label made it easier to explain why they were not reaching him.

3. *We cannot expect skilled performance without adequate and appropriate opportunities for practice in a way that develops proficiency.* We cannot expect learners like Michael to acquire and then demonstrate their knowledge and skill with the same success as learners with other styles unless we offer these learners the opportunity to acquire, practice, and affirm their growth using strategies with which *they* can learn successfully. Michael's "intelligence" emerged to his teachers when he finally had the opportunity to learn in a way that was natural and made sense to him: through discussion, verbalization, and personalization of abstract ideas. These opportunities unleashed his potential.

4. *The mode of practice must support the desired skill if the aptitude is going to develop to its fullest potential.* Given the chance to learn in the way most natural and productive to him, a learner like Michael can and does build his literacy skills. It's not that he is unable or lacking in intelligence or ability but rather that he needs to learn and practice in ways that differ from those currently offered to him on a regular basis. The remarkable success of the boys at Chicago's Urban Prep could not be a more dramatic example of this; even though only 4 percent of entering freshmen read at grade level, 100 percent of those same boys as seniors were accepted to college (Eldeib, 2010).

In other words, where an underachieving boy and his literacy are concerned, his initial style-based deficits may be compounded by a lack of opportunity for him to practice his skills in a way that actually allows him to learn them successfully. His diminishing belief that his efforts will result in success lead to a gradual disengagement from learning, and when, somewhere in the midst of this disengagement, we also label him as incapable, slow, or lazy, we further undermine his and our belief in his ability to be a capable learner (Reichert & Hawley, 2006). As his literacy deficits become more and more glaring, his perception of himself as a failure may become a self-fulfilling prophecy. With neither hope nor insight, he may give up entirely, which is, I suspect, precisely the case for the increasing numbers of boys dropping out of schools earlier and earlier and ending up on our streets and in our prisons (Barton, 2005). Ask any prison educator how many of his boys or young men read, write, and speak proficiently, and you will sense the gravity of the situation.

Thus, to build an underachieving boy's literacy, we must focus equally on rebuilding him as a learner. In Michael Oher's story, we saw how a boy with little hope was able to develop his literacy skills, even after years of failure and neglect, as a result of changed perspectives (his own and his teachers') about his ability to learn, opportunities to learn in a manner that made sense and was comfortable for him, and support that helped him to persist. The message in Michael's story is that by providing the conditions for an underachieving boy to re-engage successfully in literacy learning, we empower him as a learner—and a learner who believes he is capable will persist to develop the skills he needs.

The Code. Again. As we think about the problems associated with boys' widespread underachievement in literacy, let's also take a moment to revisit the issue of the negative perception many boys have of literacy proficiency as a "feminine" skill and, thus, one to be avoided. This attitude is directly related to the Code, and although we can easily recognize that it further complicates the style-based issues confronting struggling learners like Michael Oher, we also know that it has the power to affect boys of all styles.

In Chapter 3, I shared four factors that contribute to the pervasive power of this negative attitude, and I'd like to address each again, this time keeping in mind what we now know about responding more effectively to our underachieving boys.

1. *The growing absence of positive role models.* One of the more contentious issues related to this factor is the lack of male teachers entering the education field and the preponderance of women teaching in our classrooms. This is particularly the case in lower grades, where the focus on building literacy skills through explicit instruction is most intense. In other words, at the very time when boys are most directly involved in building literacy skills, they are least likely to have the benefit of male role models. Though we know having a male teacher does not guarantee that a boy will become more literate, the *presence* of positive male role models in the classroom may offer powerful, real-world exemplars for boys about the ways in which real men use and value literacy on a daily basis. And that is the relevant point.

Fortunately, there are many ways for female teachers to provide the boys in their classrooms with positive male role models who view literacy as an essential attribute of their masculinity. For example, many teachers encourage fathers (stepfathers, grandfathers, uncles, big brothers) to get involved at their child's school. Interestingly, the simple presence of these male figures *in school* communicates support for literacy learning ("Canberra," 2002). To make this connection even stronger, teachers can ask fathers (and other male role models) to read aloud to their students (either a passage of their own choosing or one selected by the teacher) or, if they are not comfortable with reading aloud, to simply talk about why reading and writing have been important in their own lives. We can see how the strength of the adult male reader's relationship with at least one boy in the class might enhance the impact of his message to all of the boys, because it is natural to give greater credence to the words and actions of those we know and trust. This holds true, though to a lesser degree, when the male role model is, for example, a familiar businessman from the local community or a recently graduated former student.

One school built on this principle by developing a "catch men reading" project. Students (boys and girls) took pictures of willing male volunteers reading and used the pictures to create a series of "Real Men Read" posters ("Canberra," 2002, p. 165). The project heightened boys' awareness about the real-world value of literacy and resulted in the ongoing involvement of many of the male volunteers in literacy activities throughout the year.

2. *A concurrent overabundance of hypermasculine, antihero models in the media.* The effect of seeing familiar and respected men talk about and demonstrate the importance of literacy cannot be underestimated for its ability to counteract the media's restrictive definition of masculinity. The greater the variety of male exemplars, the more a boy may be able to see and understand that literacy is not only appropriately masculine but also valuable in the real world, no matter a man's profession. It may, in fact, be especially powerful for boys to see men in professions they associate with hypermasculinity (e.g., sports heroes, construction workers, firemen, policemen, soldiers) using, enjoying, and relying on literacy skills. To aid in fostering this revised perception, teachers can use easily available online images of "real men reading" to create posters for their classrooms.

3. *An unspoken understanding that boys who follow the Code do not enjoy or make public their literacy.* One of my favorite examples of a teacher

helping her boys understand the folly of this line of thinking happened when she invited a dad, who happened to be a helicopter pilot, to speak to her class about the role of literacy in his life ("Canberra," 2002). When he chose to read a poem he had written and then talked about how writing had helped him to work through the grief of losing a close friend, he communicated the value of literacy as a fully masculine task in ways that spoke volumes to his male listeners. Granted, we may not all have poetry-reading, journal-writing, helicopter pilot dads available, but chances are that many dads (or other male role models) have something they can share about the ways in which literacy has helped them to deal with life.

4. *An acute fear of being labeled as different.* Hopefully, the implementation of many of the strategies shared in previous Pathways will go a long way toward reducing an underachieving boy's concerns about being seen as different. For example, developing a trusting teacher-student relationship, establishing a nonthreatening learning environment, and helping boys acquire and use communication and collaboration skills all contribute to the kind of learning community in which all students know one another well and come to respect one another's unique gifts. It's much harder to label or exclude someone when we see him as a human being with rights and abilities worthy of respect.

In fact, in a very real way, every previous Pathway and Access Point counteracts the attitude that literacy learning is not a masculine pursuit by meeting the four goals I set forth at the very beginning of this book:

• *Replace* a boy's negative attitudes about learning with productive perspectives about the role of risk (and even failure) as a necessary and valued part of the learning process;

• *Reconnect* him with school, with learning, and with a belief in himself as a competent learner who is capable, valued, and respected;

• *Rebuild* life skills and learning skills that lead to academic success and also lay the groundwork for success in life; and

• *Reduce* his need to use unproductive and distracting behaviors as a means of self-protection.

Each of these goals helps to build an underachieving boy's sense of competence as a learner, and this, in turn, may help him to take a less defensive stance toward learning in general and especially toward literacy learning. Confident, connected, skilled, resilient, and supported learners are less vulnerable to the fears that the Code works so hard to promote.

In this, the final Access Point, we will explore three new strategies. Each is designed to provide a boy who continues to struggle with literacy a chance to build the skills he so desperately needs in order to succeed academically and to do so in a way that not only makes sense to him as a learner but also honors his need for appropriate masculine identity building. We are reconfiguring our classrooms as "active and embodied" spaces for literacy learning in which underachieving boys and literacy thrive, side by side (Alloway et al., 2002, p. 133).

Access Point: Engaging Literacy-Building Activities

A teacher who understands the conditions that make people want to learn— want to read, to write, and do sums—is in a position to turn these activities into flow experiences. When the experience becomes intrinsically rewarding, students' motivation is engaged, and they are on their way to a lifetime of self-propelled acquisition of knowledge.

—Mihaly Csikszentmihalyi, psychologist and author

It's probably safe to say that most of us enjoy doing what we do well. The problem for a boy who struggles with literacy is that the very thing that would most help him to develop those literacy skills is also the very thing he least enjoys or wants to do.

Figure 10.1 lists some of the most common reasons that a struggling reader might resist re-engaging in literacy activities, and you will see the influence of both the Code and school-versus-style conflicts in evidence: sensitivity to his lack of skill, fear of public failure, lack of confidence in his ability to be successful, a need for support but an unwillingness to ask for it, lack of opportunities to practice, and, most debilitating of all, a feeling of hopelessness. These, we know, are powerful adversaries, culturally entrenched and reinforced daily.

FIGURE 10.1
Criteria for Re-Engagement in Literacy Learning

Barriers to Literacy Learnings		Criteria for Re-Engagement
• Sensitivity to his lack of skill	→	*(1) High personal interest*
• Fear of public failure	→	*(2) Rapid success*
• Lack of confidence in his ability to succeed	→	*(3) Evidence of growth*
• A need for support but an unwillingness to ask for it	→	*(4) Access to support*
• Lack of opportunity to practice in ways that are helpful	→	*(5) Companionable learning*
• A feeling of hopelessness	→	*(6) Choice and control*

Yet if we can somehow help a boy who struggles with literacy to see himself as a capable learner *while* he continues to build his literacy skills, his motivation to continue may propel him forward, even in spite of his limitations. The sense of growing competence may help to overcome his understandable resistance in the face of his previous failures.

Thus, our challenge in finding an effective response to the somewhat paradoxical problem of providing effective literacy learning experiences to underachieving boys is twofold. First, we must find ways to engage a boy who struggles with a process from which he often feels estranged and about which he has an acute sense of incompetence. We can achieve this by meeting the criteria for re-engagement laid out in Figure 10.1. Second, we must offer him access to skill-building literacy learning through participation in activities that make sense to him, seem achievable, and—despite his lack of skill—offer him the elusive success that will motivate him to persist. In other words, we must provide opportunities for effective practice.

Criteria for re-engagement. In answer to the first part of this challenge (i.e., finding ways to engage a boy who struggles with a process from which he often feels estranged and about which he has an acute sense of incompetence), we can look to the barriers listed in Figure 10.1 and use them to identify ideal qualities of literacy-based activities that have the potential to counteract their negative influence and eliminate or reduce their power.

- To overcome sensitivity to his lack of skills, the struggling literacy learner needs to experience **high personal interest.**
- To overcome fear of public failure, he needs to experience **rapid success.**
- To overcome lack of confidence in his ability to be successful, he needs to experience **evidence of growth.**
- To overcome a need for support but an unwillingness to ask for it, he needs to experience **access to support.**
- To overcome lack of opportunities to practice, he needs to experience **companionable learning.**
- To overcome a feeling of hopelessness, he needs to experience **choice and control.**

These six antidotes to disengagement are our criteria for re-engagement, and we can use them to identify activities that address the second part of the challenge—offering access to skill-building literacy activities.

Opportunities for effective literacy practice. The following three Key Resources each exemplify a unique approach to literacy learning that meets the *criteria for re-engagement* and also provides *opportunities for effective practice.* As opportunity, engagement, and support join forces, a struggling boy begins to see himself as a capable learner. When he begins to see improvement and feel a sense of mastery, no matter how small, his motivation to keep learning is strengthened, even when he is fully aware that he has a long way to go yet. This is resilience in action.

Key Resource: Graphic Novels

Literacy Challenge: Lack of interest in free reading

Criteria for Re-Engagement:
1. High personal interest
2. Rapid success
3. Evidence of growth
6. Choice and control

In *Misreading Masculinity* (2002), longtime literacy advocate Thomas Newkirk explains that unless boys read, they "will not develop the skills that make them good readers" (p. 65), and that is the crux of the issue. If we are serious about wanting to re-engage struggling boys in literacy, we

> "*Appeal* means that students are free and encouraged to read information that they find highly interesting. This factor is not as straightforward as it seems. In addition to being interesting to students, the selected books should be at appropriate levels of reading difficulty" (Marzano, 2004, p. 44).

need to give them access to the kinds of books they will truly enjoy reading, so that they rediscover reading as a pleasurable pastime and continue to build their skills as a result.

There is some excellent and surprising research in regard to what these materials should include. It turns out that because getting a boy to read is far more important to his academic success than *what* he actually reads (Marzano, 2004), the salient qualities to look for in ideal literature for under-achieving boys are *readability* and *relevance.* It's the enjoyment of the reading experience that engages him and helps him persist, and because he persists, he builds both his literacy skills and the background knowledge he needs to achieve academically in all subject areas.

The problem, of course, is that as educators, our notions about what makes for appropriate reading material are often in conflict with the kinds of materials that disengaged readers find most appealing. Fortunately, a solution to this conflict exists: the graphic novel. This literacy-building resource encompasses both high interest (for the struggling boy) and high quality (for his teacher).

Graphic novels to the rescue. Graphic novels provide a range of choices to meet an underachieving boy's desire for relevant topics and enjoyable stories, and what makes this a particularly happy circumstance in terms of the task of literacy-building is that graphic novels are also good literature. Despite their superficial similarity to the comic books of our youth, graphic novels possess qualities for developing literacy that put them on equal footing with the more traditional titles in our classroom libraries and media centers. The fact that armies of librarians and teachers recommend them is a powerful endorsement of their potential for re-engagement (NCTE, 2005;

Schwartz, 2006), and fortuitously, the list of high-quality titles available for boys ages 7 and older continues to expand exponentially.

We can use the criteria for re-engagement to understand what makes graphic novels both engaging and effective for resistant and struggling literacy learners.

• *High personal interest.* I'm convinced that graphic novels' visual appeal for struggling boys lies in the fact that the images they employ resonate with them on a personal level. Many graphic novel artists use an artistic style similar to that of a young person's. That is, the art has a uniquely kid-friendly feel to it and doesn't necessarily have the slickness that one might expect from a professional publication. This familiarity offers boys an instant sense of connection. In addition, the absence of formality common to more traditional texts invites a boy into the reading experience, lowering his defenses and keeping his interest high.

• *Rapid success.* Simply put, graphic novels are easier for a reluctant or struggling reader to "get into" than traditional texts. They provide a shortcut to the fun part of reading, and this is due to the many differences inherent in the experience of reading a graphic novel.

Rather than line by line, the narrative in a graphic novel is depicted scene by scene, with each scene fitting into a "panel" (often one panel per page). To understand the scene, a boy must simultaneously make sense of the images and the words, which are organized within the panel to convey not only plot progression but also sounds, setting, character, dialogue, pacing, perspective, and virtually any other element imaginable. The tale is told via every single aspect possible within the limitations of the form: spatial, organizational, pictorial, and textual (Rudiger, 2005).

Like a storyboard, each panel connects various story elements in a way that helps a boy's brain make multiple associations within each segment of the story. To comprehend each panel, he processes all of these elements together, making sense of them in a holistic and personalized (and therefore brain-friendly) manner. Rather than merely receiving information word by word, he is constructing his understanding scene by scene.

If the language in the previous two sentences reminds you of the principles of active learning from Pathway No. 5, you're right. Reading graphic novels is active learning at its best, and that's precisely the point. This format may be especially helpful for any boy who ordinarily is put off by trying to make sense of details and sequence in text-dense writing. Because graphic novels provide a variety of clues to meaning, he "reads" in a much different way that helps him actively make sense of the content on many levels. From the outset of his reading experience, his comprehension soars along with his confidence as a reader.

• *Evidence of growth.* The chief feat of graphic novels is that they make the engaged reading experience accessible to even the least accomplished of readers. As one reviewer explains, they "relieve the tension of reading expectation for kids who are not natural readers," giving them equal opportunity to experience the confidence and engagement felt routinely by more experienced and successful readers (Brenner, 2005, p. 1). By drawing in a struggling reader and motivating him to persist, graphic novels provide an empowering reading experience that supports a boy in building his reading skills along with his background knowledge, both of which contribute to his potential for academic success. He "gets" what he's reading and enjoys the subtle but powerful sense of accomplishment that comes as a result.

• *Choice and control.* Reading a graphic novel offers a boy choice and control from beginning to end. He is free to peruse each frame at his own pace, and his interpretation is necessarily unique because no two readers will synthesize the elements within a panel in exactly the same manner, nor do they have to. This lack of expectation of an exact interpretation of the text helps boys who struggle with literacy to engage in reading and to feel more relaxed about their ability to grasp the story's message. In fact, many teachers report that boys who were unresponsive to text-based literature are highly responsive to graphic novels.

Graphic novels involve a struggling boy in literacy learning in a manner that makes sense to him, builds his literacy skills, and helps him feel successful while doing so. For recommendations of graphic novel titles organized by grade level, check out the *School Library Journal*, a great online resource for educators. You'll find suggestions for appropriate titles for each grade level at multiple levels of reading readiness.

Key Resource: Jeffrey Wilhelm's Enactments

Literacy Challenge: Poor comprehension, especially while reading literary texts

Criteria for Re-Engagement:
1. High personal interest
2. Rapid success
3. Evidence of growth
4. Access to support
5. Companionable learning
6. Choice and control

As expectations for a boy's ability to comprehend a variety of genres continue to grow with each grade level, so, too, does his need to make sense of language that is less and less concrete. In literary genres (e.g., prose, poetry, and drama), words convey much more than factual information, and their greater meaning is hidden among intertwined elements of plot, character development, and figurative language. The process of interpreting this kind of language can, understandably, be especially difficult for a boy who lacks strong reading skills.

> "Facilitating student interaction not only increases the amount of exposure students have to information, but also dramatically expands their base of language experience. Additionally, dialogue [among learners about what they have learned] is apparently a natural consequence of developing expertise in a topic" (Marzano, 2004, p. 59).

In addition to the challenge of interpretation, the very process of reading a literary text may consume so much energy that a boy with weak reading skills simply tunes out. How many of us, at some point in college (or even more recently), had the similar experience of getting to the end of an assignment only to discover that we had no clue what we'd just read? Interestingly, then as now, reading the same passage over and over isn't necessarily all that helpful, because rereading words is not the same as comprehending their meaning. Adding to a struggling boy's frustration is the fact that, even with effort, he simply may not "get" what he's reading.

As educators, we can easily do two things on a regular basis to support a struggling boy who is faced with the dual obstacles of limited reading proficiency and a challenging text. First, we can chunk the reading into smaller, more accessible segments, which reduces the level of fatigue a struggling reader experiences and gives the brain time to relax and recover; second, we can make sure to process each chunk actively before proceeding to the next one, which helps the brain make sense of the complex language and the meaning "hidden" within it. And although the length of each "chunk" may vary from as little as a sentence or a paragraph for young readers to as much as a chapter for older readers, the opportunity for a boy of any age to stop briefly and actively make sense of what he has just read increases his comprehension dramatically, thereby building his sense of competence as a reader and encouraging him to persist. In other words, we can support a boy's competence as a *learner* even while he struggles to understand what he has read.

In *Action Strategies for Deepening Comprehension* (2002), Jeffrey Wilhelm shows us how to accomplish both of these goals at the same time using Enactments, a strategy that allows a boy to pause after reading and respond creatively and energetically to what he has just read. Sometimes Enactments look like dramatizations, but that simple description belies both the breadth of their scope and the potential depth of their impact. Their greatest power lies in their ability to make the hidden elements of literature visible for boys who struggle to comprehend them. Enactments are about making sense of the meaning that's hidden between the lines: the possible motivations for a character's actions, the emotions that lead to decisions, the elements of the situation that aren't overtly explained but which plainly affect the plot. As he imagines the world of the story and its characters, contemplates the similarities between the story and his real life, and grasps the story's message, a boy develops a personal connection to what he is reading that builds both comprehension and competence, motivating him to persist as well as expanding his ability to discuss and write about what he now understands.

Notice in the following examples of Enactments that students aren't simply reading the lines of the story aloud. They're developing an understanding of what's *not* on the page by imagining it and then actively bringing those imaginings into reality.

Before Reading (Grade 11)

Prior to a lesson on *Romeo and Juliet*, the teacher divides the class into groups that represent two familiar rival sports teams. Students brainstorm the kinds of taunts they would typically hear shouted at a game. After moving desks to the side of the room to clear a space, students face off and shout their taunts at one another, gradually increasing their volume as they are urged to move closer and closer by the teacher. As emotions and energy reach a fever pitch, the teacher calls a halt and introduces their next unit of study: *Romeo and Juliet.* Students (especially boys) begin their study of the play with a visceral sense of conflict that is connected to their own experience. They will be able to relate to the complexities of Shakespearean language as they filter the unfamiliar words through this lens, making sense of it by translating it through their own perceptions of strong, entrenched, real-world conflict (Wilhelm, 2002).

During Reading (Grade 6)

To help students understand interactions among characters in a novel about the Salem witch trials, students enact coming before a town council. Each student is assigned a character and must justify that character's actions and explain the reasoning behind his or her behaviors, both of which insights a boy must infer from the story. He must figuratively step into the shoes of his character. As he prepares for the Enactment, he generates reasons for his character's behavior, using his own experience to understand the character better. During the Enactment, the town council members' questions (to which he must respond), the statements of other characters (to which he must react), and his moment-by-moment experiences help him make sense of the story through his character's eyes by feeling, hearing, and seeing it on a personal level. His perspective and vocabulary are both enhanced as a result, and when it's time to write an essay comparing his character to another, he has much to draw from.

After Reading (Grade 3)

After reading *Charlotte's Web*, students take on the roles of several of the main characters: Wilbur (the pig), Fern (the 8-year-old girl who first saves Wilbur from being butchered), and Templeton (the gluttonous rat). Other lesser characters may be involved as well (e.g., the lamb, the goose, and the old sheep). For the Enactment, students take on the job of explaining to Joy, Aranea, and Nellie—Charlotte's offspring who remain on the farm after she has died—what their mother Charlotte was like and how she saved Wilbur. Students stay in character and tell their story through their own perspective. Each character chooses the one word he or she would have Joy, Aranea, and Nellie write in their own webs to describe Charlotte.

We can use the criteria for re-engagement to see why underachieving boys respond so positively to this kind of literacy activity.

> "I find that the more practical something is the more I'll get out of the underachievers whether they be boys or girls; they're more stimulated especially in writing if they've actually experienced something; they're keener to write" (Alloway et al., 2002, p. 103).

• *High personal interest.* The now-familiar principles of active learning explain what makes Enactments so inviting. This single strategy incorporates many of the principles that most engage reluctant learners: *active involvement, compelling situations, direct experience, enjoyable setting, informal learning,* and *patterns of connection.* And throughout an Enactment experience, a boy continues to develop personal interest as a result of the connections he forms with his character and the story, engaging him further as he reads subsequent segments.

• *Rapid success.* Just as graphic novels provide a degree of familiarity that eases a struggling reader into the reading process, Enactments provide a similarly familiar and comfortable route to deeper comprehension. The simplest way to explain this phenomenon is with the phrase "experience first." A boy's engagement in a concrete experience helps him actively process the mystifying abstract elements of what he has read and thereby generate language he can use to express his ideas about it. He develops both comprehension and a sense of competence without his fear of failure getting in the way. Research tells us lots of boys truly enjoy this kind of dramatized learning. It's great when something this much fun is so effective.

• *Evidence of growth.* A great benefit of Enactments is that by bringing a story to life, a boy with weak literacy skills is able to access and give voice to the inner language and feelings he discovers as a result. Because Enactments are performed at junctures between reading assignments, they help the boy who has difficulty absorbing and understanding long written passages of text to understand the current "chunk" of information before having to try to understand the next one. He recalls and understands each previous segment of what he has read and can connect it to the next. Instead of layering confusion upon confusion, he builds insight and depth of understanding with each successive Enactment experience.

- *Access to support.* As a result of seeing his teacher model the Enactment process and working with others in a relaxed and spontaneous manner, a struggling boy finds continuous support, which leads to reduced anxiety.

- *Companionable learning.* As he works with others and responds to them "in character," a boy shares a part of who he is and what he thinks, and he learns about others at the same time. Shades of active learning's *enjoyable setting* and *informal learning* abound here, too, along with an added benefit that some authors call "social capital"—when a boy's participation gives him a common experience about which he can talk to other students. Of course, when he talks about his experiences, he continues to refine and develop his understanding of the literature.

- *Choice and control.* During Enactments, a boy has both the choice of how to respond as well as control over what his Enactment will look like. There is no right or wrong answer, just a chance to see what will happen. The spontaneous nature of the experience frees him to respond without fear of failure.

Not just for language arts. Enactments aren't restricted to language arts use, and this flexibility is part of their attractiveness as a literacy-building tool across disciplines. It's easy to adapt the Enactment approach in other content areas. Recall Karen Washer Everly's Coordinate Plane lesson from Pathway No. 5, in which students became points on a floor-sized coordinate plane; Christi Caronis-Pomeroy's lesson about the civil rights movement in which students sat in the back of a bus while listening to their teacher read a story about Rosa Parks's experience; and Patrick McNeeley's lesson on car buying, specifically the role-plays in preparation for visiting the credit bureau. All three of these lessons include elements that offer students a physical way to process abstract language and concepts (coordinate planes, segregation, and credit, respectively) in a manner that makes them more concrete—the very essence of using Enactments.

Wilhelm takes this familiar but underused strategy to the level of an art form, and part of what makes it so effective for underachieving boys in any grade level or subject area is that it combines physical activity with mental activity to engage the entire psyche. As one of Wilhelm's book titles says so perfectly, *"You Gotta BE the Book"* (1997). In so doing, the underachieving boy re-engages in literacy and affirms himself as a competent learner *while* he continues to build his skills.

Key Resource: Talking Cards

Literacy Challenge: Difficulty generating descriptive language (written or spoken)

Criteria for Re-Engagement:
  1. High personal interest
  2. Rapid success
  3. Evidence of growth
  4. Access to support
  5. Companionable learning
  6. Choice and control

Underachieving boys may have difficulty in generating their own descriptive language for many of the same reasons they struggle to comprehend language in literary texts. It's not uncommon to hear teachers at all grade levels complain that their boys write easily about action sequences or factual information but less capably about anything descriptive or remotely emotional. Although the "F(eeling)" qualities possessed

"Expressive writing is one of the best ways to deepen students' understanding and enhance their language experience. Free-response writing... accomplishes multiple goals that include facilitating the storage of information in permanent memory, enhancing language experience, and promoting self-expression" (Marzano, 2004, p. 55).

"Processing... information in linguistic and nonlinguistic forms while in working memory [provides]... multiple by the SF/Interpersonal or NF/Self-Expressive boy may help him to see and understand aspects of the human condition with greater sensitivity, he may be no better equipped to express those insights than boys with other styles. Neither he nor his peers have had much practice. Talking Cards can provide a simple, flexible way for boys to access descriptive language using images to jump-start the process.

> exposures to the information. . . . They also increase the language experience of students in the context of something they are excited about" (Marzano, 2004, p. 54).

The Talking Cards approach was developed by Peter Mortola, Stephen Grant, and Howard Hiton for their BAM! (Boys Advocacy and Mentoring) groups to help boys build fluency in emotional expression (an outcome I affirm and admire for reasons that are no doubt abundantly clear by this point). I have adapted their basic approach as a way for teachers to support literacy building in a more general way that is suitable for a heterogeneous classroom. For our purposes here, Talking Cards work in a manner somewhat akin to Enactment's "experience first" approach, using "images first" to unlock a boy's ability to generate descriptive language in response to chosen images (Mortola, Grant, & Hiton, n.d.). To understand how Talking Cards work, it is first important to understand how the cards are made.

Talking Cards

Talking Cards are a set of 80 to 100 images laminated on large index cards or half-sheets of card stock. A teacher creates the cards using images culled from common materials such as photos, magazines, calendars, or other graphic resources. The images share one of several key characteristics, each of which is designed to stimulate descriptive language:

• *Variations in nature* (e.g., shapes [anything from a cloud to a bird's beak]; heights [from a towering redwood to a sapling]; intensity [high winds, waves, lightning]; and denseness [trees in a forest, a flock of migrating geese, a field of wildflowers]).

• *Uniqueness* (e.g., people, places, things, and art from other countries and cultures).

• *Commonalities and differences* (e.g., members of a family, clothes in a closet, food at the grocery store, bugs on a tree, flowers in a vase, boats at a marina).

· *Openness to interpretation* (e.g., a set of tools [Who would use these tools? Which would you pick? What other tools do you have in your life?], a bowl of fruit [How might it taste? Who put it there?], a door with peeling paint [What's in the next room? Why is the door shut? Where is this door located?]).

· *Complexity* (e.g., a scene in which multiple events happen simultaneously or many different characters are present; a design with many colors, shapes, or patterns).

· *Cognitive dissonance* (e.g., a lion as a pet, the moon and sun shining at the same time) (Mortola et al., n.d.).

Using the Talking Cards is a delightfully uncomplicated process. All a teacher needs is the cards, a place to spread them out (for ease in choosing), and an opportunity for students to select and discuss them. We can use the criteria for re-engagement to explain what makes this Tool so effective in re-engaging a struggling boy in this aspect of his literacy learning.

• *High personal interest.* After the cards are made available, a boy selects a card that catches his interest. The first few times students use the Talking Cards, the teacher may provide a prompt before students make the selection (e.g., Pick a picture that reminds you of... what to do when you are scared; what it is like to get a surprise; doing something you hate to do; getting bad news). This helps boys begin to find language to describe their chosen images. At other times, the teacher will let the students pick a card and then will ask them to answer a series of open-ended questions about the card they've chosen, and with practice and a growing familiarity and comfort with the process, the teacher can make the use of Talking Cards fully and freely associative, without any prompts or guiding questions.

• *Rapid success.* The goal of the activity is to help students talk freely about the image they have selected. By connecting to personal experience or memory, the image helps a boy who has difficulty expressing himself find the language to do so. The realization that his seemingly ordinary observations are a genuine resource in this regard is a bit like discovering a treasure he didn't know he was looking for.

• *Evidence of growth.* Once a boy is familiar with the process of choosing and then talking about an image, his descriptive language may increase in variety as well as clarity. As he becomes increasingly comfortable talking about experiences or memories associated with each picture, he acquires a broader range of language, notices the growing ease with which he can generate it, and begins to use that language in his writing. Before he even fully comprehends what he is doing, he may begin forming characterizations and potential plot elements. A boy who never would have imagined himself capable of writing a story suddenly finds that he has both the ability and the confidence to do so. It's a bit like turning on a faucet that has been long out of use. Initially, water comes out in spurts, but before long, there is a steady stream.

• *Companionable learning.* In small groups (which may be either single-gender or heterogeneous, as best fits the situation), students take turns talking about their cards, responding to the teacher's prompt (or making free associations, depending on what the framework of their sharing calls for). There are no right or wrong answers, and the setting is relaxed and conversational.

• *Access to support.* As with any new or unfamiliar skill, the teacher models how the cards will be used and scaffolds their use so that students feel comfortable and can enjoy the freedom of choice. Since the learner's emotional awareness is essential to the success of this strategy, the teacher builds in success each step of the way by making sure that the challenge of the "stretch" between the familiar and the new feels safe enough to be engaging and fun, yet not great enough to induce fear of failure.

For example, the teacher might initiate the Talking Cards process very informally, as a simple, low-risk game (e.g., What picture do you like best?). Gradually, the teacher may offer prompts that require the students to describe what they have selected and then why they have selected a particular image. When students are comfortable with the process of selecting and discussing an image and are able to freely generate descriptions for their chosen images without prompting or questioning, the teacher may integrate the Talking Cards process into literacy lessons, for example, to jump-start a prewriting brainstorming session. In all cases, the teacher remains attuned to the struggling boy's sense of comfort and safety during the Talking Cards activity, thereby maintaining a productive balance between challenge and enjoyment, with neither being sacrificed for the other.

• *Choice and control.* As with his initial choice of image, a boy is free to respond however he wishes. There is no expectation for how much or how little he must say; how many nouns, verbs, or adjectives he has to use; or whether he has to speak in complete sentences. By removing these restrictive and more formal expectations from the process, he is free to generate natural and spontaneous responses in a manner that feels comfortable and manageable to him.

Talking Cards "prime the pump" for a boy's ability to access his inner language resources. His halting initial response to a picture he has selected might be as simple as a one-sentence comparison between the look of surprise he sees on the face of the monkey in his picture and the one he remembers seeing on his brother's face: "The look of surprise on the monkey's face is like the one I saw on my brother's face when he opened his birthday present and found a doll." For a boy who struggles with descriptive language, even this rough beginning is a much easier route to accessing such language than sitting at his desk and trying to write about a topic with which he has no familiarity or in which he has no interest. Instead of having to dig for ideas and words, his brain generates them automatically, "image first"—perhaps slowly initially, but eventually with more ease and competence. The combination of *informal learning* in an *enjoyable setting* gives a relaxed, game-like quality to the experience and sets the stage for continued active learning. With practice and experience, the same card at another time might generate a far more detailed response.

The look of surprise on the monkey's face is like the one I saw on my brother's face when he opened his birthday present and found a doll. Sam knew he had to be polite and say something nice, but he had no idea how. His face and ears got really red and he sort of started sputtering. He couldn't figure out what to say. The funny thing was that my grandma said later that she thought asking for a Barbie doll was pretty weird in the first place, but she got it for him because she thought that's what he wanted. We finally figured out that Grandma had misunderstood Mom when she told her what Sam wanted. When Mom said "BB," Grandma heard "Barbie."

In the same way that a boy struggling to read must read, a boy struggling to write must write. The genius of Talking Cards is that they stimulate this process by making it fun as well as empowering.

Literacy Activities in Other Disciplines

One of the great things about each of the Tools I've shared in the three Key Resources of Pathway No. 6 is that they can be used to enhance literacy-based elements in almost all subject areas. In the following lesson, notice how high school teacher Marion James integrates aspects of all three Key Resources to deepen her students' comprehension of math's real-world problem-solving capacities, engaging them in the learning experience and building their literacy skills at the same time.

Building Literacy into a Mathematics Lesson

1. High personal interest

2. Rapid success

3. Evidence of growth

4. Access to support

5. Companionable learning

6. Choice and control

Marion wants to support literacy development in her math classroom. She decides to do this by tapping into her students' love of drawing, which is usually offered as a reward for hard work. To appeal to their interests, emotions, humor, and creativity, she builds a lesson around the development of their own graphic novels. The subject for these novels is "real-world problem solving using math."

To begin the lesson, Marion provides students with copies of a graphic novel that will eventually serve as a model for the graphic novels they will develop. Rather than reading through the novel, she asks students to thumb through its pages and note whatever catches their attention. In a subsequent discussion, students generate vocabulary drawn from their personal experience to describe elements of the graphic novel that they found interesting or helpful. Some mention the quality of the art, whereas others talk about the image-to-text ratio, the various ways that the images are organized within the frames on each page, or the way that the various patterns and sizes of the images convey action (or lack of action). After discussing the more visual elements of the graphic novel, Marion asks students to talk about the content, specifically the problem(s) around which the story was developed. Students gradually identify the ways in which math concepts they have been working with were used in the story.

Marion then challenges students to develop their own graphic novels, building their story line around a real-world problem that can be solved with math. Students select their problem and work in groups to create the story line, characters, dialogue, and images.

During their group work, students interact continually within and among groups, sharing ideas and feedback. Using a rubric and a clearly defined time line, Marion facilitates their creative process by helping them to find resources, get the technical help they need, and dialogue with individuals and groups along the way. She encourages groups to act out their stories when they hit a roadblock in their thinking, and as a result, students are usually able to find a solution to the problem.

At the end of the unit, groups publish their graphic novels and share them with other groups. Marion asks students to reflect on their group and individual learning processes, focusing especially on how their understanding of a mathematical concept was reinforced or deepened as a result of the task.

Why it works: In this rich and innovative literacy lesson, Marion engages her students in a task that connects them to math content and helps them to make sense of it in a way that is uniquely meaningful to them (*high personal interest*). As students discuss what they found interesting about the graphic novels they explored individually, the class collectively develops a vocabulary to describe the most important characteristics of the novels they will eventually complete (*companionable learning, elaboration*). No one is "right" or "wrong" (*rapid success*). Making decisions about the topic, characters, dialogue, plot, and format puts students in charge of the processes they use to develop their graphic novels (*choice and control*). Their work in groups adds to the fun of the project—which is unusual for a "serious" course like upper-level math—as do their more informal discussions in and outside of class (*companionable learning*). As students grapple with the task, they experience a sense of developing competence because they are learning to meet a significant challenge (*evidence of growth*). Groups receive continuous support from Marion during the development of their novels, as well as substantial peer support during the creation process and sharing of their final products (*access to support, elaboration*). As a result of Marion's innovative lesson, students build literacy skills (i.e., reading, writing, organization, planning, illustrating, dialogue and plot development, etc.) along with mathematical knowledge. The motivation inherent in the learning experience enhances the depth of students' understanding as well as their willingness to persist. All of the pieces of this complex puzzle play a critical role. Individually, they are important; together, they are transformational.

 TAKE FIVE

How has your understanding of engaged literacy learning changed since you started reading this chapter? Which of the criteria for re-engagement do you use most often and successfully? If you were to pick just one criterion that you could work on implementing immediately, what would it be? How might you use it, and who might benefit most as a result?

Milepost

In Pathway No. 6: Empower and its Access Point, Engaging Literacy-Building Activities, we explored ways to support an underachieving boy in surmounting perhaps the most challenging of all obstacles in his journey toward academic achievement: literacy learning. We looked at six criteria for re-engagement that outline the ideal qualities of effective literacy-based activities. Such activities help a struggling boy overcome barriers to literacy learning and re-engage him in the process of reading and writing so that he can continue to develop these essential skills.

We explored three Key Resources that meet the criteria for re-engagement in a way that also addresses a common literacy challenge: finding reading materials and activities that struggling readers *want* to read and participate in. Graphic novels make the experience of reading more accessible and engaging; Enactments help readers deepen their comprehension by providing opportunities to process what they are reading in an active manner; and Talking Cards generate authentic descriptive language, which expands students' capacity for verbal and written expression.

Each Key Resource can also be adapted to other subject areas and multiple grade levels.

• Excellent graphic novels written by respected authors are available for readers as young as 1st grade, and equally engaging graphic novels with diverse storylines and compelling plots are available to engage older boys, especially ones who still struggle to read. Whatever the topic, the format of the graphic novel draws the struggling reader in, supports his comprehension, and motivates him to persist. As a result, his literacy skills grow.

• Enactments can help a 3rd grader imagine the realities of life in a faraway country and a high school student to imagine the way in which a virus is transmitted from one person to another. In both cases, the Enactment process makes an abstract concept concrete and offers a boy who struggles with literacy a way to develop comprehension as well as competence. As a result, his literacy skills grow.

• Talking Cards can jump-start a middle school science discussion about genetic mutation or a kindergarten class's identification of primary colors. In both situations, a boy who struggles with literacy discovers that a simple response to an image helps him generate the language he needs to express his ideas. As a result, his literacy skills grow.

Although the use of these three Key Resources as tools for re-engaging an underachieving boy may appear at first glance to generate only small positive outcomes in any given moment, their benefits are cumulative. The more a struggling boy invests himself in the process, the greater his interest in continuing to learn. As his proficiency continues to develop, so, too, does his potential to see himself as a successful learner. As Marzano tells us (and as we may perhaps appreciate more fully now), reading is the key to academic achievement.

There are many other wonderful literacy-related resources available that meet the criteria for re-engagement which I was not able to share in detail here. Among my favorites, and in addition to those already mentioned, I recommend *Reading, Writing, and Gender* (2002) by Gail Lynn Goldberg and Barbara Sherr Roswell, *Teenage Boys and High School English* (2002) by Bruce Pirie, and *"Reading Don't Fix No Chevys": Literacy in the Lives of Young Men* (2002) and *Going with the Flow: How to Engage Boys (and Girls) in Their Literacy Learning* (2006) by Michael Smith and Jeffrey Wilhelm. Each looks at the complex task of building literacy skills through the eyes of boys and offers an invaluable perspective on the problems, the challenges, and the joys of teaching literacy skills to struggling and reluctant boys. Their collective enthusiasm is part of why I wrote this book, and I urge you to tap into their energy and ideas.

BUILDING A REPERTOIRE OF RESPONSES

Before you move on, pause to take note of any "aha!" moments you've had along the way.

1. What do you now understand about how struggling boys learn best that you didn't know before?

2. Of the strategies you are currently using, which could be tweaked or used more intentionally for an even greater positive outcome?

3. Which ideas or strategies caught your attention the most?

4. Choose one idea or strategy related to this Pathway that you could implement right now.

Epilogue

There comes that mysterious meeting in life when someone acknowledges who we are and what we can be, igniting the circuits of our highest potential.

—Rusty Berkus, author

What I didn't mention at the beginning of this book is that the Pathways on this journey toward enabling underachieving boys to succeed are but first steps in a much longer adventure. And though much of the territory in this complex journey remains to be discovered and thoughtfully explored, I believe that we can at least look at the problem through a new set of lenses. We have set off on a path that addresses underachievement in boys without stereotyping boys or their problems, without needing to separate them from girls, and without needing to blame boys, their teachers, or our best efforts made thus far.

Often, solutions to the challenges of addressing underachievement in boys are right under our noses, and we need only use them more intentionally. In other words, we may find new ways to tweak what we are already doing well or add to our practices in ways that build on the foundations we already have in place. Other times, however, we may need to close a door on a response that we now know isn't helpful, turning instead to the selection of ideas you have encountered in this book to find a fitting replacement. The best news is that each step we take in the Pathways to Re-Engagement model puts us one step closer to getting it right.

I heard a wonderful saying several years ago, and I have thought of it often while writing this book: "Fifty miles in; fifty miles out." Simply put, the problem of underachievement didn't develop overnight, and we need to recognize that finding solutions will take time, too. It isn't meant to be a fast process. We live in an age of speed and access; the Internet has made more information available to more people in less time than at any other point in history. But none of these factors have helped us solve the problem of underachievement. Hence, it makes sense to slow down for a change and really take a hard look at the complex variables that make up the problem of underachievement in boys. Yes, this takes time, but it's time well spent.

What I hope most of all is that this book will generate new and lively conversations. My goal has always been to stimulate discourse about this hugely important issue. I hope that the information and ideas I've shared here will help each of you to think more broadly and speak more confidently about the complexity of what is happening, who is affected, and how we can respond in new ways. I hope that you will continue to ask questions of yourselves and others and that you will generate your own Pathways, Access Points, and Tools. Remember that the more you examine the problem, the more you will see, not just in your struggling boys, but in yourself, as both learner and educator.

Something that touched me deeply as I was researching and writing this book is the simple fact that everything counts; every effort matters. Often, by embarking on one Pathway and implementing its Access Points or Tools, we set the benefits of others in motion as well, supporting learning on many levels at one time. We build skills while reducing fears and anxieties, minimize distractions while enhancing focus, offer outlets for physical activity while reinforcing content and procedural knowledge, and provide comfort while developing self-awareness. These strategies lift the spirit and open the doors to a fresh perspective and a renewed sense of energy and commitment born of little successes achieved along the way.

This process is not a linear task; it is not a quest for information that leads directly from the identified problem to the desired outcome. Rather, it is akin to the process of weaving, in which the crisscrossing tracks of an educator's journey into and across the Pathways, Access Points, and Tools overlap and strengthen one another, each effort threading its way into the fabric of our teaching and the lives of the underachieving boys we are trying to help.

As you contemplate which Pathways you will choose, I will leave you with the wise words of educator Laurent Daloz: "For good teaching rests neither in accumulating a shelf of knowledge nor in developing a repertoire of skills. In the end, good teaching lies in a willingness to attend and care for what happens in our students, ourselves, and *the space between us*" (emphasis added).

May your journey lead to practical and effective solutions to the problems of underachievement you see in the boys you teach, helping you to understand who they are, how they are struggling, and what you can do to help them move from a position of weakness to one of strength.

References

Alloway, N., Freebody, P., Gilbert, P., & Muspratt, S. (2002). *Boys, literacy and schooling: Expanding the repertoires of practice.* Canberra, Australia: Commonwealth Department of Education, Science, & Training. Available: http://www.dest.gov.au/sectors/school_education/publications_resources/profiles/boys_literacy_schooling.htm

Armstrong, T. (1999). *ADD/ADHD alternatives in the classroom.* Alexandria, VA: ASCD.

Assessment Reform Group. (1999). *Assessment for learning: Beyond the black box.* Cambridge, UK: University of Cambridge. Available: http://www.assessment-reform-group.org/AssessInsides.pdf

Assessment Reform Group. (2002a). *Assessment for learning: 10 principles.* Cambridge, UK: University of Cambridge Faculty of Education. Available: http://www.assessment-reform-group.org/CIE3.PDF

Assessment Reform Group. (2002b). *Testing, motivation and learning.* Cambridge, UK: University of Cambridge Faculty of Education. Available: http://www.assessment-reform-group.org/TML%20BOOKLET%20complete.pdf

Barnett, R. C., & Rivers, C. (2006, October 2). The boy crisis—fact or myth? [Electronic version]. *Teachers College Record.* (Publication ID Number 12750). Available: http://www.tcrecord.org

Barton, P. E. (2005). *One-third of a nation: Rising dropout rates and declining opportunities* (Policy Information Report). Princeton, NJ: Policy Information Center, Educational Testing Service. Available: http://www.ets.org/research/policy_research_reports/pic-onethird

Bernard, L. C., Mills, M., Swenson, L., & Walsh, R. P. (2005). An evolutionary theory of human motivation. *Genetic, Social, and General Psychology Monographs, 2005, 131*(2), 129–184. Available: http://www.drmillslmu.com/publications/Bernard-Mills-Swenson-Walsh.pdf

Black, P., Harrison, C., Lee, C., Marshall, B., & Wiliam, D. (2004, September 1). Working inside the black box: Assessment for learning in the classroom. *Phi Delta Kappan, 86*(1), 8–21. Available: http://datause.cse.ucla.edu/DOCS/pb_wor_2004.pdf

Black, P., & Wiliam, D. (1998a, March). Assessment and classroom learning. *Assessment in Education: Principles, Policy & Practice, 5*(1), 7–74.

Black, P., & Wiliam, D. (1998b, October 1). Inside the black box: Raising standards through classroom assessment. *Phi Delta Kappan, 80*(2), 139–148.

Boston, C. (2002). The concept of formative assessment. *Practical Assessment, Research & Evaluation, 8*(9). Available: http://pareonline.net/getvn.asp?v=8&n=9

Boyd-Franklin, N., Franklin, A. J., & Toussaint, P. (2000). *Boys into men: Raising our African American teenage sons.* New York: Penguin.

Brenner, R. (2005, March 6). Graphic novels 101: FAQ. *The Horn Book Magazine.* Available: http://www.hbook.com/magazine/articles/2006/mar06_brenner.asp

Brightman, H. J. (n.d.). *GSU Master Teacher Program: On learning styles.* Available: http://www2.gsu.edu/~dschjb/wwwmbti.html

Caine, R., Caine, G., McClintic, C. L., & Klimek, K. J. (Eds.). (2008). *12 brain/mind learning principles in action: Developing executive functions of the human brain.* Thousand Oaks, CA: Corwin Press.

"Canberra." (2002). *See* House of Representatives Standing Committee on Education and Training.

Clark, R. (2004). *The essential 55: An award-winning educator's rules for discovering the successful student in every child.* New York: Hyperion.

Cleveland, K. (2008). *Boys and school: Challenging underachievement, getting it right!* [Online graduate course]. Available: http://teacheronlineeducation.com/courses.asp

Conlin, M. (2003, May 26). The new gender gap: From kindergarten to grad school, boys are becoming the second sex. *BusinessWeek.* Available: http://www.businessweek.com/magazine/content/03_21/b3834001_mz001.htm

Corbett, C., Hill, C., & St. Rose, A. (2008, May 20). *Where the girls are: The facts about gender equity in education.* Available: http://www.aauw.org/learn/research/WhereGirlsAre.cfm

Cox, A. (2006a, July/August). Lost in electronica. *Psychotherapy Networker,* 50–57. Available: http://www.ohio.edu/ohiotoday/print/upload/LostInElectronica.pdf

Cox, A. (2006b). *Teaching boys pragmatic communication.* Available: http://www.dradamcox.com/pdf/PragmaticCommunication.pdf

Daloz, L. A. (1986). *Effective teaching and mentoring: Realizing the transformational power of adult learning experiences* (Jossey-Bass Higher and Adult Education Series). San Francisco: Jossey-Bass.

DePorter, B. (2009). *The 8 keys of excellence: Principles to live by* (Rev. ed.). Oceanside, CA: Learning Forum Publications.

DePorter, B., Reardon, M., & Singer-Nourie, S. (1999). *Quantum teaching: Orchestrating student success.* Boston: Allyn and Bacon.

Eldeib, D. (2010, March 5). Every Urban Prep senior is college-bound. *Chicago Tribune* [Online article collections]. Available: http://articles.chicagotribune.com/2010-03-05/news/ct-met-urban-prep-college-20100305_1_metal-detectors-college-school-leaders/2

Eliot, L. (2009). *Pink brain, blue brain: How small differences grow into troublesome gaps—and what we can do about it.* New York: Houghton Mifflin Harcourt.

Gardner, J., Harlen, W., Hayward, L., & Stobart, G. (2008). *Changing assessment practice: Process, principles, and standards.* Cambridge, UK: University of Cambridge Faculty of Education. Available: http://www.assessment-reform-group.org/ARIA%20English.pdf

Goldberg, G. L., & Roswell, B. S. (2002). *Reading, writing, and gender: Instructional strategies and classroom activities that work for girls and boys.* Larchmont, NY: Eye on Education.

Guild, P. B. (2001). Diversity, learning style and culture. *New Horizons for Learning.* Available: http://www.newhorizons.org/strategies/styles/guild.htm

Gurian, M. (2001). *Boys and girls learn differently! A guide for teachers and parents.* San Francisco: Jossey-Bass.

Gurian, M., & Ballew, A. C. (2003). *The boys and girls learn differently action guide for teachers.* San Francisco: Jossey-Bass.

Gurian, M., & Stevens, K. (2005). *The minds of boys: Saving our sons from falling behind in school and in life.* San Francisco: Jossey-Bass.

Hannaford, C. (2005). *Smart moves: Why learning is not all in your head* (2nd ed.). Arlington, VA: Great Ocean Publishers.

Hanson, J. R., & Dewing, T. (1990). *Research on the profiles of at-risk learners: Research monograph series.* Moorestown, NJ: Institute for Studies in Analytic Psychology.

Hattie, J. (1999, August 2). *Influences on student learning.* Inaugural lecture: Professor of Education, University of Auckland, New Zealand. Available: http://www.education.auckland.ac.nz/webdav/site/education/shared/hattie/docs/influences-on-student-learning.pdf

House of Representatives Standing Committee on Education and Training. (2002, October). *Boys: Getting it right. Report on the inquiry into the education of boys.* Canberra, Australia: AGPS (Australian Government Publishing Service). Available: http://www.aph.gov.au/house/committee/edt/eofb/report.htm

Jackson, D. (1998). Breaking out of the binary trap: Boys' underachievement, schooling and gender relations. In D. Epstein, J. Elwood, W. Hey, & J. Maw (Eds.), *Failing boys? Issues in gender and achievement* (pp. 77–95). Buckingham, UK: Open University Press.

James, A. N. (2007). *Teaching the male brain: How boys think, feel, and learn in school.* Thousand Oaks, CA: Corwin Press.

Jensen, E. (2005). *Teaching with the brain in mind* (Rev. 2nd ed.). Alexandria, VA: ASCD.

Jensen, E. (2008). *Enriching the brain: How to maximize every learner's potential.* San Francisco: Jossey-Bass.

Jensen, E. (2009). *Teaching with poverty in mind: What being poor does to kids' brains and what schools can do about it.* Alexandria, VA: ASCD.

Johnson, B., Kosove, A., Netter, F. (Producers) & Hancock, J. L. (Director). *The blind side* [Motion picture]. United States: Warner Brothers.

Kagan, S. K. (1992). *Cooperative learning.* San Juan Capistrano, CA: Resources for Teachers.

Kagan, S. K., & Kagan, M. (2009). *Kagan cooperative learning.* San Clemente, CA: Kagan Publishing.

Kindlon, D., & Thompson, M. (2000). *Raising Cain: Protecting the emotional life of boys.* New York: Ballantine.

Kunjufu, J. (2007). *Raising black boys.* Sauk Village, IL: African American Images.

Martin, A. J. (2002, December). *Improving the educational outcomes of boys: Final report to ACT Department of Education, Youth and Family Services.* Tuggeranong, Australian Capital Territory: Department of Education, Youth and Family Services. Available: http://www .det.act.gov.au/__data/assets/pdf_file/0005/17798/Ed_Outcomes_Boys.pdf

Marzano, R. J. (2004). *Building background knowledge for academic achievement.* Alexandria, VA: ASCD.

Mead, S. (2006, June 27). *The evidence suggests otherwise.* Washington, D.C.: Education Sector.

Mortola, P., Grant, S., & Hiton, H. (n.d.). *Images before words: Honoring a boy's indirect style of contact in counseling.* Available: http://bamgroups.com/bam_site/Resources_files/ Images%20Before%20Words.pdf

MSNBC (Producer). (2006, January 22). The boy crisis: Why are boys falling behind? [Archived video of aired television broadcast]. Available: http://www.bing.com/videos/watch/video/ whats-happening-to-your-sons-education/6gav69b?from=00

Myers, I. B., McCaulley, M. H., Quenk, N. L., & Hammer, A. L. (2003). *MBTI manual: A guide to the development and use of the Myers-Briggs Type Indicator* (3rd ed.). Mountain View, CA: CPP.

Narvaez, M. L., & Brimijoin, K. (2010). *Differentiation at work, K–5: Principles, lessons, and strategies.* Thousand Oaks, CA: Corwin Press.

NCTE (National Council of Teachers of English). (2005, September 5). Using comics and graphic novels in the classroom [Electronic version]. *The Council Chronicle.* Available: http://www.ncte.org/magazine/archives/122031

Neall, L. (2002). *Bringing out the best in boys: Communication strategies for teachers.* Stroud, UK: Hawthorne Press.

Neu, T. W., & Weinfeld, R. (2007). *Helping boys succeed in school: A practical guide for parents and teachers.* Waco, TX: Prufrock.

Newkirk, T. (2002). *Misreading masculinity: Boys, literacy, and popular culture.* Portsmouth, NH: Heinemann.

Partnership for 21st Century Skills. (2009). *The MILE guide. Milestones for improving learning & education* [Online publication]. Available: http://www.p21.org/index.php?option=com_ content&task=view&id=800&Itemid=52

Petty, G. (n.d.). *Black and Wiliam 1998.* Available: http://www.geoffpetty.com/downloads/ WORD/BlackandWiliam.doc

Pirie, B. (2002). *Teenage boys and high school English.* Portsmouth, NH: Heinemann.

Pleasants, R. K. (2007). Teaching young men in correctional education: Issues and interventions in male identity development. *Journal of Correctional Education, 58*(3), 249–261. (ERIC Document Retrieval No. EJ789182). Available: http://findarticles.com/p/articles/ mi_qa4111/is_200709/ai_n21100696/

Promising practices at Urban Prep Charter School for Young Men [Web log post]. (2010, January 11). Available: http://usinetworkschools.org/2010/01/11/promising-practices-at-urban-prep-charter-school-for-young-men

Reichert, M. C., & Hawley, R. A. (2006, October 25). Confronting the "boy problem": A self-study approach to deepen schools' moral stance [Electronic version]. *Teachers College Record* (Publication ID Number 12813). Available: http://www.tcrecord.org

Reichert, M., & Kuriloff, P. (2004). Boys' selves: Identity and anxiety in the looking glass of school life. *Teachers College Record, 106*(3), 574–576.

Rennie Center for Education Research and Policy. (2006, October). *Are boys making the grade? Gender gaps in achievement and attainment.* Cambridge, MA: Author. Available: http://renniecenter.issuelab.org/research/20

Robinson-English, T. (2006, December). Saving black boys: Is single-sex education the answer? *Ebony Magazine.* Available: http://findarticles.com/p/articles/mi_m1077/is_2_62/ai_n27094615

Rudiger, H. M. (2005, March). Reading lessons: Graphic novels 101. *The Horn Book Magazine.* Available: http://www.hbook.com/pdf/articles/mar06_rudiger.pdf

Salomone, R. C. (2003). *Same, different, equal: Rethinking single-sex schooling.* New Haven, CT: Yale University Press.

Salomone, R. C. (2006a, November 20). Single-sex schooling and the language of difference [Electronic version]. *Teachers College Record* (Publication ID Number 12845). Available: http://tcrecord.org

Salomone, R. C. (2006b, December 6). Putting single-sex schooling back on course. *Education Week, 26*(14), 32–33, 44. Available: http://www.edweek.org/ew/articles/2006/12/06/14salomone.h26.html

Sax, L. (2005). *Why gender matters: What parents and teachers need to know about the emerging science of sex differences.* New York: Broadway Books.

Schwartz, G. (2006, July). Expanding literacies through graphic novels. *English Journal, 95*(6), 58.

Sciutto, M. J., & Eisenberg, M. (2007, September). Evaluating the evidence for and against the overdiagnosis of ADHD. *Journal of Attention Disorders, 11*(2), 106–113.

Silver, H. F. (2007a, October 20). *Why students fail and what we can do about it* [Conference handout]. Presentation at the ASCD Conference on Teaching & Learning: Connecting Instruction and Assessment, Atlanta, GA.

Silver, H. F. (2007b, October 21). *Boredom and its opposite: The role of active engagement in improving student achievement* [Conference handout]. Presentation at the ASCD Conference on Teaching & Learning: Connecting Instruction and Assessment, Atlanta, GA.

Silver, H., & Hanson, J. R. (1996). *Learning styles & strategies.* Ho-Ho-Kus, NJ: Thoughtful Education Press.

Silver, H. F., Strong, R. W., & Perini, M. J. (2007). *The strategic teacher: Selecting the right research-based strategy for every lesson.* Alexandria, VA: ASCD.

Smith, M. W., & Wilhelm, J. D. (2002). *"Reading don't fix no Chevys": Literacy in the lives of young men.* Portsmouth, NH: Heinemann.

Smith, M. W., & Wilhelm, J. D. (2006). *Going with the flow: How to engage boys (and girls) in their literacy learning.* Portsmouth, NH: Heinemann.

Smith, R. (2004). *Conscious classroom management.* San Rafael, CA: Conscious Teaching Publications.

Sousa, D. (2006). *How the brain learns* (3rd ed.). Thousand Oaks, CA: Corwin Press.

Taylor, J. F. (2001a). *From defiance to cooperation: Real solutions for transforming the angry, defiant, discouraged child.* New York: Three Rivers Press.

Taylor, J. F. (2001b). *Helping your ADD child* (3rd ed.). Roseville, CA: Prima Publishing.

Taylor, J. F. (2007, March 19). *Please sit still, pay attention, and get your homework done* [Conference handout]. Presentation at the 2007 ASCD Annual Conference, Anaheim, CA (Session 3328).

Terry, R., & Churches, R. (2009). *The NLP toolkit: Activities and strategies for teachers, trainers and school leaders.* Williston, VT: Crown House Publishing.

Toch, T. (Moderator), Wattenberg, R., Holzer, H., Mead, S., & Whitmire, R. (2006, September 21). Education Sector debates: Are boys *really* in crisis? [Transcript and audio]. Available: http://www.educationsector.org/publications/are-boys-ireallyi-crisis-transcript [transcript] and http://www.educationsector.org/audio/audio-file-are-boys-really-crisis [audio]

Tomlinson, C. A. (1999). *The differentiated classroom: Responding to the needs of all learners.* Alexandria, VA: ASCD.

Tyre, P. (2006, January 30). The trouble with boys. *Newsweek.* Available: http://www.msnbc.msn.com/id/10965522/site/newsweek/

University of Northern Iowa College of Education (Producer). (n.d.). InTime project videos. Available: http://www.intime.uni.edu

Vygotsky, L. S. (1978). *Mind in society: The development of higher psychological processes.* Cambridge, MA: Harvard University Press.

Weaver-Hightower, M. (2005). Dare the school build a new education for boys? [Electronic version]. *Teachers College Record* (Publication ID Number 11103). Available: http://tcrecord.org

Wiggins, G. (2004, March). Assessment as feedback. *New Horizons for Learning.* Available: http://www.newhorizons.org/strategies/assess/wiggins.htm

Wilhelm, J. D. (1997). *"You gotta BE the book": Teaching engaged and reflective reading with adolescents.* New York: Teachers College Press.

Wilhelm, J. D. (2002). *Action strategies for deepening comprehension.* New York: Scholastic.

Wolfe, P. (2001). *Brain matters: Translating research into classroom practice.* Alexandria, VA: ASCD.

Younger, M., & Warrington, M. (with Gray, J., Rudduck, J., McLellan, R., Bearne, E., Kershner, R., & Bricheno, P.) (2005). *Raising boys' achievement* (Research Report No. 636). Cambridge, UK: Department for Education and Skills. Available: http://www.dfes.gov.uk/research/data/uploadfiles/RR636.pdf

Index

Information in figures is denoted by *f*.

About the Author

Kathleen Palmer Cleveland is president and CEO of TeacherOnlineEducation.com. During the last 20 years of her 30-year career in education, she has designed, written, developed, and produced content, materials, and graphic art for more than 30 graduate-level site-based and online courses for K–12 teachers. As a former K–12 teacher and longtime instructor of practicing educators, she works with universities and colleges across the United States to meet mid-continuum professional educators' needs for rigorous courses that speak to both the teacher's need for practical relevance and the profession's need for research-based best practices.

Cleveland received a bachelor of arts degree in English education from St. Olaf College in Northfield, Minnesota, a master of music degree in vocal performance from Washington University at St. Louis, and a doctor of education degree in adult education with an emphasis in curriculum and instruction from Nova Southeastern University in Fort Lauderdale. She may be contacted at (800) 861-2295 (T), (706) 268-3478 (F), or kcleveland@teacheronlineeducation.com.

Related ASCD Resources: Educating Boys

At the time of publication, the following ASCD resources were available (ASCD stock numbers appear in parentheses). For up-to-date information about ASCD resources, go to www.ascd.org.

ASCD Professional Interest Communities

Exchange ideas and connect with other educators interested in gender in education on the social networking site ASCD EDge™ at http://ascdedge.ascd.org.

Print Products

ASCD Express, March 18, 2010: Does Gender Matter in Education?

ASCD Express, November 25, 2010: Teaching Boys

Educational Leadership, November 2010: Closing Opportunity Gaps
  (#111031)

Motivating Black Males to Achieve in School and in Life by Baruti K. Kafele
  (#109013)

THE WHOLE
CHILD

The Whole Child Initiative helps schools and communities create learning environments that allow students to be healthy, safe, engaged, supported, and challenged. To learn more about other books and resources that relate to the whole child, visit www.wholechildeducation.org.

For more information: send e-mail to member@ascd.org; call 1-800-933-2723 or 703-578-9600, press 2; send a fax to 703-575-5400; or write to Information Services, ASCD, 1703 N. Beauregard St., Alexandria, VA 22311-1714 USA.

TEACHING
BOYS

WHO STRUGGLE IN SCHOOL

SUSTAINABLE
FORESTRY
INITIATIVE

Certified Sourcing

www.sfiprogram.org